The Great Plains

"The natural environment is more than stage or setting. It offers opportunities and imposes limitations or restraints. The reactions to an area, including adaptations to it, are conditioned by the attitudes, technology, and experience of the society of which the inhabitants are a part. Individuals and groups, by processes of trial and error, discover opportunities existing in an area. Likewise, through living in an area, its occupants encounter its limitations, some of which may prove flexible. Thus, man-land relationships are developed and may change significantly through time."

LESLIE HEWES

The Great Plains

Environment and Culture

EDITED BY
Brian W. Blouet and Frederick C. Luebke

Published by the
UNIVERSITY OF NEBRASKA PRESS ● LINCOLN AND LONDON
for the
CENTER FOR GREAT PLAINS STUDIES   University of
Nebraska–Lincoln

Copyright © 1979 by the University of Nebraska Press
Manufactured in the United States of America

Library of Congress Cataloging in Publication Data

Cultural Heritage of the Plains Symposium, University
    of Nebraska–Lincoln, 1977.
    The Great Plains.

    1. Great Plains–History–Congresses.
2. Anthropo-geography–Great Plains–Congresses.
3. Agriculture–Great Plains–History–Congresses.
I. Blouet, Brian W., 1936–   II. Luebke,
Frederick C., 1927–   III. Title.
F591.C84   1977   978   79–1152
ISBN 0-8032-1155-4

Contents

Preface

The essays in this volume were presented at the Cultural Heritage of the Plains Symposium, which was held on April 13–15, 1977, at the Nebraska Center for Continuing Education at the University of Nebraska–Lincoln. One of the major purposes of the conference was to launch the newly created Center for Great Plains Studies and to establish what has become a series of annual symposia treating plains topics and problems.

The idea of a Center for Great Plains Studies had been discussed for some years. In 1976 Dr. Max Larsen, Dean of the College of Arts and Sciences, developed the proposal to the point where it was given concrete form. The establishment of the center was approved by the Board of Regents on December 11, 1976, and in 1977 the University of Nebraska Foundation began its support of the scholarly activities of the center.

It is not possible to name all the people who helped with the arrangements for the Cultural Heritage of the Plains Symposium. Without the financial help of the Montgomery Lectureship fund, the UNL Convocations Committee, the UNL Research Council, and particularly the S & H Foundation, the program could not have been so rich and broad as it became. Because of the diversity of the program it was not possible to publish all the papers presented at the symposium. A number of those for which we could not find a place in the present volume have already appeared in scholarly journals. Papers treating literary topics are to be published in a separate volume.

We owe a collective debt to our colleagues on the program committee and particularly to Kathleen Avery, who acted as administrative assistant to the Center for Great Plains Studies during its formative months.

BRIAN W. BLOUET
FREDERICK C. LUEBKE
University of Nebraska–Lincoln

Introduction

Frederick C. Luebke

A century ago, in 1878, Major John Wesley Powell presented his *Report on the Lands of the Arid Region of the United States* to his superiors in the Department of the Interior in Washington. The noted explorer and surveyor described the physical characteristics of the American West and advocated a series of fundamental changes in the land system of the federal government to bring policy into conformance with environmental realities. Writing only sixteen years after the passage of the Homestead Act, Powell pointed out that the agricultural frontier had extended westward by 1878 to the limits of where farming was possible without irrigation. Old laws based on experience in the humid East were obsolete; new laws appropriate for the semiarid West were needed. Solidly grounded in scientific fact as understood at that time, the report challenged widely held myths and fantasies that served the interests of persons devoted to the rapid exploitation of western resources. Political opposition was therefore intense and Powell's legislative proposals were never enacted.[1]

Although Powell may have been ignored by the legislators of his own time, his work has had substantial influence upon later interpretations of the Great Plains region. For many years most scholars, like Powell, interpreted the region as having an essential unity dictated by characteristics of physical geography. In Powell's view, the region was integrated by rainfall patterns of less than twenty inches per year, even though it displayed a notable variety in topography, soils, and climate.[2] His report implied that the physical forces of the Great Plains environment were so powerful that people could settle the region permanently and successfully only if they conformed or adapted their ways appropriately.

In contrast to Powell's environmentalism, other students of the American West have emphasized factors of time and culture. They have argued that the Great Plains must be analyzed in relation to other parts of the country and of the world and that these relationships have changed notably with the passage of time. In their view, the question of whether the Great Plains possesses unity as a region is less significant than what actually happened there, because major events and developments are strongly and sometimes primarily conditioned by circumstances as they existed in the East or elsewhere at a particular time. Moreover, students of American regionalism have tended to ignore physiographic or climatic consistencies and to focus on the cultural characteristics of the people. They argue that regional unity emerges, not from the facts of physical geography, but from the values, attitudes, behaviors, and life-styles of the people who live there. For them the analytical key is found in historic patterns of migration and settlement.[3]

In the pages that follow I have summarized the views of certain selected scholars whose emphases seem to illustrate changing and contrasting interpretations of the interaction of environment and culture on the Great Plains. I have grouped their writings into two inclusive categories. First come those whose conceptual schemes suggest the primacy of environmental variables. I refer to these scholars, perhaps simplistically, as environmentalists, even though this term has acquired a different meaning in recent years. In the second group are several scholars, selected more arbitrarily than the first, whose writings seem to accord more importance to cultural factors. For present purposes I refer to them as culturalists. Then follow brief introductions to the essays included here, in which I suggest relationships to the environmentalist and culturalist views. Because of the diversity of concept and method employed by the several essayists, I make no effort to define the Great Plains or to delineate its boundaries.

The most influential scholar to build on the foundation laid by Powell was Walter Prescott Webb, a native of Texas and a professor of history at the University of Texas. Reading Powell's observations on the inhibiting effects of climate and topography confirmed Webb in his own environmentalist views. His book, *The Great Plains,* was published in 1931 and remains to this day the most widely read single volume on the region.[4]

At the heart of Webb's interpretation was his conception of the Great Plains as an environment unified by its flatness, lack of trees, and semiaridity. He argued that the methods used by Americans to master the wilderness had been developed in areas where trees and water were abundant. The frontier of agricultural settlement moved steadily westward until it reached the Great Plains; there it faltered

for several decades in the middle of the nineteenth century, unable
to overcome the natural obstacles of the region or to displace its
fierce and hostile Indian tribes. In the East "civilization rested on
three legs—land, water, and timber," wrote Webb; but in the West
"not one but two of the legs were withdrawn,—water and timber,—
and civilization was left on one leg—land. It is small wonder that it
toppled over in temporary failure."[5] Successful settlement of the
plains had to await the development of suitable tools and techniques,
such as the revolver, the railroad, the windmill, and the barbed-wire
fence, as well as methods of irrigation, dry farming, and the evolution of appropriate land and water laws. In the meantime, according
to Webb, agricultural settlement bypassed the Great Plains for out-
posts on the Pacific Coast. A second attempt at settlement was made
after the Civil War. This time it was successful, and the Great Plains
region was populated rapidly, especially after 1880.

Webb also insisted that the West could be understood only
through appropriate contrasts with the East. "In history," he wrote,
"the differences are more important than the similarities," for the
West was no "mere extension of things Eastern." The comparisons
he made, based as they were on physical differences between the
plains and the woodland East, tempted him to ignore important
contrasts within the region and to accord it greater geographical
unity than most geographers would be willing to accept. The thesis
required that sharp distinctions be drawn; he insisted that the eastern
boundary of the plains was definite even though "when people first
crossed this line they did not immediately realize the imperceptible
change that had taken place in their environment." Webb located this
line in the vicinity of the 98th meridian. So clearly did he discern the
break that he compared it to a geological fault and asserted that at
this line "practically every institution that was carried across it was
either broken or remade or else greatly altered."[6]

In a passage reminiscent of Frederick Jackson Turner, Webb
romanticized his thesis:

> Let us visualize the American approach to the Great Plains by imagining
> ourselves at the point where the ninety-eighth meridian cuts the thirty-
> first parallel [a few miles north of Austin, Texas]. As we gaze northward
> we see on the right side the forested and well-watered country and on the
> left side the arid, treeless plain. On the right we see a nation of people
> coming slowly but persistently through the forest, felling trees, building
> cabins, making rail fences, digging shallow wells, or drinking from the
> numerous springs and perennial streams, advancing shoulder to shoulder,
> pushing the natives westward toward the open country. They are nearing

the Plains. Then, in the first half of the nineteenth century, we see the advance guard of this moving host of forest homemakers emerge into the new environment, where there are no forests, no logs for cabins, no rails for fences, few springs and running streams. Before them is a wide land infested by a fierce breed of Indians, mounted, ferocious, unconquerable, terrible in their mercilessness. They see a natural barrier made more formidable by a human barrier of untamed savagery. Upon this barrier of the Great Plains the pioneers threw themselves, armed and equipped with the weapons, tools, ideas, and institutions which had served them so long and so well in the woods that now lay behind them. Inevitably they failed in their first efforts, and they continued to fail until they worked out a technique of pioneering adapted to the Plains rather than to the woodland.[7]

From his vantage point in Austin and perhaps with the Cross Timbers in his mind's eye, Webb projected the Texas experience onto the entire Great Plains region, where the idea was less applicable. If the agricultural frontier halted anywhere north of Texas in the first half of the nineteenth century, it was not in the vicinity of the 98th meridian but rather at the western boundaries of Arkansas and Missouri. It was not because pioneering techniques had failed in a new and strange environment but because the land to the west was reserved at that time for Indian tribes, some of whom had been brought there by the federal government from the East. The area was closed by law to settlement until the Kansas and Nebraska territories were organized in 1854 and treaties with indigenous tribes were negotiated. Meanwhile, the agricultural frontier moved steadily up the Missouri River valley, north and west across Missouri and Iowa into Nebraska, and later into Dakota. In 1860, when Nebraska Territory encompassed the entire northern Great Plains to the Canadian border, the census registered fewer than twenty-nine thousand inhabitants, all but a few hundred living within twenty miles of the Missouri River in the southeastern corner of the territory. Not until the 1870s, a decade stricken by economic depression, drought, and grasshopper plagues, did the agricultural frontier reach Webb's institutional fault line. Demographic studies have shown that at no time did the westward sweep of settlement falter or hesitate as it approached the 98th meridian on the central or northern plains. At no time had civilization "toppled over in temporary failure."[8]

Although historiographers have customarily placed Webb in the tradition of Frederick Jackson Turner, the Texas historian properly objected to that easy classification. Turner taught that the American historical experience and character derived from a continuous process in which each generation built upon the experiences of its predecessor until the continent was crossed. Webb insisted that Turner's thesis was valid for woodlands only, and that the Great Plains experience was qualitatively different: previous frontier experiences were largely irrelevant, as the alleged hesitation at the 98th meridian demonstrated.

In 1939 Webb's most severe critic, Fred A. Shannon, attacked *The Great Plains* on Turnerian grounds, although he did not invoke Turner's name. A University of Illinois historian who subsequently included Great Plains agriculture in his 1945 book, *The Farmer's Last Frontier,* Shannon disputed Webb's interpretation of the Great Plains as having regional unity and he rejected the description of the 98th meridian as an institutional fault line. Each frontier, Shannon insisted, was different from its predecessors and required the pioneers to make adjustments in their farming methods. If Webb had "shown how the problems of a relatively treeless country started at the edge of the eastern prairies and became more intensified, step by step, till the actual deserts of Arizona, Utah, and California were occupied, he would have performed a far greater service." But what distressed Shannon most was Webb's tendency, as he saw it, to use only evidence that supported his thesis and to ignore the rest.[9]

In 1947, sixteen years after the publication of *The Great Plains,* James C. Malin, a historian at the University of Kansas, published a volume intended as an interdisciplinary preface to the history of the Great Plains. Malin drew upon studies in biology, geography, and soil science to describe the ecology of *The Grassland of North America,* as he titled his highly unconventional book.

To Webb the Great Plains environment was a powerful, dominating force that required men to conform to its dictates; to Malin the environment was the physical setting in which plants and animals, if undisturbed, naturally existed in harmonious relationships—a delicate ecological balance. The important question for Malin was how well men fit their "culture into conformity with the requirement of maintaining rather than disrupting environmental equilibrium."[10] In order to understand the history of human occupance of the region, one needed first to understand its plant and animal life, climate, geology, geography, and soils. Then one could go on to evaluate the adaptations that men had made to them. Thus, the first half of *The Grassland* treats plant and animal ecology, climate, geology, soils, and factors in grassland equilibrium; the second summarizes the individual contributions of pioneers in the study of the Great Plains, analyzes Webb and his regionalism, presents sample population and agricultural studies, and concludes with an exhaustive bibliography.

Unlike Webb's environmentalism, Malin's ecological interpretation left no room for determinism. He was especially sensitive on this point because during the Great Depression of the 1930s social and biological scientists were strongly attracted to determinist views in order, Malin wrote, to justify social policy. "At every turn one meets the dictum that low-rainfall climate makes necessary a collective form of society." In Malin's view, the existence of more than one possibility for action eliminated the element of determinism—there were always several ways to achieve a specific end. Culture often influenced the choices men made, he wrote, and alternatives were often consciously developed. Moreover, technological improvements from time to time were being discovered and utilized. Indeed, he observed, it was the peculiar combination of technology and culture in a particular place, such as the Great Plains, that could distinguish one region from another. Thus, while Malin's interpretation of the Great Plains was primarily rooted in environment, he insisted that culture was also of fundamental importance, even though he did not pursue the matter in the book.[11]

Interregional dependency, however, was a theme that infused Malin's criticism of Webb's *The Great Plains*. Although Malin hailed the book as a landmark in the regional approach to the West and recognized it as an implicit criticism of Turner's frontier thesis, he thought that Webb had insufficiently related the rapid settlement of the plains after 1870 to eastern technological developments. "It is beside the point," wrote Malin in an illustrative passage, "to argue that windmills did not come in quantity until the 1880s. To place windmills within the financial reach of the average pioneer farmer awaited cheap steel, mass production methods, as well as mechanical refinements of machine design."[12] Moreover, the devices used by the frontiersmen to conquer the plains were developed independently of, not in response to, their needs. Once they became available, they were applied successfully to the specific problems of the plains region. Thus, Malin's work is profoundly environmentalist and, at the same time, free of environmental determinism.

The last of the environmentalist interpretations in the tradition of John Wesley Powell to be considered here is Carl Kraenzel's *The Great Plains in Transition*, first published in 1955. A Montana sociologist, Kraenzel echoed Webb in asserting that the Great Plains was a clearly distinguishable region. But its unity had been virtually destroyed by the forest-land culture imported by settlers from eastern, humid areas. Kraenzel describes the settlers' failure to adjust their ways to new circumstances:

> Inexperienced in the conditions that made for uniqueness of a semi-arid land, they did not look for the explanation of their hardships in the inappropriateness of the forest-land way of living. They failed to see the need for fitting their institutions and their philosophy to the facts of semi-aridity in the Plains. And there was no help to be found in any of the customary, traditional patterns of contending with the environment.[13]

Institutions, which naturally lack plasticity, were transferred from the forest lands and imposed upon the plains environment without needed modifications. Now firmly entrenched, these institutions have stoutly resisted adaptation.[14]

Kraenzel's basic assumption is "that a humid-area type of civilization cannot thrive in the semi-arid American Plains without constant subsidy, or, lacking this, without repeated impoverishment of the residents." Throughout its history, the Great Plains has remained an exploited hinterland and its residents have displayed the attitudes and conduct typical of minority groups. Kraenzel's solution to the problem of the Great Plains was strongly deterministic. Writing in a vein reminiscent of William Graham Sumner ("root, hog, or die"), Kraenzel's message was a blunt "adapt or get out." People who cannot or will not make the appropriate adjustments must leave, and the few who remain will have to choose between "a feast-and-famine type of existence or a standard of living well below that of most other parts of the country."[15]

How should the people of the plains adapt? Kraenzel's answer was in the development of a thoroughgoing regionalism. By this he meant "the unique but democratic ordering and programming of economic, social, and living activities of a common area, through political and all other avenues, so that the greatest possible advantages can accrue to these residents."[16] In this way, Kraenzel believed, the Great Plains could once again attain the essential unity it had lost.

Although as a sociologist Kraenzel was not wedded to a spatial interpretation, his commitment to regionalism led him to accept uncritically Webb's notion that the agricultural frontier had hesitated at a cultural fault line. "For several decades prior to 1880," wrote Kraenzel, "in spite of the Homestead Act, the westward push of settlement was almost stationary and came to a halt along the ninety-eighth meridian. Following the Civil War, cattlemen established themselves in the region and sheepmen roamed about in it, but the agriculturists appeared to hesitate." This was "not only because of the Indians on the Plains, but because of a basic recognition that this vast area was different from the humid and forested area through which the settlers had come."[17]

Yet there are important differences between Webb's and Kraenzel's interpretations. In Webb's schema, agriculturalists from the forested lands of the East were unable to cross the cultural fault line successfully or permanently until appropriate adaptations had been made; Kraenzel more or less assumes that the region had been occupied by easterners, the inappropriateness of their forest-oriented institutions notwithstanding, and that their continued occupance depended upon present and future adjustments to environmental realities. For Webb hesitation at the 98th meridian was essential to his thesis; for Kraenzel it was a matter of only incidental importance.

Few scholars like to be tagged as determinists and Kraenzel was no exception. He described his own interpretation as a middle position between environmental and cultural poles. While the environment established limits beyond which culture could not go, he wrote, within those limits culture could produce much variety.[18]

If Kraenzel was willing to admit the theoretical importance of culture, other scholars eagerly used cultural concepts in their research designs. This is especially true of geographers, folklorists, linguists, and others who have studied the regional diversity of the United States. Although they have not entirely ignored environmental factors, they have focused on cultural variables such as religious belief, political behavior, folk architecture, and speech. Since a given place often remains imprinted with the characteristics of its first settlers, patterns of migration have become central in their research, and they have shown that the flow of culture has normally followed parallel east-to-west lines.[19] The culture of North Dakota, for example, more closely resembles that of Minnesota and Wisconsin than that of Nebraska and Kansas; similarly, the culture of the Southern Plains has more in common with that of Arkansas and Tennessee than with that of northern states. Hence, for the purposes of most culturalists, the Great Plains, with a north-south orientation, are not a useful unit of study and therefore they have tended to ignore the region.[20]

Historians also have found the concept of environmentalism inadequate for their purposes. In 1955, the same year that Kraenzel's book appeared, Earl Pomeroy wrote an influential essay entitled "Toward a Reorientation of Western History: Continuity and Environment." Pomeroy criticized historians for their tendency to study aspects of western experience in which environmental influences were obvious. "They argue the importance of environmental influences in the West while demanding that the West qualify as West by being the place where the environment predominates."[21] Echoing Shannon's criticism of Webb, Pomeroy also charged that they tend to avoid evidence that does not fit the environmentalist formula. He insisted that the facts testifying to the continuity of culture brought to the West cannot be ignored and that fundamentally westerners have been imitators, not innovators; conformists, not radicals.[22] In Pomeroy's view, economic historians had charted the new course as they shifted attention from the pageantry of adventurous trappers, prospectors, and cowboys to questions of investment capital and management. Western radicalism was a reaction to the concentration of eastern economic power, Pomeroy suggested, not to western atmosphere. Similar orientations were needed in social and cultural studies in order to illuminate relations between the settled East and frontier West and to reveal continuities in religion, education, class structures, elites as culture bearers, and the army as an ingredient in western society and economy.

Although Pomeroy's essay, with its emphasis on continuities rather than contrasts, shares in the neoconservatism that infused American historiography during the 1950s, it is more than that. It reflects as well the long-term emphases of Pomeroy's own work and that of his students.[23] Pomeroy, like Webb and the environmentalists, also stressed the importance of interdisciplinary research and the use of comparative methods in the study of social and political developments in the West. But his essay was especially a criticism of scholars whose emphasis was on space rather than on time, differences instead of similarities, and on the West as "no mere extension of things Eastern."[24]

Pomeroy's plea for a reorientation of western history was carried forward in 1964 by Robert Berkhofer in an article entitled "Space, Time, Culture, and the New Frontier." Berkhofer agreed that the history of the West in every period had to be placed in a larger context, but his main purpose was to show "how the American frontier should be viewed in the perspective of modern social theory." Much of Berkhofer's analysis pivots on changing concepts of culture. He shows first that Frederick Jackson Turner and the environmentalists who followed him were naturally influenced by contemporary thought to accord space premier importance as a causative agent, with time and culture in secondary positions.[25] For them culture referred essentially to behavior and artifact—"an inherited part of the social organism." But in more recent times, Berkhofer pointed out, culture has come to mean a normative system serving as a blueprint for behavior, rather than the behavior itself:

> Thus a person's culture prescribes what ought to be done, delimits what may be done, and defines what exists, or concerns what are frequently called values, norms, and beliefs. Culture, then, shapes the nature of the institutions in a society and the roles a person plays in them. Culture also filters the perception of reality. What a person accepts as "fact" is highly conditioned by his value-orientation. It is assumed that the various cultural by-patterns, such as subsystems and institutions, fit into an overall configuration that provides that culture's unique integration.[26]

Lacking such an understanding of culture, the environmentalists overestimated the effect climate, terrain, and vegetation have in human affairs. While a person may alter his behavior, wrote Berkhofer, he may do so reluctantly and his conception of what is desirable may not change at all. Thus, if we are to explain the American West in terms of modern social theory, we must consider the prevailing cultural system of the time as the fundamental determinant, because the ways in which man responds to environmental forces are "highly conditioned by the cultural screen through which the stimulus passes."[27]

Berkhofer noted further that technological improvements enhance the ability of a society to transcend the limitations imposed by the physical environment. This was the real message hidden in Webb's environmental thesis; it was a relationship largely ignored by Kraenzel. Berkhofer further observed that political, social, and religious institutions are far less subject to environmental influence than economic institutions, since the latter are dependent upon environmental products much more than the former. When Webb asserted that "practically every institution" was transformed in the flat, treeless, semiarid Great Plains environment, he was in fact analyzing the more easily influenced economic institutions. But, observed Berkhofer,

> More important than lush grass in the rapid spread of cattle ranching on the plains was expanding industrialism which provided eastern workers' mouths to eat beef and railroads to get it to their tables. Furthermore, the railroad speeded up the settlement of the plains by farmers and ended the open range grazing. Railroads gave these same farmers access to market and brought them the new farm machinery which enabled them to stay in business. Environment did alter some manifestations of the economic institutions of the time, but commercialized farming and the pursuit of

profit determined the main outline of plains capitalism. Except for water and land laws, this frontier would seem to have had no effect on political institutions.[28]

Berkhofer concluded that the frontier should not be viewed, as Webb had seen it, as an area or space that demanded innovation, but rather as an opportunity within a time framework for the proliferation of imported institutions that "enabled a greater number of people to participate at higher levels in them than would have been possible in a society without a frontier."[29]

E. Cotton Mather provides another variation of the culturalist point of view. In an article on the Great Plains as a geographic region, he flatly rejects the notion that the Great Plains are characterized by physiographic unity. Instead, Mather describes the unexpected diversity of the region and then shows that such unity as it possesses emerges from cultural traits that have persisted throughout its history and remain prominent today. In Mather's interpretation, Great Plains culture derives from its character as a transit region. The temperament of the people, for example, has been conditioned historically by Texas drovers moving cattle to railheads in Kansas, migrants headed for farms or mines farther west, and builders of great transcontinental railroads and more recently of interstate highways. For such persons the Great Plains have been a place to move through rather than to. Moreover, tourists, suitcase farmers, migrant laborers, and combine crews have imprinted the region with nomadism. Billboards, truck stops, motels, and fast-food restaurants testify to the dominance of great space without centers. Moreover, the cowboy image, symbolic of past and present, has become transcendent in Great Plains culture as western garb, rodeos, "frontier day" celebrations, and the widespread ownership of horses demonstrate. Finally, Great Plainsmen have become addicted to what Mather calls megalophilia—a passion for bigness. Texans in particular are promulgators of a distinctive Great Plains culture characterized by preoccupation with innovation on a grand scale ranging from the world's biggest drive-in theater to immense cattle ranches and feedlots.[30]

Mather makes the additional point, almost in passing, that most students of the Great Plains have ignored its culture because of self-imposed restrictions. They fetter themselves with statistical concepts and market psychology, asserts Mather; if they could free themselves, for example, from the limitations of visual perception and listen to the distinctive sounds and smells of the region they would more readily perceive the uniqueness of Great Plains culture.[31]

To environmentalists like Webb, the question of place or region is paramount; to culturalists like Berkhofer, that which people brought to a place or region is most important. In the former view, the validity of studying the Great Plains as a region with more or less uniform characteristics is taken for granted; in the latter, the unity of the Great Plains is almost inconsequential, since such topics as railroad development, the immigration of ethnic groups, the cattle industry, or architectural forms are studied with only secondary reference to place. It would be a mistake, however, to draw too heavy a line between the two conceptual structures because they are subject to effective synthesis in the hands of a skilled analyst, as Donald W. Meinig illustrates in his *Imperial Texas: An Interpretive Essay in Cultural Geography,* published in 1969. His purpose is to show how Texas, both "a distinct culture area" and "an autonomous functional region," evolved historically from an early simple framework to its present complexity—a neat blend of Berkhofer's space, time, and culture. Meinig's concern for culture leads him to emphasize who the people of Texas are, "where they came from, where they settled, and how they are proportioned one to another and from place to place." His concern for spatial relationships leads to emphases "upon strategies of territorial organizations, how areas have been brought into focus, connected to another, and bound up into larger networks of circulation." Both in turn are applied to "the successive layers of Texas history." Thus the uniqueness of Texas history is interpreted as emerging from the confluence of environmental and cultural factors. What distinguishes Meinig's view from that of the environmentalists is the working assumption that race, ethnicity, language, religion, and custom continue to identify and separate Americans in fundamental ways and that the Texas environment, itself highly varied, has not produced a composite or homogenized Texan, popular lore to the contrary.[32]

The twelve essays included in this volume demonstrate that both the environmentalist and culturalist points of view continue to have vitality and that it is possible to integrate the two successfully. How one's essay is to be organized—spatially, temporally, or culturally—depends upon the question being asked. For some contributors the Great Plains is an environment that strongly influenced human behavior and modified it in important ways. For others the Great Plains is merely the place where the cultural phenomena under study occurred. Each scholar employs a methodology that is appropriate to his inquiry and none debates the validity of the Great Plains as an organizing concept.

In the initial essay, Waldo Wedel, an anthropologist, approaches his topic—cultural adaptations in the Republican River basin of Colorado, Nebraska, and Kansas—in the manner of the environmentalists. First he establishes the spatial and temporal limits of his investigation and then, beginning with the earliest known inhabitants of the area, he traces changes in the ways of life of mammoth-hunting societies of more than twelve thousand years ago, through forager groups, to horticultural communities that began to occupy the valley a thousand years ago. Lacking the technology to surmount unfavorable environmental conditions, prehistoric inhabitants were entirely dependent upon the plant and animal life of the valley. Climatic fluctuations account for most of the changes in their way of life, but with the advent of Woodland culture about two thousand years ago, social and technological skills were introduced from the east that led to a village tradition. Subsequently horticulture was supplemented by seasonal bison hunts. Wedel concludes his account with the changes wrought by the arrival of white culture in the area.

The second essay, by G. Malcolm Lewis, a geographer, illustrates Berkhofer's point that culture as understood in modern social theory filters perceptions of reality and that culture, rather than space, should serve as the starting point for the study of a frontier. Lewis first draws on psychophysiology to show how varied and selective human perceptions of stimuli may be. He then reviews the various ways in which Indians and early explorers of the eighteenth century cognized the Great Plains, how the region acquired its name, and what images were associated with this appellation in more recent times, especially in the nineteenth century.

The problem of environmental cognition is developed further by Bradley Baltensperger, a geographer, in his study of late-nineteenth-century agricultural adaptation in the Republican River valley, the same general area studied by Waldo Wedel. Baltensperger analyzes first the origins of migrants into the area in order to determine the character of their previous farming experience and, second, the preconceptions the settlers had about the Great Plains region and its agricultural possibilities. Although the earliest farmers, who had experienced the drought of the mid-1870s, diversified their crops in order to survive, the second wave of migrants arrived in a period of ample rainfall and, influenced by boomer literature and the slogan "rain follows the plow," relied excessively on crops of corn. By the end of the devastating dry cycle of the 1890s, farmers of the Republican River valley had abandoned concepts of weather modification and had begun experiments with irrigation and dry-farming techniques. It was a case, as Kraenzel put it, of "adapt or get out."

Ever since the 1880s the Great Plains has produced substantial agricultural surpluses for the world market. Naturally the prices farmers received were determined partly by conditions external to the region. Questions of agricultural income and government support during times of environmental and economic adversity have inevitably dominated much of the political life of the plains. In his study of Nebraska Populism, David S. Trask, a historian, notes that the third-party movement was strongest in counties located along the eastern edge of the Great Plains, an area in which agricultural practice was often inappropriate for the marginal amounts of rain that could be expected there. Trask specifically links the Populist movement to the effort of farmers to sustain a corn-hog operation in parts of Nebraska where the climate rendered it unsuitable. During the 1890s, Trask shows, farmers in the Populist belt made an accommodation to the environment by increasing their production of wheat. Populism as an expression of agrarian discontent disappeared accordingly. Trask also shows that ethnocultural issues such as prohibition, which were entirely unrelated to questions of environment, also influenced the agrarian political reform movement of the 1890s.

At the same time that the Populists were advocating political solutions to the problems of farmers in the transitional area between the humid East and arid West, a group of propagandists advanced irrigation as the key to development in the Great Plains. Timothy Rickard, a geographer, analyzes these ideas and explains their fate. He describes how these men, in their enthusiasm, enlarged the area requiring irrigation eastward to the 97th meridian, denigrated dry-farming techniques along with rain-making schemes, rejected ranching as wasteful of the region's resources, and projected an image of the Great Plains as a potentially rich, heavily populated Western Empire. In effect, the irrigationists urged an accommodation so extreme that it was unrealistic in terms of the water, land, and technology available at the time. Hence, as memories of the drought of the 1890s faded, irrigationist propaganda ceased and dry-farming methods won wide acceptance on the Great Plains early in the twentieth century.

Among the essays of this volume that best illustrate the culturalist point of view is John Hudson's study of the development of country towns on the Great Plains. Hudson, a geographer, shows that the characteristics that distinguish these communities from their eastern counterparts were due to time of settlement as much as to environmental forces. "The later the settlement," he writes, "the larger the accumulated stock of material and nonmaterial cultural traits that are of potential importance." The internal geography of these towns and their functions, number, and spacing emerged from the special circumstances of settlement in the late nineteenth and early twentieth centuries, of which the technology of transportation was most important. Town life was strongly influenced by the standardization in American business practice, manufactured goods, and buildings that had occurred by the time most plains towns were founded. Standardization reached its fullest development in the architecture of the railroad depot, which on the plains replaced the courthouse as the focal point of the country town.

Roger Grant, a historian, details the origin and development of the standardized railroad station as an architectural form. Although the designs of these structures were obviously imports brought to the region from the eastern railroad headquarters, they also were outstanding examples of architectural adaptations to the Great Plains environment. The cheaply constructed, stylistically sterile buildings were centers of town activity. The combination freight and passenger depot of wooden construction with living quarters for the agent was especially distinctive to the region because the railroads were usually constructed before the area served was settled. It was only on the Great Plains that railroad companies made extensive use of prefabricated, portable depots.

The essay by Douglas Hurt, a historian, is clearly in the environmentalist tradition of Malin and Kraenzel. Hurt describes how farmers of the Great Plains tried to protect their land from severe drought and destructive winds during the 1930s. During the previous two decades farmers had violated the ecological balance of the area by cultivating marginal lands; they retained inappropriate agricultural practices brought to the region from the East; and they abandoned practices capable of checking blowing soil that had been known to them for several decades. With the advent of Dust Bowl conditions in 1932 farmers either had to adjust or get out. Hurt then reviews the agricultural technology that farmers, encouraged by government agencies, employed to cope with wind erosion—methods including the use of farm implements such as listers and harrows, terracing and contour plowing, and the revegetation of plowed land with native grasses.

Leslie Hewes, a geographer, returns to the problem of harmonizing agricultural practice with environmental conditions that concerned James Malin. In his essay on agricultural risk in the modern era, Hewes makes imaginative use of the rates charged by insurance companies to measure the hazards perceived for specific areas within the Great Plains. Significant differences exist within the area; the

100th meridian generally serves as a warning line from Kansas southward. In order to reduce risk, farmers have adopted a variety of interrelated practices, especially summer fallow, protective covers of crop residue, and alternating strips of crops and fallow. In general, farmers have adjusted well to the physical conditions of the Great Plains, but important ecological imbalances remain, manifested in continued high-risk farming in the Dust Bowl, saline seep on fallowed land in the northern plains, and excessive use of underground water resources in the central and southern plains.

The contribution of historian Gilbert Fite is in the environmentalist tradition of Webb and Kraenzel. After surveying the cycles of hope and despair that have been associated with alternating periods of abundant rainfall and severe drought, Fite illustrates how people of the plains have adapted their agricultural practices, governmental relationships, and institutional arrangements to environmental realities. Like Hewes, Fite believes that they have adjusted reasonably well, even though modifications are made reluctantly and only when forced by crisis and necessity. These adaptations, however, have caused an increase in farm size, a corresponding decrease in population, and thereby new and severe problems in local government, education, health care, and highways. Since the 1930s the federal government has provided important help through relief payments, reclamation programs, military installations, and farm stabilization and conservation programs, but the Great Plains will continue to produce raw materials and retain its "colonial status" in relation to the rest of the United States. As pressure for institutional change increases, appropriate adjustments are likely to be made.

Mary Hargreaves, a historian, examines the impact of sparse population on Great Plains institutions, a topic introduced in the preceding essay by Gilbert Fite. Throughout its recent history, Hargreaves shows, Great Plains society has had to adjust to changing spatial relationships. Like Roger Grant, she illustrates the interplay of environmental and cultural forces. The geographic characteristics of the plains, independent of technology, have dictated a farm size much larger than eastern norms. But this tendency has been immensely strengthened by the subsequent introduction of automobiles, trucks, and air travel, as well as sophisticated farm machinery. Sidewalk and suitcase farming has long since become the dominant pattern in some areas of the High Plains. Hargreaves details the disruption of established institutions that has resulted from decreasing population and changing residential patterns. Although space, rather than time or culture as defined by Berkhofer, is her organizing concept, she is not concerned with establishing the spatial unity of the plains, as Webb was. Her analysis is in some respects a postscript to Kraenzel, although she does not outline regional solutions to the problem of low-density population.

Changes in the location and size of population are central to the essays by both Fite and Hargreaves. Glen Fuguitt, a rural sociologist, studies city and village population trends since 1950. In contrast to John Hudson's essay, which treats town formation and development, Fuguitt's analysis concerns patterns since 1950 only. He notes that since most plains towns were established to serve an agricultural population of greater density than prevails today, they are declining at extremely high rates compared to towns in other parts of the nation. Even though the rate of decline has been slowed since 1970, Fuguitt reports, loss of population and an increasingly aged population require that planning for the future of these communities must be undertaken so that appropriate adjustments may be made in institutional structures and functions.

Taken collectively, these contributions to our knowledge and understanding of the Great Plains reveal that, ever since the earliest human habitations in the region, environmental forces have compelled men to adjust their ways to climatic changes, topography, and locational relationships. At the same time, cultural traits, imported in migrant streams, frequently survived in unfamiliar and sometimes uncongenial environments. Prehistoric inhabitants had few options compared to modern society, which has developed complex technologies that have greatly enlarged the range and choice of possible behaviors. The adjustments of the past century have generally been successful, though in times of ample rainfall memories have been unfortunately short and practices often wasteful. Although none of the essayists presumes to predict the future, it seems clear that periods of severe climatic and economic distress will occur and that yet unknown accommodations will have to be made, especially if water resources are depleted and if drought exceeds anything so far experienced in the modern era.

Notes

1. John Wesley Powell, *Report on the Lands of the Arid Region of the United States*, 45th Cong., 2d sess., House Executive Document 73, serial 1805 (Washington, D.C.: Government Printing Office, 1878). Wallace Stegner has produced a modern edition published by Harvard University Press in 1962. For the

political and scientific context of the report, see Stegner's biography of Powell, *Beyond the Hundredth Meridian* (Boston: Houghton Mifflin, 1953), pp. 202–42. For others among Powell's contemporaries who identified the insufficiency of rainfall for agriculture on the Great Plains, see Walter M. Kollmorgen, "The Woodman's Assaults on the Domain of the Cattleman," *Annals of the Association of American Geographers* 59 (June 1969): 224.

2. Powell, *Report*, pp. 2–4.

3. The classic regionalist study is Howard W. Odum and Harry E. Moore, *American Regionalism: A Cultural-Historical Approach to National Integration* (New York: Holt, 1938). An effective recent study is Raymond D. Gastil, *Cultural Regions of the United States* (Seattle: University of Washington Press, 1975), but see also Wilbur Zelinsky, *The Cultural Geography of the United States* (Englewood Cliffs, N. J.: Prentice-Hall, 1973), Daniel Elazar, *American Federalism: A View from the States* (New York: Crowell, 1966), and Carle C. Zimmerman, "The Great Plains as a Region," in *Symposium on the Great Plains of North America*, ed. Carle E. Zimmerman and Seth Russell (Fargo: North Dakota Institute for Regional Studies, 1967), pp. 3–9. No effort is made in the pages that follow to provide a comprehensive bibliography of Great Plains studies. I have selected a small number of books and articles that seem to have special importance for studying the interplay of environment and culture in the Great Plains region.

4. Walter Prescott Webb, *The Great Plains* (Boston: Ginn, 1931); Gregory M. Tobin, *The Making of a History: Walter Prescott Webb and "The Great Plains"* (Austin: University of Texas Press, 1976), pp. 87-96.

5. Webb, *Great Plains*, p. 9.

6. Ibid., pp. 507, 9, 8.

7. Ibid., pp. 140f. Cf. Frederick Jackson Turner, "The Significance of the Frontier in American History," in *The Frontier in American History* (reprint ed., New York: Holt, Rinehart and Winston, 1962), p. 12.

8. David J. Wishart, "The Changing Position of the Frontier of Settlement on the Eastern Margins of the Central and Northern Great Plains, 1854–1890," *Professional Geographer* 21 (May 1969): 153-57. See also Fred A. Shannon, *The Farmer's Last Frontier: Agriculture, 1860-1897* (New York: Holt, Rinehart and Winston, 1945), especially chapter 2, "Agricultural Settlement in New Areas," pp. 26-50.

9. Tobin, *Making of a History*, pp. 110f., 116-26; Fred A. Shannon, *An Appraisal of Walter Prescott Webb's "The Great Plains"* (New York: Social Science Research Council, 1940), p. 12 and passim. John W. Caughey wrote a brief rejoinder to Shannon in defense of Webb, *Mississippi Valley Historical Review* 27 (December 1940): 442–44.

10. James C. Malin, *The Grassland of North America: Prolegomena to Its History* (Lawrence, Kans.: published by the author, 1947), p. 154; reprinted with addenda by Peter Smith, Gloucester, Mass., 1967.

11. Malin, *Grassland*, pp. 163, 265. See also Robert G. Bell, "James C. Malin and the Grasslands of North America," *Agricultural History* 46 (July

1972): 414-24, and Thomas H. LeDuc, "An Ecological Interpretation of Grasslands History: The Works of James C. Malin as Historian and as Critic of Historians," *Nebraska History* 31 (September 1950): 226-33. LeDuc shows that Malin's work generally is integrated by time relationships; but this is not true of *The Grassland of North America.*

12. Malin, *Grassland,* p. 266.

13. Carl F. Kraenzel, *The Great Plains in Transition* (Norman: University of Oklahoma Press, 1955), p. 6.

14. Ibid., p. 165.

15. Ibid., p. 283 and especially chapter 21.

16. Ibid., p. 8.

17. Ibid., pp. 125f.

18. Ibid., p. 285. Scholars in various disciplines continue to find the environmentalist approach to the problems of the Great Plains to be useful. As an outstanding example, see the volume by Howard W. Ottoson and his colleagues, *Land and People of the Northern Plains Transition Area* (Lincoln: University of Nebraska Press, 1966). Another excellent contribution is Leslie Hewes, *The Suitcase Farming Frontier: A Study in the Historical Geography of the Central Great Plains* (Lincoln: University of Nebraska Press, 1973), which treats nonresident wheat farming in western Kansas and eastern Colorado.

19. As examples, see Fred Kniffen, "Folk Housing: Key to Diffusion," *Annals of the Association of American Geographers* 55 (December 1965): 549-77; Wilbur Zelinsky, *The Cultural Geography of the United States* (Englewood Cliffs, N. J.: Prentice-Hall, 1973); idem, "An Approach to the Religious Geography of the United States," *Annals of the Association of American Geographers* 51 (June 1961): 139-93; John Hudson, "Two Dakota Homestead Frontiers," ibid. 63 (December 1973): 442-62; idem, "Migration to an American Frontier," ibid. 66 (June 1976): 242-65; Henry Glassie, *Pattern in the Material Folk Culture of the Eastern United States* (Philadelphia: University of Pennsylvania Press, 1968).

20. To illustrate, in Gastil's recent book the Great Plains are not identified as a separate region and are accorded less than three pages, interestingly enough, as a district within the Rocky Mountain region (Gastil, *Cultural Regions,* pp. 234-36).

21. Earl Pomeroy, "Toward a Reorientation of Western History: Continuity and Environment," *Mississippi Valley Historical Review* 41 (March 1955): 581.

22. Cf. Webb: "The innovations of the Great Plains are more remarkable than the survivals" (*Great Plains,* p. 510).

23. Among Pomeroy's works are *The Territories and the United States, 1861-1890* (Philadelphia: University of Pennsylvania Press, 1947; *In Search of the Golden West: The Tourist in Western America* (New York: Knopf, 1957); and *The Pacific Slope* (New York: Knopf, 1965). See also Gene M. Gressley, *Bankers and Cattlemen* (New York: Knopf, 1966). Gressley has also edited a volume of essays that are illustrative of this point of view entitled *The American*

West: A Reorientation (Laramie: University of Wyoming, 1966). For a useful historiographical review, see Harry N. Scheiber, "Turner's Legacy and the Search for a Reorientation of Western History," *New Mexico Historical Review* 44 (July 1969): 231–48. For a recent article in this category by a geographer, see David Wishart, "The Fur Trade of the West, 1807–1840," in David H. Miller and Jerome O. Steffen, eds., *The Frontier: Comparative Studies* (Norman: University of Oklahoma Press, 1977), pp. 161–200.

24. Cf. Webb: "In history the differences are more important than the similarities. When one makes a comparative study of the section, the dominant truth which emerges is expressed in the word *contrast*" (*Great Plains,* p. 507).

25. Webb, for example, asserted that "land is the matrix out of which culture grows" (Tobin, *Making of a History,* p. 151, n. 21).

26. Robert Berkhofer, Jr., "Space, Time, Culture, and the New Frontier," *Agricultural History* 38 (January 1964): 25. Geographers have had a long-standing interest in the role of culture in the history of specific areas. Among the earliest exponents of cultural geography were Paul Vidal de la Blache and Lucien Febvre. See the latter's *A Geographical Introduction to History* (New York: Knopf, 1925) or, more briefly, Carl Sauer, "Foreword to Historical Geography," *Annals of the Association of American Geographers* 31 (March 1941): 1–24.

27. Berkhofer, "Space, Time, Culture," p. 24.

28. Ibid., p. 29.

29. Ibid., p. 30.

30. E. Cotton Mather, "The American Great Plains," *Annals of the Association of American Geographers* 62 (June 1972): 237–57.

31. Ibid., p. 246, n. 7.

32. Donald W. Meinig, *Imperial Texas: An Interpretive Essay in Cultural Geography* (Austin: University of Texas Press, 1969), pp. 7, 8, 17, 121–24. Since the mid-1960s a variety of materials on the Great Plains have been published that blend, with varying degrees of success, cultural and environmental variables. One of the most important is a volume of essays edited by Brian Blouet and Merlin Lawson, *Images of the Plains: The Role of Human Nature in Settlement* (Lincoln: University of Nebraska Press, 1975). See also Terry G. Jordan, *German Seed in Texas Soil: Immigrant Farmers in Nineteenth-Century Texas* (Austin: University of Texas Press, 1966); Robert R. Dykstra, *The Cattle Towns* (New York: Knopf, 1968); Frederick C. Luebke, *Immigrants and Politics: The Germans of Nebraska, 1880-1900* (Lincoln: University of Nebraska Press, 1969); and David Wishart, "Cultures in Cooperation and Conflict: Indians in the Fur Trade on the Northern Great Plains, 1807–1840," *Journal of Historical Geography* 2 (1976): 311–28.

Holocene Cultural Adaptations in the Republican River Basin

Waldo R. Wedel

The spatial setting from which the principal data for this study have been drawn is an area of some twenty-six thousand square miles, centering on the 100th meridian west and on latitude 40° north (fig. 1). The time span is roughly the last fifteen thousand years, beginning with the waning Pleistocene and continuing upward to the historic present. Within these temporal and spatial limits, which may be transgressed from time to time in the interest of clarity or comparison, there occurred a series of cultural events whose sequence, duration, and relationships to the contemporary environmental setting have engaged the attention of archeologists for half a century. In broadest outline, these events involved a slow progression from heavy reliance by man on the specialized hunting of big game of species now extinct through a forager stage to settled maize-growing communities whose latest representatives were the

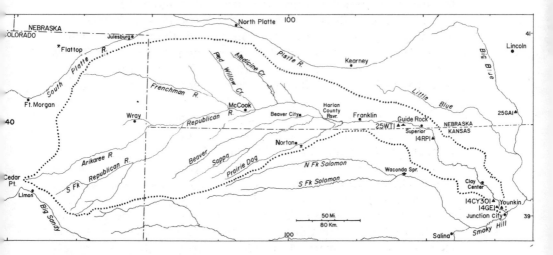

Figure 1. Map of Republican River Basin (heavy dotted line), Showing Modern Towns (solid circles) and Archeological Features

1

Indians met by the invading Europeans and Americans. The nature of these changes and the climatic fluctuations that may have been in large part responsible for them are the subject of this paper.

Our knowledge, as is ever the case with the data of archeology, is fragmentary and one-sided. The events of prehistory are reconstructed by the archeologist from bits of stone, bone, and other materials, from house structures and skeletons, and from other debris left in relatively meager quantities in and on the streamside terraces and around the upland ponds by people who had no ability to make written records. So much more has been lost than remains!

We are confronted, in truth, with more questions than answers. Still, it seems increasingly apparent already that the human prehistory of the Republican River drainage, with all its shadowy corners and blank spots, is probably synoptic of the story of native man in a much larger portion of the North American Great Plains. Even as a synopsis, there is far more information at hand than can be adequately treated here, but our survey will indicate, I hope, the direction in which archeologists are moving and what they are learning about the human experience during some thousands of years before the white man arrived on the scene.

In approaching this material, I shall first review the environmental setting in some detail, since it bears directly on man's activities. The human adaptations to that setting, insofar as archeologists and their coworkers have interpreted them, will then be reviewed in historical perspective—not so much in terms of the several named cultural complexes by which the specialists handle their data but rather in terms of the subsistence economies or lifeways or traditions we can recognize. By tradition I mean a distinctive way of life, traceable through a long period of time, varying somewhat in details from time to time or from place to place but with a basic overall consistency throughout. Radiocarbon or other dates are used where available to provide guidance, not absolute time limits. Between traditions there are only transitions, not sharp breaks.

The Republican River, as Parker pointed out, is "of the plains."[1] It heads far from the Rocky Mountains, on the high tablelands of northeastern Colorado. Its principal headwaters—the South Fork and the Arickaree—both rise in Lincoln County, respectively east and north of Limon, and trend generally northeastward in shallow valleys ten to twenty miles apart. At Haigler, Nebraska, the Arickaree joins the North Fork some thirty miles from its source ten or twelve miles southwest of Wray, Colorado, to form the Republican; less than thirty miles to the east, the South Fork enters at Benkelman. Fed by Frenchman, Red Willow, Medicine, and many lesser creeks from the north and Beaver, Sappa, and Prairie Dog creeks from the south, the Republican then pursues an easterly course through southern Nebraska to Superior, where it turns southward into Kansas to join the Smoky Hill River at Junction City and thus form the Kansas (Kaw) River.

East to west, the Republican basin measures some 360 miles air-line. In elevation, it declines from 6,000 feet m.s.l. at Cedar Point, where the Arickaree heads, to 1,100 feet m.s.l. at Junction City. Main river distances approximate 150 miles in Colorado, 250 miles in Nebraska, and less than 200 in Kansas. Of the area drained, 40 percent is in Nebraska; the remainder is almost equally divided between Colorado and Kansas. The 1970 census counted in the Republican basin about 175,000 people, largely an agricultural population engaged in stock raising, cultivation of cereal crops, and supporting activities.

Around the headwaters of the Republican River, the climate is semiarid, with annual precipitation averaging approximately fourteen inches. Eastward there is a rise in rainfall of about one inch for every twenty miles, so that at Junction City the annual average approaches thirty-two inches. Throughout, most of this falls during the crop-growing season; but west of the 100th meridian, sometimes regarded as the line separating the arid west from the humid east,[2] maize growing without irrigation is an increasingly uncertain venture. Hot, dry summers, cold, dry winters, with frequent unpredictable and often wide short- and long-term fluctuations in the precipitation pattern, and strong wind movement, are notable characteristics of the setting that directly affect man's welfare in the region. Temperature maxima of 110° F. and minima of −25° F. have been recorded in every county in the basin; the extreme recorded temperatures basin-wide are 118° F. and −38° F.

Native vegetation, as generally throughout the Great Plains, consisted originally of grasses, with trees limited to narrow belts of gallery forest along the stream valleys.[3] The short grasses (blue grama and buffalo) typical of the western steppe in Colorado gave way in the sandy areas north of the Arickaree and east to the Medicine Creek basin to sand sage and bluestem. Prickly pear and yucca are locally abundant. Farther east, in northern Kansas and southern Nebraska, wheatgrass, needlegrass, and bluestem occurred in varying proportions, finally shading into tall-grass prairies at the end of the basin.

The floodplain forest consisting of cottonwood, willow, elm, ash, and box elder is an extension of the eastern oak-hickory forest. Underbrush and vines, including woodbine and wild grape, are often heavy along stream banks. Stands become progressively thinner and the trees smaller as they ascend the Republican. Yellow pine and red cedar formerly grew along the south rim of the valley; the former has long since been cut away by early settlers, but juniper still flourishes from Franklin County, Nebraska, westward. The hardwood forests substantially end at about 101° west longitude except for scattered open stands of cottonwood and willow that have returned to the Colorado valleys in the past half century. West of the 100th meridian, the occasional development of "big timers"—extensive concentrations of large cottonwoods, good grass, and strong springs—at certain localities to which Indians and bison alike retired during hard winters, are a notable feature.[4]

Although itself of secondary import as a cross-country thoroughfare in the days of westward expansion by the white man, especially by comparison with the Platte Valley to the north or the Smoky Hill and Arkansas valleys to the south, the Republican had several notable advantages for residence from the standpoint of native man. For one thing, throughout much of its course, it was exceptionally well supplied with good water.[5] In Colorado, its valleys are cut mostly in porous Tertiary and Quaternary deposits; in Nebraska, they have been deepened into the impervious Cretaceous beds. The Tertiary materials include the Ogallala formation, long recognized as one of the nation's outstanding aquifers. Its waters are collected from precipitation in the plains and sandhills north of the Republican, and as underflow from the Platte River. The accumulated groundwaters tend to move south and southeast, with the general slope of the land surface, appearing as springs and seeps wherever the underlying impervious bedrock forces the water to the surface along the valley margins. Springs are, or formerly were, abundant and strong all along the north side of the Republican in Nebraska, particularly at and near the heads of the tributaries, long and short, that enter at intervals of a few miles.[6] Other fine springs were scattered along the upper reaches in Colorado, west on the South Fork to the vicinity of Flagler at 103° west longitude, and on the Arickaree; but over much of this westerly region, the surface flow diminishes sharply or disappears entirely into the deep, sandy beds during the heat of midsummer. Alternate dry and running stretches are characteristic of many of these watercourses, and this behavior is enhanced today by the greatly intensified use of pump and reservoir irrigation. By withdrawing groundwater in marked excess of its recharge rate,[7] irrigation in the past decade or two has significantly lowered the water table to the point where many springs are dried up or run at a greatly reduced volume, and there is only intermittent stream flow even during the nonirrigation season.

Away from the streams and associated springs, surface water was available to native man only in the innumerable undrained ponds (widely termed "buffalo wallows") scattered freely over the uplands. A notable characteristic of the High Plains, they occur by the thousands, "as many as 20 per square mile in Kit Carson County [Colorado]."[8] Usually dry except after heavy rains, they range in size from a few tens to several thousands of yards; the larger and deeper ones may form more or less permanent ponds and lakes. These, as Frémont and Bryan reported, were favorite spots for bison, attracted to their grassy margins by the lush grass, and for waterfowl, either nesting or gathering for seasonal migrations.[9] That these were major foci of interest to hunting peoples, afoot or ahorse, over a very long period of time is indicated by recent finds along their margins of bones of mammoth, native horses, camels, peccaries, and other now extinct fauna, unmistakably butchered, beside the ancient waterholes where thirsty, sick, injured, aged, or dying animals became particularly vulnerable to the onslaughts of that master predator—man.

Besides the bison for which the Republican country was so renowned in the nineteenth century, there was also an abundance of pronghorn, elk, deer, bear, wolf, beaver, and other, lesser fur bearers. Grouse and prairie chicken swarmed the region. Ponds and streams sheltered resident waterfowl, easily harvested during the flightless molting period from June to August, and migrating species greatly increased the potential supply. The valley bottoms and adjacent uplands could also provide a wide variety of wild plant foods, among them the prairie turnip in May and June, ground bean, ground nut, sunflower and Jerusalem artichoke, bush morning glory, and prickly pear. Wild plums and chokecherries could be gathered in season during the summer.

Mineral resources were there, too. Of prime importance in the manufacture of chipped stone implements—points, hide scrapers, knives, and so on—was the distinctive yellow to brown, and sometimes red, green, or black, Graham jasper.[10] Often referred to as Alma or Republican River or Smoky Hill jasper, it was available in the upper beds—the Smoky Hill chalk—of the Cretaceous Niobrara formation. As laminae or nodules, of widely varying quality for chipping, this stone is found on many of the small creeks tributary to the Republican in Nebraska from Webster County west as far as McCook, north along Medicine Creek and its tributaries, and south to Sappa, Beaver, and Prairie Dog creeks. At probable quarries near Norton, Kansas, the jasper is associated with a soft whitish, pinkish, to yellowish chalk suitable for pipe making or for pigment. Near

Cambridge, Nebraska, a light greenish quartzite seems to have been quarried for rougher tools. Farther downstream, in Republic and Cloud counties, Kansas, there are several salt marshes which may have been utilized by the Indians, as they were extensively by the nineteenth-century white settlers.

The Early Big Game Hunting Tradition

No date can yet be set for the beginning of man's occupancy of the Great Plains (fig. 2). Until very recently, the oldest evidence with consistent and acceptable radiocarbon dates began with the Clovis mammoth hunters at ca. 11,000–11,500 years BP (before the present), followed by the Folsom bison hunters of ca. 10,000–10,500 years BP, and these, in turn, by a succession of bison-hunting folk running up to ca. 7,000 years BP.[11] From their distinctive projectile points, the Clovis and Folsom complexes have sometimes been lumped together as Fluted Blade cultures, in contrast to the unfluted, or "lanceolate," points used by later hunters.

The "sea of grass" teeming with herds of large game animals apparently came into being as a habitat for man in the waning millennia of the last continental glaciation. As something other than the present short-grass steppe, it provided potential pasturage when the Des Moines lobe of the ice sheet still lay in central Iowa and a boreal spruce forest extended from Iowa across northeastern Kansas into Nebraska and the Dakotas.[12] In the High Plains, under a progressively drying climate but with frequent alternations of wet and dry episodes, the upland depressions were fresh-water lakes and ponds sprinkled through a lush grassland with belts of timber along the streams. It is around these fossil lakes in the Colorado plains that the earliest traces of man in the Republican Valley—and, indeed, perhaps in the Great Plains generally—have been coming to light in recent years.

Far too little is yet known about these ancient materials, for several reasons; but briefly, in deposits clearly associated with former lake sediments and in the still unidentified (Peoria?) loess underlying them, the remains of a grassland fauna including mammoth, camel, horse, peccary, dire wolf, sloth, and other forms, and showing clear evidence of butchering and of purposeful fracturing of the bones while still green in search of marrow or to get tool-making material have been unearthed recently in central Yuma County, Colorado.[13] Pointed, edged, and otherwise modified bone tools, with marked wear polish and retouch scars analogous to those on flint, have all been recognized. The apparent stacking of certain

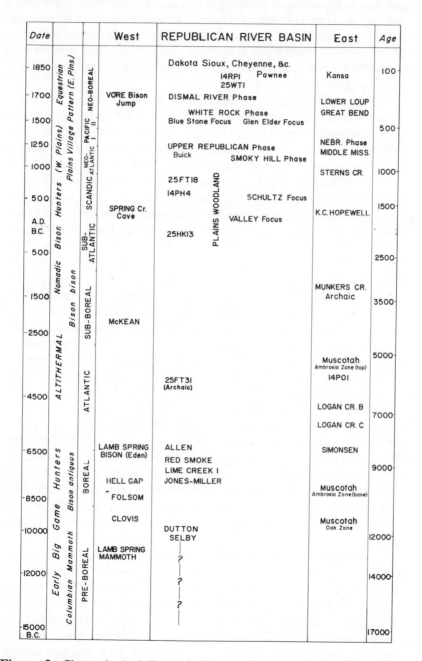

Figure 2. Chronological Relationships of Certain Republican River Basin Archeological Sites and Complexes

selected bone elements is strongly suggested. Curiously, there are as yet no stone tools or chips, no fireplaces, and the known occurrences cannot be categorized as camp or kill sites. The fractured condition of the bone, including the mammoth, suggests that the animals were totally butchered and utilized, in contrast to the limited use made of them in Clovis times.

These materials occur stratigraphically, and in several levels, well below the Weld soil, equivalent to the Brady soil farther east and to the Clovis archeological horizon. They may correlate in time with the find of a worked *Camelops* phalanx found beneath a pile of disarticulated mammoth bones at the stratified Lamb Spring site 5DA201 near Littleton, Colorado.[14] From a mammoth bone sample there came a radiocarbon date of $13,000 \pm 1,000$ years. This date has not been confirmed or corrected by additional dates; it is pre-Clovis, however, as is a date of $11,710 \pm 150$ years BP from Dutton mammoth site.

Not much is known about the lifeway of these early plains elephant hunters, either Clovis or pre-Clovis, or about the great beasts with whom their traces are usually linked in our thinking. The finds are nearly always associated with water situations of one sort or another—i.e., with springs, streams, lake margins, upland ponds and waterholes, and the like. No campsites have been identified, and the nature of the shelters, hearths, and any other structures or features these people may have used is not known. Neither are there any skeletons from which their stature and general appearance might be judged or their burial practices and religious concepts inferred. A sparse and scattered population, perhaps based on wandering family units with seasonal coalescence into larger units, may be suggested. Nor can we do more than guess at the habits, social behavior, and psychology of their proboscidean quarry, unless perhaps through guarded analogy with the modern elephants of Africa and Asia, none of which now live in the sort of unrestricted pristine wild shared thousands of years ago by the American mammoths and their hunters.

Aside from the problem of brute size, there is the fact that they probably traveled normally in herds. Thus, there is first the problem of isolating a potential victim. Then, how to kill an elephant without a high-powered rifle.[15] In historic times African natives killed isolated adult bulls in various ways, for example, using razor-sharp metal-tipped spears and working in teams, spearing the animals in the belly, or hamstringing them with metal knives. But our ancient plainsmen had no metal weapons. The task of killing an adult animal eleven or twelve feet tall and weighing up to five or six tons[16] with only a flaked stone on a stick would seem to pose some major problems. There is no evidence of traps, pitfalls, poisoning, surrounds or drives, or other special techniques or devices. Not unexpectedly, however, a considerable proportion of the animals from these kill sites were females or immature. According to Russell Graham, a paleontologist, there is some evidence that group cohesiveness may have been looser among mammoths than among modern elephants, so that under stress the adults were perhaps concerned more with their own survival and less about the safety and survival of their young. In such circumstances, it might have been easier to isolate calves and immature animals, weighing up to two and one-half or three tons by the age of ten years, which could then have been dispatched by the combined efforts of several hunters armed with stone-tipped thrusting or throwing spears. It has been pointed out, too, that the foot of the elephant is extremely sensitive to injury, and that with one foot rendered useless by a well-directed or lucky hit from a hunter, the animal is essentially immobilized and can be dispatched with relative ease. The usual association of butchered animals with water may reflect recognition by the hunters that the elephants, and indeed the associated fauna, whether sick or healthy, could be more easily found and taken at their watering places than by extended search elsewhere. The development of meat-preserving techniques, for example, drying, can probably be inferred.

Soon after 11,000 years BP, the mammoth seem to have vanished, and with them went the native horse, camel, sloth, and peccary. The hunters' meat-getting operations were then directed against the smaller but far more abundant bison. Like the mammoth earlier, the bison was doubtless taken singly or in small numbers by stalking, ambush, or other methods available to individual hunters or to small hunting parties, working around waterholes, along game trails, from blinds, perhaps with grass fires, or in deep snow. The need for water every day or two kept the herds near the ponds and lakes in the interstream areas, and here, too, the grass and forage would have been more abundant. The activities of small groups or individual hunters would have disturbed the herds little, and the killing of an animal or two as needed by such low-key methods may not have alarmed the surviving animals unduly.

It is now abundantly clear from archeology that long before the reintroduction of the horse by the Spaniards in the sixteenth and seventeenth centuries, followed by the development of the well-known surrounds and noisy drives of the mounted Indians, the natives of the plains had learned to exploit the herd instincts of the bison and their penchant for headlong flight en masse when they considered themselves endangered. The organization of cooperative hunts, carried out by a number of individuals from extended family groups and bands, resulted in the mass destruction of dozens to hundreds of animals and the harvesting of an abundance of hides, bones for tool making, and especially food for immediate feasting and for drying and storage against future needs. The techniques followed varied widely, depending on circumstances. The archeological evidence of such practices consists of bone beds representing the dismembered, broken, and tool-marked remains of the butchered victims. With these bones are associated weapon points, skinning and butchering tools, and occasionally hearths and the like. In the Northern Plains, such bone beds are commonly associated with cliffs, cut banks, or other topographic breaks over which the herds were stampeded to fall to their death in the drop. At other times, the animals were driven through converging lines of rock, turf, or bison chips into strong log corrals, there to be dispatched with bow and arrows, spears, and later guns. From at least nine or ten thousand years ago, post molds probably to be identified as medicine poles were sometimes associated with these structures.[17]

The most carefully studied of the bison kills in the Republican River basin is the Jones-Miller site south of Wray, Colorado.[18] Here the disarticulated and broken bones of at least three hundred bison, mostly cows and young animals identified as *Bison antiquus,* are believed to represent several different fall-through-winter kills. The exact methods used are unclear; if a corral was involved, no definite traces have survived, although the mold of a post analogous to the medicine post used by historic Northern Plains tribes with a pound were identified. Among the bones were numbers of projectile points, cutting, scraping, and chopping tools of stone, and bone implements, all assignable to the Hell Gap complex of approximately 10,000 years ago. The kills were of nursery herds, consisting of cows, calves, and yearlings, with very few bulls, and disarticulation was total. At fifty to one hundred animals per kill, with an average meat yield of three hundred to five hundred pounds per animal, there would have been the problem of disposing of as much as fifteen thousand to fifty thousand pounds of meat. A few dog-sized canids were also represented, along with meadow voles, fox squirrels, small lizards, snakes, frogs, and small shore and song birds. The climate at the time is believed to have been colder and moister than at present, with snowy winters and dry summer-to-fall seasons. The microfauna suggest a partially wooded river valley with well-grassed uplands. The stone used in tool making included Spanish Diggings quartzite from eastern Wyoming, Graham (Republican River) jasper from farther east in the Republican drainage, grayish purple Flat Top cherts from a large quarry site eighteen miles north of Sterling, Colorado, Bijou Basin petrified wood from central Colorado, and Alibates dolomite from the Texas Panhandle. Whether this diversity reflects widespread regional trade, the travels of a single peripatetic band on its yearly round, the coming together of several normally widely scattered bands at a central kill site, or some other mechanism is not clear.

No traces of an associated campsite have been found. Possibly brush shelters, or perhaps skin-covered lodges, were scattered along the floor of the nearby Arickaree Valley, and from these were drawn the manpower needed for the kills when circumstances were appropriate.

An important but still incompletely described group of early big game hunter campsites is located farther east, at the Lime Creek sites in Medicine Creek Reservoir, Frontier County, Nebraska.[19] Relatively permanent or frequently reoccupied hunting and gathering camps seem to be indicated, but there is no evidence of communal mass kills. In addition to bison, there are remains of a wide range of large and small plains animals, including reptiles, amphibians, and birds. Burned nests of the mud dauber wasp were found in the debris; apparently broken in pursuit of the larvae for food, these suggest a summertime (May to September) residence, though they do not exclude occupation at other seasons. Leaf-shaped projectile points, grinding stones, eyeletted bone needles, crude bone awls, and other items reflect an economy—or at least a task orientation—aimed at meat getting, skin working, and the maintenance of a general hunting-gathering subsistence economy.

If mass kills were customary at Lime Creek, no evidence of the fact has been reported. It seems likely that the animals here were ambushed singly or in small bunches as they came to the springs and pools along the creeks or perhaps fed afterward in the lush meadows and streamside grassy flats. Historical documents briefly but cogently describing bison hunting by sixteenth-century foot Indians in the southern Plains, as witnessed by early Spanish exploring expeditions, abundantly testify to the relative ease with which meat could be obtained by stealth rather than by the "brass band" techniques of the later horse-riding Indians with firearms.

Note should be taken of the wide and varied assortment of smaller animals revealed by the bone refuse at the more completely worked early big game hunter sites. Here is clear evidence that the heavy predominance of mammoth or giant bison bones commonly noted at the ancient kill sites in the first half of the century is a one-sided glimpse into the native subsistence economy. At stations other than these communal kills, where other necessary activities were carried on, the small game includes birds, reptiles, and amphibians as well. One suspects that, were preservation conditions more favorable, appropriate recovery techniques might also disclose a wide range of roots, tubers, fruits, seeds, and other vegetal products that must certainly have been utilized in season or under proper circumstances. In this light, aside from the specialized hunting of large mammals by single hunters or cooperatively, the early big game hunters were pursuing an essentially Archaic, or forager, life-style in which the edible resources of every ecological niche within reach were drawn upon as needed. The communal hunts, besides periodically providing massive amounts of meat and hides, doubtless served an important social function also as integrative devices by which the individual foraging family groups, perhaps wide-ranging at other times, came together on occasion for ritual, mate-getting, and other purposes.

The Archaic Foragers

The archeological record shows a striking dearth of sites between ca. 5000 and 2000 B.C. throughout much of the western plains region, though they do occur in the mountain front zone to the west and in the eastern plains. This interval of limited occupancy by man, variously dated by different observers and strongly doubted by some, corresponds to the Altithermal. This was a period of inferred higher aridity and temperatures, which is thought by some to have reduced large parts of the region to near-desert conditions, greatly diminishing the vegetative cover and its carrying capacity for grazing animals, and reducing the game herds or displacing them to unaffected areas around the periphery of the stricken region.

The Altithermal is not well known in the plains. Its effects may be partially reflected in the heavy overburden of aeolian materials at the Lime Creek sites, reaching in one instance a depth of over forty feet. Surface finds of projectile points and other artifacts attributed to Archaic foragers during the Altithermal have been found in the Republican River drainage, but few sites have been studied. One that has been is the lowest of three occupation levels at the Spring Creek site 25FT31 on Red Willow Creek, Nebraska, radiocarbon dated at 3900 B.C. (M-1364). The artifacts are reportedly similar to those from Logan Creek in eastern Nebraska and Simonsen in northwestern Iowa.[20] The projectile points in all cases are side-notched, distinct from the earlier lanceolate and fluted forms and reminiscent of the eastern United States. At all sites, bison bones are abundant. Undoubtedly many other Archaic sites remain to be discovered, especially in the lower portions of the Republican Valley.[21] The bone refuse suggests that small game and, inferentially, plant foods played at least as important a role as the larger animals, which were doubtless utilized when and where available.

In the closing century or two of the pre-Christian era, discernible changes in the material culture inventory of the Central Plains Archaic hunters and foragers began to appear. Their particular nature suggests derivation from people and cultures to the east, beyond the prairie margin. These changes ushered in the Plains Woodland culture of the archeologists.[22] The basic subsistence tradition was still one of creek valley hunters and gatherers, probably living in small communities of temporary brush, bark, or skin lodges, and shifting their location from time to time as local resources were exhausted to allow them to recover. In addition, pottery appeared for the first time, as did burial of the dead in mounds, and finally, the first efforts at crop

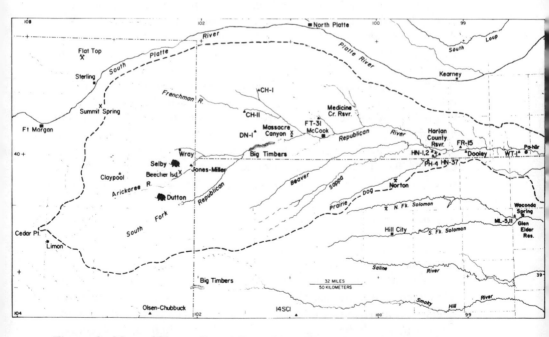

Figure 3. Map of Upper Republican River Basin (heavy broken line), Showing Certain Archeological Sites and Localities

growing in the plains. Pottery was mostly a thick utility ware, but with local variations in paste, surface finish, and other minutiae of concern mainly to archeologists. Likewise, burial methods varied greatly, from mounds in the lower Republican Valley to large communal ossuaries, or bone pits, to which were consigned the disarticulated remains of several to many corpses, often with thousands of accompanying shell disk beads, a few pendants, and other simple offerings.[23] There may have been class distinctions.

At none of the Woodland sites in the Republican River basin has evidence of horticulture been recognized, although charred maize and beans indicate its practice by contemporary Hopewellian people around Kansas City and also in eastern Nebraska Woodland sites.[24] It is possible that the Republican River groups were still relying largely or entirely on hunting and gathering. At any rate, no clearly horticultural tools of stone, bone, or other materials have yet been identified in their remains, in contrast to the situation among their immediate successors.

One other change in the archeological record has interesting implications. This is the matter of the projectile points. In Woodland times, they tend to become smaller and lighter with the passage of time, and the term *arrowhead* may be a misnomer. The bow and arrow was demonstrably preceded in North America by the spear thrower and dart or throwing spear. Of the spear thrower there is no direct evidence in the plains; but fragments have been found in rock shelters from the Big Horn basin in levels dated at ca. A.D. 350.[25] It is possible that Woodland peoples in the Republican Valley after the fifth or sixth century, if they still used the spear thrower, might have witnessed or participated in the introduction of the bow and arrow to the region. The advantages of the latter were several and significant—it was quieter and less disturbing to the quarry, easier to handle and operate in brush cover, and more accurate at a distance, and it provided more firepower for follow-up shots.

The Plains Village Tradition

By the eighth or ninth century A.D., far-reaching changes had taken place in the lifeways of the Central Plains Indians. The poorly marked and perhaps halting attempts at plant cultivation in the late Woodland economy had been replaced by a small-scale but more deeply committed sort of gardening, with special tools and a notable change in the Indians' life-style. Just where, when, or how cultivation first reached the plains is not yet clear. The practice seems to appear about the time of the Neo-Atlantic climatic episode, a period

when moist tropical air is thought by some climatologists to have
flowed into the Great Plains, encouraging the westward spread of
prairies and of corn culture at the expense of the western steppe.[26]
In any case, to the gardening peoples who followed the Woodland
hunters in the culture sequence, the designation of Plains Village
tradition has been given. Their settled way of life, with many variations through time and space, was to dominate the eastern plains
for almost a thousand years. It may be divided into an Early Village
and a Late Village period, with A.D. 1500 the approximate time of
transition.

In the Republican River basin, the Early Village period is relatively well known from extended researches in and around Harlan
and Medicine Creek reservoirs, and elsewhere in Franklin, Frontier,
and Harlan counties.[27] More limited investigations have been made at
other, widely scattered sites in Nebraska and Kansas. The sites indicate a small-village or hamlet life pattern, with square or round-
cornered rectangular earth-covered lodges scattered singly, in pairs,
or in small clusters along the banks of the secondary creeks. Houses
averaged from 150 to 600 square feet in floor area and most probably were limited to no more than five or ten persons each. It is
doubtful that many of these ill-defined communities exceeded fifty
or sixty persons, and most were probably much smaller. Small trash
heaps and storage pits were associated.

Charred maize, beans, squash, and sunflower indicate the staple
crops. The bison scapula hoe was the hallmark of this period, and the
wooden digging stick may be inferred. Probably no household tilled
more than two or three acres at most from which a yield of no more
than fifteen to twenty bushels per acre might have been expected.
Beans and cucurbits probably furnished 5–10 percent of the vegetable food. Bison were regularly utilized; as many as thirty-four other
species of large and small mammals, reptiles, and amphibians, and at
least ten species of birds have been identified from Medicine Creek
Upper Republican sites. Quantities of fresh-water mussel shells in a
few cache pits reveal another source of animal protein, but in decidedly limited amount compared to the land animals. Curved bone
fishhooks occur at most sites, with catfish and buffalo fish bones in
small numbers. The bow and arrow was the common hunting weapon;
scrapers, knives, perforators, and the like were fashioned from stone;
needles, awls, and other items from bone, all utilized in a strictly
home industry contrasting sharply with the commercially oriented
activities of the later historic fur-trade days. Much of the stonework
involved the locally available Graham jasper. The reddish to grayish
purple Flat Top flint from ancient quarries northwest of Sterling,

Colorado, some 175 miles from Medicine Creek, may have been acquired via a route along Frenchman Creek. Chalcedony, quartzite, and other materials were also in use. Shells included marine and Gulf Coast forms, as well as fresh-water species.

In the Republican Valley, the Early Village period, as represented by the Upper Republican settlements, seems to have ended soon after ca. A.D. 1250–75, though scattered radiocarbon dates continue for a century or more later. It is not yet clear why these western communities were given up—whether because of the arrival of hostile nomads in the region or on account of deteriorating climatic conditions that made maize growing increasingly difficult. The terminal dates are not far from the estimated end of the Neo-Atlantic and beginning of the Pacific I climatic episode, in which changed circulation patterns are thought to have brought cool, dry westerly air into the plains, resulting in lowered temperatures and decreased rainfall, both factors adverse to corn growing. The destination of the émigrés is also uncertain. There are good reasons to believe that the Upper Republican people were directly ancestral to the historic Pawnees, but the intermediate stages between ca. A.D. 1300 and 1550 remain undiscovered or unrecognized and the presumed transition apparently took place elsewhere than in the Republican River country.

The ability to produce food, supplementing its collection by hunting and gathering, led to increased and more stable populations, with more, larger, and longer-lived settlements whose inhabitants perhaps enjoyed a more secure and affluent lifeway than that of pre-horticultural groups in the plains. Equipped only with such rudimentary hand tools as the scapula-bladed hoe and the simple digging stick, and lacking draft animals large enough to draw soil-turning equipment, the pre-Columbian Indians limited their crop growing largely to the mellow and easily worked soils of the valley bottoms and the floodplains. Theirs was a strictly garden or horticultural technology, without known irrigation, fertilizers, or other technological adjuncts of the mechanized modern dryland farmer. All gardening and related activities were women's work.

Around most prehistoric settlements west of the Missouri River, this technology required the modification of only a few acres—perhaps no more than a third to half acre per person, or one and one-half to two acres for a family of four or five. Later, around the opening of the white contact period in the 1600s and 1700s, with the concentration of the population into large communities of hundreds or even thousands of individuals, several hundreds of acres were required, but with emphasis still on family plots and hand tools rather than field-scale operations. The nearby uplands were left unbroken, their tightly sodded surface continuing to support large numbers of bison and other plains game animals. At all times the economy was a subsistence, or kitchen, rather than a commercial one such as the white man brought in. There was probably no large-scale, long-enduring, or otherwise significant modification of the natural setting by these early native crop growers of the trans-Missouri grasslands.

Archeology has shown us what crops were grown, but tells us little about the varieties used and nothing of the methods practiced. Planting, tillage, and harvesting are unknown except as they can be guessed at from analogy with historic Pawnee methods. On their nineteenth-century reservation near Genoa, Nebraska, the hoe-using Pawnees seem seldom to have produced harvests of more than twenty-five bushels of corn per acre from their individual plots. On the Republican River one hundred to two hundred miles farther west, smaller yields would have been more likely among the thirteenth-century maize growers. Here, too, the bell-shaped storage pits in which crop surpluses were carried over from one harvest to the next seldom exceed one meter in depth and diameter, with an estimated capacity of perhaps twenty-five to thirty bushels. Among the sixteenth- and seventeenth-century Pawnees on the lower Loup and Platte rivers, storage pits reached depths and diameters of six to eight feet, with a capacity of two hundred bushels or more. By the nineteenth century, among the Pawnees with whom the Americans were coming into contact, smaller storage pits were again more characteristic. Whether these size variations reflected increasing and then declining crop yields, improved technology, or fluctuating climatic conditions is still conjectural. One supposes that the Indians on the western margin of maize growing, as along the Republican, may well have developed special deep-rooted, early maturing, or otherwise drought-resistant strains of maize to cope with the increasingly uncertain environment.

The Republican River Valley cuts through the zone where the usually ample rainfall of the cornbelt on the east declines westward to a deficiency for maize. We know little about the thirteenth-century climate, but recurrent droughts and crop shortages or failures can doubtless be inferred. The hazards may be illustrated, in oversimplified form, by table 1. Here, as a crude index, the 8-inch summer (June, July, August) isohyet is suggested as the line beyond which maize growing without irrigation or other special techniques is likely to be unrewarding. The table indicates the annual summer

Table 1
Long-Term Summer Rainfall Averages
and Frequency of Deficiencies for Selected Stations
in and around the Republican River Basin

Station	Dates of Record	No. of Years	Average June–August Rainfall (in Inches)	No. Years below 8 Inches	% Years below 8 Inches
Leavenworth, Kans.	1836–1975	139	13.26	16	12.0
Clay Center, Kans.	1902–1975	73	12.13	13	18.0
Superior, Nebr.	1879–1975	79	10.97	17	22.0
Genoa, Nebr.	1876–1975	100	10.90	25	25.0
North Loup, Nebr.	1875–1975	92	10.39	24	26.0
Beaver City, Nebr.	1882–1975	94	9.90	29	31.0
Alma, Nebr.	1896–1975	80	9.80	27	34.0
Curtis, Nebr.	1894–1975	78	9.37	32	41.0
McCook, Nebr.	1882–1975	87	8.86	40	46.0
Wauneta, Nebr.	1898–1975	76	8.55	36	47.0
Norton, Kans.	1890–1975	81	9.56	32	40.0
Scott City, Kans.	1889–1975	80	8.56	41	51.0
Julesburg, Colo.	1888–1975	72	7.30	43	60.0
Wray, Colo.	1890–1975	83	7.84	47	57.0
Yuma, Colo.	1890–1971	81	7.63	48	59.0
Limon, Colo.	1907–1975	65	6.73	45	69.0
Ft. Morgan, Colo.	1867–1975	88	5.42	77	88.0

rainfall for each of seventeen selected stations in and around the Republican River basin, the number of years of record in which the summer rainfall has been below 8 inches, and the percentage of sub-normal years. Thus, for example, the summer average at Leavenworth, Kansas, on the Missouri River is 13.26 inches and in only one year in every 8.6 is the rainfall less than 8 inches. At McCook, Nebraska, the average is 8.86 inches and nearly every other year is subnormal. At Fort Morgan, Colorado, the average is 5.42 inches and nearly nine years of every ten are subnormal. In this increasingly hostile setting may lie the explanation for the fact that the prehistoric maize growers in the Republican basin did not extend their permanent settlements or leave unmistakable signs of horticulture—tools, crop remains, and the like—west of the longitude of McCook, the approximate line at which summer rainfall drops below the 8-inch line and the chances of subnormal precipitation approach 50 percent. It may explain, too, why these people made provision to store food for a year or so ahead, against the strong probability of a short-term but crop-killing drought. I am fully aware that this point can be challenged on the perfectly valid grounds that I am applying twentieth-century figures on crop yields and climate in a commercially oriented culture to thirteenth-century conditions in a noncommercial culture about whose climatic setting we are largely in ignorance.

While the Pawnees of the fifteenth, sixteenth, and seventeenth centuries were developing and elaborating their culture elsewhere and having their first confrontations with the Euro-American invaders, other groups were occupying portions of the Republican River basin. Best known are the Apachean groups identified archeologically with the Dismal River culture.[28] Widespread in the western plains of Nebraska, Kansas, and Colorado, and showing considerable variability in many details, the Dismal River people left several important sites in the Republican drainage—for example, the Lovitt site (25CH1) on Stinking Water Creek in Chase County, Nebraska, and White Cat village (25HN37) in Harlan County, Nebraska, but none east of Franklin County and the 99th meridian. Probably descended from some of the bison-hunting dog-nomads encountered by Coronado in the Southern Plains in 1540–41, these people around A.D. 1700 were raising maize and other crops in seasonally occupied villages of semi-permanent houses at and beyond the western limits of the earlier permanent Upper Republican village range. The hunting of bison was probably the main subsistence base, with other animals and plant foods perhaps a lesser item. Bison meat, hides, and tallow were traded with the Pueblo Indians of the Rio Grande in exchange for maize, turquoise, pottery, and other goods. During the hard winters, these Plains Apaches appear to have moved west and southwest to the vicinity of the pueblos or eastward to the neighborhood of the permanent villages and food stores of the Pawnees and Wichitas. Their material culture shared much with that of the Village tribes; but the five-pole semipermanent houses and bell-shaped baking pits were distinctive in the plains. Their lifeway may be termed intermediate between that of the western nomadic bison hunters and the eastern Village Indians. It ended with the displacement of the Plains Apaches by the horse-riding Comanche invaders from the west in the first half of the eighteenth century.

Roughly contemporaneous with the Plains Apaches but perhaps slightly earlier were several sites of a little-known pottery-making complex termed the White Rock aspect.[29] To it have been attributed hunting camps in the Harlan County district and more permanent village remains in Jewell County, Kansas. No tribal identification has yet been made, and the nature of the lifeway is very imperfectly known.

The Late Village Indians are represented in the Republican River basin by several historic Pawnee communities, all of which date after the mid-eighteenth-century heyday of Pawnee culture. The Republican band, from which the river takes its name, first appears in history in a Spanish report on tribes who received presents in 1777 at Saint Louis. They are credited with 350–400 warriors, or roughly 1,600–1,800 individuals, whose main activity was hunting to provide beaver, bison, otter, and deer skins for the Saint Louis trade. In 1804, Lt. Zebulon Pike visited a village of the same band on the south bank of the Republican near present Red Cloud, Nebraska, facing down the truculent Pawnees and persuading them to replace the Spanish flag they were then flying with the Stars and Stripes. Pike reported forty-four lodges and 1,618 inhabitants, a far higher ratio of persons to houses than can be imagined for the small thirteenth-century Upper Republican houses. Archeological excavations in the burial grounds at this site, designated 25WT1 or the Hill site, have yielded English, French, Spanish, and American medals, with dates beginning as early as 1762. Located about one hundred miles overland from the mouth of Blue River, this may have been the village of the Republican Pawnees at the time of Lt. Governor Francisco Cruzat's report in 1777. In 1825–26, Jedidiah Smith spent an uncomfortable winter at a temporarily deserted Pawnee village about forty miles downstream that can almost certainly be identified with the Kansas Monument site (14RP1) in Republic County, Kansas.[30] There is at least one other probable Pawnee site (14GE1), apparently fortified as the Republic County site was, on the lower Republican River,[31] and others have been reported. All of these communities, one suspects, sustained themselves not only by gardening with maize, beans, and so on, but also with seasonal hunts twice yearly when the entire tribe abandoned the earth-lodge village and spent weeks hunting bison in the western plains. The dire straits, often verging on starvation, in which the Pawnees found themselves when the tribal bison hunt was unsuccessful indicates the heavy reliance on that food source even with their gardens. In historic times, as doubtless in the thirteenth-century days on Medicine Creek, droughts repeatedly brought distress to the Pawnees, and the stored crops seem never to have been adequate. Grasshoppers were a nineteenth-century scourge of the Pawnee gardeners, as they may have been previously to earlier gardening people.

By 1825 the Pawnees had to all intents and purposes abandoned the Republican River as village habitat, and had withdrawn northward to join their more numerous kindred on the Platte for greater security against their many enemies. Strong ties to the Republican were maintained, however. It was prime bison-hunting country as long as the Pawnees resided in Nebraska. Only five miles downstream from the Hill site, on the south bank of the river, was Pa-hŭr, "the hill that points the way," one of the five sacred places of the Pawnees.[32] Now badly defaced by road and ditch building, this landmark has given its name in anglicized form to the town of Guide Rock, Nebraska, across the river. Another shrine, Kitz-a-witz-uk, "water on a bank," lay thirty-five miles south of the Hill site at Waconda Spring on the Solomon River southeast of Cawker City, Kansas, now submerged by the waters of Glen Elder Reservoir.

The Pawnees were under the necessity of contesting for the Republican country as hunting territory with other tribes. These included their inveterate enemies, the Oglala and Brulé Sioux, as well as the Cheyennes and Arapahos, sometimes the Kiowas and Comanches, and eventually a number of eastern tribes who had been transplanted to reservations west of the Mississippi by the government. These were difficult years, made more so by the waves of white settlement moving westward up the rivers across Kansas and Nebraska, particularly after the Civil War.

Confrontations were inevitable, both intertribal and between whites and the natives. Some have become notable—or notorious. At Beecher's Island on the Arickaree, Col. George A. Forsyth and fifty-one scouts stood off a war party of nearly 1,000 Cheyenne and Sioux in September 1868. A year later, in 1869, U.S. Army troopers scattered a Cheyenne band consisting largely of Dog Soldiers at Summit Springs in Colorado. Of the intertribal encounters, probably the most notable one took place in August 1873 near present Trenton, Nebraska. Participants were a Pawnee hunting party of about 400 persons, including 150 women and children, and a 600-man war party of Oglala and Brulé Sioux. Surprised while butchering animals from a recent kill, the Pawnees lost at least 69 persons, 100 horses, and all the bison meat and hides from a month of successful hunting. Within two years of this incident, the Pawnees abandoned their lands on the Loup River and moved to Oklahoma, thus ending a stay of at least several centuries on the prairies of Nebraska and Kansas.

In this brief review, a number of interesting points have been slighted. A particularly intriguing one is the matter of aboriginal populations in prewhite days, about which a few comments seem appropriate here. The Republican basin cuts across three tribal territories as delineated by Kroeber in his discussion of population densities in early contact days.[33] The lower portion is in Kansa territory, the middle is Pawnee, the upper is Cheyenne-Arapaho. In all cases, the Republican section is but a small portion of the lands assigned to each tribe. The total population of the three tribal groups is estimated at 19,500, their combined territory at 3,916 "metric townships" (= 100 km^2), and the average density at 5 persons per "township." Adjusting these figures to the 26,000 square miles of the Republican basin, which is about 17 percent of the area assigned to the three groups by Kroeber, we get a total population of 3,315 persons for the entire basin of 675 "metric townships," or 7.8 square miles per person. This total is about 40 percent of the 1970 census figure for the city of McCook, Nebraska. For the Republican River basin, the 1970 census shows a total population of about 175,000, roughly 7 persons per square mile, or 270 per "metric township." Stated in still another way, the Kroeber-Mooney figures give the Republican basin a population shortly after its discovery of less than one-fiftieth that of the 1970 census count. That the basin at any time in prewhite days ever held a much larger population than the estimated figure of 3,315 seems to me unlikely.

Some thousands of years have passed since the mammoth provided the pièce de résistance for man in the Republican River basin, more than a century since the bison served similarly. The black angus and whiteface have replaced both. In favored spots, where advanced technology has enabled modern man to draw without stint on deep-lying underground waters which have been gathering during uncounted centuries, the maize grows with an exuberance unmatched by anything the ancient native Americans here ever dreamed of. The corn and the beef alike, of course, are designed to feed a population many times greater than that which drew on the mammoth, the bison, and the low-yielding Indian corn in the past. Were one of the thirteenth-century Upper Republican pioneers or even one of the nineteenth-century Pawnees to walk through the irrigated cornfields in Harlan or Franklin county, Nebraska, or in Republic County, Kansas, he would surely marvel at what he saw.

Our hypothetical visitor would be much less impressed if he revisited some of the springs and clear-flowing creeks from which he once drank freely and refreshingly, and which today are choked with silt, deadwood, and other debris—if indeed they still carry water! As drought returns again to the plains and signs multiply that continued uncontrolled pumping is relentlessly lowering the groundwater levels at rates in excess of the recharge, one wonders what will be man's next adaptation to the beautiful valley whose human history during the past fifteen thousand years has been briefly sketched here.

Notes

1. H. N. Parker, *Quality of the Water Supplies of Kansas*, U.S. Geological Survey Water Supply Paper no. 273 (Washington, D.C., 1911), p. 228.

2. A. L. Kroeber, *Cultural and Natural Areas of Native North America*, University of California Publications in American Archaeology and Ethnology no. 38 (Berkeley, 1939), p. 208.

3. A. W. Küchler, *Potential Natural Vegetation of the Coterminous United States*, Special Publication no. 36 (New York: American Geographical Society, 1964).

4. Waldo R. Wedel, "The High Plains and Their Utilization by the Indian," *American Antiquity* 29 (1963): 1-16.

5. Robert Hay, "Water Resources of a Portion of the Great Plains," in U.S. Geological Survey, *Sixteenth Annual Report* (1895), pt. 2, pp. 535-88; G. E. Condra, *Geology and Water Resources of the Republican River Valley and Adjacent Areas, Nebraska*, U.S. Geological Survey Water Supply Paper no. 216 (Washington, D.C., 1907).

6. Wedel, "High Plains," p. 5.

7. Arnold J. Boettcher, *Ground-Water Developments in the High Plains of Colorado*, U.S. Geological Survey Water Supply Paper no. 1819-I (Washington, D.C., 1966), p. 19; E. G. Lappala, *Changes in the Water Supply in the Upper Republican Natural Resources District, Southwest Nebraska, from 1952-75*, Open File Report 76-498 (Lincoln, Nebr.: U.S. Geological Survey, 1976).

8. Boettcher, *Ground Water Developments*, p. 14.

9. John C. Frémont, *Report of the Exploring Expedition to the Rocky Mountains in the Year 1842, and to Oregon and California in the Years 1843-44*, 28th Cong., 2d sess., House Document no. 166 (1845), p. 110; F. T. Bryan, "Explorations for a Road from Fort Riley to Bridger's Pass, 1856," *Annual Report of the War Department, 1857*, Appendix H, "Report of the Chief of Topographical Engineers," 35th Cong., 1st sess., House Executive Document no. 2, 2:469.

10. F. W. Cragin, "On the Stratigraphy of the Platte Series, or Upper Cretaceous of the Plains," *Colorado College Studies* 6 (1896):51; G. F. Carlson and C. A. Peacock, "Lithic Distribution in Nebraska," in *Lithic Source Notebook*, ed. Ronald A. Thomas (Milford, Del.: Division of Historical and Cultural Affairs, State of Delaware, 1975), p. R6.

11. C. Vance Haynes, Jr., "Fluted Projectile Points: Their Age and Dispersion," *Science* 145 (1964): 1408-13; C. Vance Haynes, Jr., *Carbon-14 Dates and Early Man in the New World*, Interim Research Report no. 9 (Tucson: Geochronology Laboratories, University of Arizona, 1965).

12. H. E. Wright, Jr., "Vegetational History of the Central Plains," in *Pleistocene and Recent Environments of the Central Great Plains,* ed. W. Dort, Jr., and J. Knox Jones, Jr. (Lawrence: University Press of Kansas, 1970), pp. 157–202.

13. Dennis J. Stanford, "Excavation of the Dutton and Selby Sites: Evidence for pre-Clovis Occupation of the Great Plains," MS, Smithsonian Institution, Washington, D.C., 1978.

14. Waldo R. Wedel, "Investigations at the Lamb Spring Site, Colorado," MS, Final Report to National Science Foundation, Project NSF-17609, 1965.

15. Sylvia K. Sikes, *The Natural History of the African Elephant* (London: Weidenfeld and Nicolson, 1971), p. 302.

16. Paul S. Martin and John E. Guilday, "A Bestiary for Pleistocene Biologists," in *Pleistocene Extinctions: The Search for a Cause,* ed. Paul S. Martin and H. E. Wright, Jr. (New Haven, Conn.: Yale University Press, 1967), p. 38.

17. Dennis J. Stanford, "The 1975 Excavations at the Jones-Miller Site, Yuma County, Colorado," *Southwestern Lore* 41 (1975): 34–38.

18. Dennis J. Stanford, "Preliminary Report of the Excavation of the Jones-Miller Hell Gap Site, Yuma County, Colorado," *Southwestern Lore* 40 (1974): 29–36; idem, "1975 Excavations," pp. 34–38.

19. Preston Holder and Joyce Wike, "The Frontier Culture Complex: A Preliminary Report on a Prehistoric Hunters' Camp in Southwestern Nebraska," *American Antiquity* 14 (1949), pt. 1, pp. 260–66; E. Mott Davis, *Archeology of the Lime Creek Site in Southwestern Nebraska,* Special Publication no. 3 (Lincoln: University of Nebraska State Museum, 1962).

20. G. A. Agogino and W. D. Frankforter, "A Paleo-Indian Bison Kill in Northwestern Iowa," *American Antiquity* 25 (1960): 414–15.

21. Thomas A. Witty, *The Woods, Avery, and Streeter Archeological Sites, Milford Reservoir, Kansas,* Anthropological Series no. 2 (Topeka: Kansas State Historical Society, 1963).

22. A. T. Hill and Marvin F. Kivett, "Woodland-like Manifestations in Nebraska," *Nebraska History* 21 (1941): 147–243; Marvin F. Kivett, *Woodland Sites in Nebraska,* Publications in Anthropology no. 1 (Lincoln: Nebraska State Historical Society, 1952); idem, "Early Ceramic Environmental Adaptations," in *Pleistocene and Recent Environments of the Central Great Plains,* ed. W. Dort and J. Knox Jones, Jr. (Lawrence: University Press of Kansas, 1970), pp. 92–102; Waldo R. Wedel, *An Introduction to Kansas Archeology,* Bureau of American Ethnology Bulletin no. 174 (Washington, D.C.: Smithsonian Institution, 1959), pp. 542–57.

23. Floyd Schultz and Albert C. Spaulding, "A Hopewellian Burial Site in the Lower Republican Valley, Kansas," *American Antiquity* 13 (1948): 306–13; Charles Eyman, "The Schultz Focus: A Plains Middle Woodland Burial Complex in Eastern Kansas" (Ph.D. diss., University of Alberta at Calgary, 1966); Marvin F. Kivett, *The Woodruff Ossuary: A Prehistoric Burial Site in Phillips County, Kansas,* Bureau of American Ethnology Bulletin no. 154 (Washington, D.C.: Smithsonian Institution, 1953), pp. 103–42.

24. Waldo R. Wedel, *Archeological Investigations in Platte and Clay Counties, Missouri,* United States National Museum Bulletin no. 183 (Washington, D.C.: Smithsonian Institution, 1943), p. 26; Kivett, *Woodland Sites in Nebraska,* p. 57.

25. George C. Frison, "Spring Creek Cave, Wyoming," *American Antiquity* 31 (1965): 81-94.

26. David A. Baerreis and Reid A. Bryson, "Climatic Episodes and the Dating of Mississippian Cultures," *Wisconsin Archeologist* n.s. 46 (1965): 203-20.

27. Marvin F. Kivett, "Archeological Investigations in Medicine Creek Reservoir, Nebraska," *American Antiquity* 14 (1949): 278-84; Waldo R. Wedel, "Contributions to the Archeology of the Upper Republican Valley," *Nebraska History* 15 (1935): 132-209; idem, *Kansas Archeology,* pp. 557-71; William D. Strong, "An Introduction to Nebraska Archeology," *Smithsonian Miscellaneous Collections* 93 (1935): 245; W. Raymond Wood, ed., "Two House Sites in the Central Plains: An Experiment in Archeology," *Plains Anthropologist* 14 (1969), memoir 6, no. 44, pt. 2; Waldo R. Wedel, "Some Observations on Two House Sites in the Central Plains: An Experiment in Archeology," *Nebraska History* 51 (1970): 225-52.

28. A. T. Hill and George Metcalf, "A Site of the Dismal River Aspect in Chase County, Nebraska," *Nebraska History* 22 (1942): 158-226; John L. Champe, "White Cat Village," *American Antiquity* 14 (1949), pt. 1, pp. 285-92; Dolores Gunnerson, "The Southern Athabascans: Their Arrival in the Southwest," *El Palacio* 63 (1956): 346-65; James H. Gunnerson, *An Introduction to Plains Apache Archeology,* Bureau of American Ethnology Bulletin no. 173 (Washington, D.C.: Smithsonian Institution, 1960), pp. 131-260; idem, "Plains Apache Archeology: A Review," *Plains Anthropologist* 13 (1968): 167-89; Wedel, *Kansas Archeology,* pp. 589-99.

29. Mary K. Rusco, *The White Rock Aspect,* Note Book no. 4 (Lincoln: Laboratory of Anthropology, University of Nebraska, 1960).

30. Louis Houck, *The Spanish Regime in Missouri,* 2 vols. (Chicago: R. R. Donnelley and Sons, 1909), 1:143; Zebulon M. Pike, *The Expeditions of Zebulon M. Pike,* ed. Elliott Coues, 3 vols. (New York: Francis P. Harper, 1895), 2:590; Waldo R. Wedel, *An Introduction to Pawnee Archeology,* Bureau of American Ethnology Bulletin no. 112 (Washington, D.C.: Smithsonian Institution, 1939), pp. 34-36; Dale L. Morgan, ed., *The West of William H. Ashley, 1822-1838* (Denver: Old West Publishing Co., 1964), p. 143.

31. Thomas A. Witty, letter to the author, March 4, 1977.

32. George B. Grinnell, *Pawnee Hero Stories and Folk-Tales* (New York: Forest and Stream Publishing Co., 1889), p. 358.

33. A. L. Kroeber, *Cultural and Natural Areas of Native North America,* map 1.

The Cognition and Communication of Former Ideas about the Great Plains

G. Malcolm Lewis

The surface of our planet is characterized by differences from place to place in both its form and material composition; spatial variations exist at each and every scale, from the whole down to the minutest part thereof. The earth's surface is nowhere homogeneous; its form and composition, the life forms and economies that it supports, and its enveloping atmosphere vary spatially in an infinitely complex, though far from random, manner. Most if not all animals are capable of cognizing spatial differences in selected aspects of those parts of the earth's surface of which they have direct experience. In establishing homes, seeking food, homing, and migrating they are known to perceive cues provided by their environments. For example, in September 1964 a homing pigeon returning to its Boston loft from a release in southern Maine followed (and therefore presumably cognized) the coast of New Hampshire and northeastern Massachusetts for a distance of fourteen miles. This was the same coast Samuel Champlain first perceived from the sea 359 years before, when he had a sketch map drawn as a means of eliciting information from the Indians about the hinterland. Much to his surprise, they inserted a major river, which was to be named the Merrimack. Because of a bar across most of its mouth, Champlain had failed to perceive it from the sea. With the benefit of an aerial perspective and endowed with a cognitive system better suited to the task, however, a second homing pigeon from the Boston loft followed (and therefore presumably cognized) that same river for a distance of eleven miles.[1]

The study of cognition and image formation falls within the field of psychophysiology, impinges on many other fields, and has implications for virtually all. It is a complex subject, in which research has only recently begun to extend beyond the controlled but impoverished world of the laboratory to the vastly more complex and emotive real worlds of animals and men in their actual environments. Even so, it will be helpful to consider briefly three relatively well known cognitive phenomena.

27

First. The same set of stimuli may be perceived by the same person in two different ways. Some of the simplest, albeit artificial, examples of this are to be found in the deliberately ambiguous drawings which appear in the literature on the psychology of visual perception. In nature, examples of something like this reversal process occur in animal camouflage, the principle behind which is to conceal the figure in relation to its background, though once perceived, the figure may become dominant. It is difficult to think of examples of figure-ground reversal in the macro world of man, but something close to it may occur, as between males and females among the Aivilik Eskimos on Southampton Island. When asked to draw maps, the men evidently produce reasonably accurate sketches of coasts, inlets, and rivers, whereas the women produce equally good point distributions showing the relative locations of settlements and trading posts.[2]

Second. Different persons perceive the same set of stimuli in different ways. In 1827, Captain Beechey met an Eskimo who sketched a very good likeness of him, correct in every essential detail except for the complete omission of his hat, which, as the Eskimo may never before have seen one, had been entirely overlooked. Even within a given culture there are wide variations between individuals in the images received from the same sets of stimuli. We all tend to perceive slopes at the earth's surface as being steeper than they really are, but the amount of exaggeration varies considerably between persons.[3]

Third. Percepts are selective. The lamb readily perceives its mother's call among the bleating of many ewes, and at a crowded reception we perceive as a conversation one sequence of sound stimuli in preference to others.

Because of the different ways in which he cognizes and organizes sense stimuli, "every man walks around in the world enveloped in a carapace of his own images. Their presence enables him to structure and to organize the multiplicity of the objects and the stimuli which throng upon him; but their presence also distorts, so no one ever perceives exactly what there is in the world."[4] In short, a person's world is not congruous with *the* world, and the worlds of specific individuals differ in varying degrees, as indeed does the world of any one person at different stages in life. Hence, it is surprising that we ever even approximately agree between or even with ourselves about the existence, nature, temporal occurrence, or geographical location of anything, and it may be that we would fail to achieve even approximate agreement in the absence of means of communication.

The measure of agreement between individuals and within groups concerning the world outside our heads cannot be understood solely in terms of perception but must be seen as the product of a larger complex of processes, including memory and communication. Not only do we perceive things when they confront our senses for the first time, but memory helps us to recognize them when we have perceived them before or when we have previously learned about them from others. In short, perception gives rise to unique images, which memory and communication together tend to group and stereotype.

Communication is a particularly vital adjunct to perception in sensing features that are too extensive or patterns that are too dispersed for a person to perceive either at a moment in time or sequentially. Prior to the launching of the first earth satellite no one had visually sensed the Mediterranean Sea, but it was nevertheless the background against which the Greeks had cognized the land masses of Eurasia and Libya some two and a half millennia before. For man, as for all nonamphibious animals, land and sea are fundamentally different, and except perhaps for the most seasoned mariner, the sea must always be the (back) ground against which the land figures. But in one widely accepted English usage, the land is also the ground, differentiated by the processes of nature and the work of man, from which we perceive figures: desiccation cracks on the dried-up bed of a reservoir; man-made clearings in a forest; buttes rising sharply above a plain. Sometimes the figures are sharply defined and clear for almost all to see, but more often they are perceived by some and not by others as they emerge from or recede into their (back) grounds. No one who has ever been to Europe will doubt that Europe exists, but it was only in the later Middle Ages that the consciousness of its distinctiveness began to emerge.[5] In 1944 in Chicago, Graham Hutton, as part of his preparation for writing *Midwest at Noon*, entertained a dozen friends to dinner. They were from a wide range of professional backgrounds and had come prepared to discuss how one could best describe the Midwest. Each came convinced that there was indeed a Midwest to be described, but beyond that agreement ceased.[6] Because they have well-known labels we talk glibly about the Midwest, the South, the Canadian Prairies, or the American Great Plains, but we cognize their extents and characteristics differently according to our personal and professional perspectives. There can be few reasonably well educated adults in the English-speaking or Western world who have not heard or seen the appellation *Great Plains*: two short words, one of West Germanic origin and the other from Old French. But what do they mean? Why, when, and by whom was a longitudinally elongated belt of land to the east of the Rocky Mountains first cognized to figure distinctively against the wider background of the North American continent? Who first applied to it the appellation *Great Plains*? With what images and concepts was it subsequently associated? These are the questions to be examined here.

Knowledge is now considered a process rather than a state. Before the Indians of the western interior of North America experienced their first contacts with Europeans, some of their chiefs had begun to cognize as a region (or, to use the terminology of mid-twentieth-century psychology, a gestalt) an area approximately coincident with what were later to be cognized by Europeans and white Americans as the Canadian Prairies and American Great Plains. Anthony Henday, who in 1754 became the first European to penetrate into the northernmost part of the area, referred to it repeatedly in his journal as the Muscuty Tuskee, a name which would seem to have been derived from two Cree words, *mos-ko-se-ah* (grass) and *as-kee* (ground). In 1802, Ki Oo Cus, a Blackfoot chief, cartographically delimited as the "woods edge" the northern and northeastern boundaries of that region. Some years later Arapooish, a Crow chief, described "Crow Country" (the hills and broken plains dissected by the Yellowstone, Powder, Wind and Little Missouri rivers) as "a good country," within which his people fared well but away from which conditions deteriorated in each direction. On the "great barren plains" to the south the water was bad and fever was prevalent. These and other groups of Algonquian- and Siouan-speaking Indians would seem to have had some concept of the distance to which the plains extended to the south. One of the two printed maps in Jonathan Carver's *Travels* has a legend to the west of the St. Pierre (now Minnesota) River indicating "The Country of the Naudowessie of the Plains. From this place the Plains are unbounded suppos'd to extend to the South Sea." To an Englishman in the last quarter of the eighteenth century, South Sea was what we now refer to as the Pacific Ocean. The legend therefore conveyed false information, but the information as communicated to Carver by the Indians was probably correct. His unpublished journal refers to "the plains which extend to the South Sea as the savages say."[7] To the Sioux Indians in the present eastern parts of the two Dakotas, the South Sea was far more likely to have been the Gulf of Mexico to the south than the Pacific Ocean to the west, and they evidently appreciated that the maximum extent of the plains was in that direction. Indeed, the alternative interpretation implies an improbability—that the Sioux Indians knew nothing of the Rocky Mountains, intermontane plateaus, Cascade, Sierra, or Coast ranges which together separate the Great Plains from the Pacific.

It would have been surprising if the Indians had not developed a fairly clear appreciation of the distinctive nature of the plains and if they had not cognized them as figuring prominently against the background of the continent as a whole. Especially to the north and northeast, where the transition was sharpest, the edge of the forest was for them what a coastline is for a maritime people; it was both a landmark and a boundary between environments that afforded different resources but necessitated different modes of life and travel. While the forests were the source of a greater range of material needs, the plains were the habitat of the buffalo, the most important single resource. Leaving the woods or the forested mountains on the western edge for the plains was an occasion to be anticipated, planned for, and even feared. In the absence of trees, kindling wood and tent poles had to be transported. In order to guarantee fresh water at campsites, circuitous routes had to be followed. To afford shelter from possible blizzards, the ideal route in winter was never far from the shelter of a valley or a clump of trees. Conversely, leaving the plains for the woods or mountains was an occasion to be anticipated with a mixture of relief at having overcome one set of potential risks, and fear at the concealed dangers ahead. For many Indians, the plains were distinctive in that they were their habitat during part only of their seasonal migrations. For example, according to Arapooish, the Crow Indians went out onto them in the autumn in search of buffalo, after spending the summer in the relatively cool foothills of the Rocky Mountains and before resorting in the winter to the wooded valley bottoms, there to find shelter and food for both horse and man.[8]

If, toward the middle of the eighteenth century, Indian chiefs from various parts of North America had had occasion to meet in a parley to prepare an inventory of natural resources, it seems probable that they would have recognized a plains region, listed its essential resources and graver deficiencies, and perhaps delimited it cartographically. For the northern and northeastern edges of the region, the essentials of such a map have survived in Peter Fidler's enhancement of original sketches made for him in his journals by Blackfoot Indians.[9] If we infer that certain information on manuscript maps drawn by the fur traders Alexander Henry the Elder and Peter Pond was obtained from Indian intelligence, then we can extend the boundary southward down the eastern edge of the region in such a way that only its southern part is somewhat in doubt (fig. 1). That at least some Indians were capable of cognizing spatial distributions on such a grand scale is suggested by the map of almost half a million square miles of southeastern North America that was drawn on deerskin by an Indian cacique for presentation to the governor of South Carolina about 1722 and by that of almost one-quarter of a million square miles drawn for William Clark by a Chopunnish Indian in 1806.[10]

The oldest surviving European accounts of the cis–Rocky Mountain West reveal a considerable vocabulary of words used to describe its landscapes. Spanish, French, English, and colonial American words were used loosely by explorers and traders, at first no doubt as conscious or subconscious attempts to convey impressions of environmental conditions analogous to those in their native lands. Confusion arose whenever, as was frequently the case, there were no close analogues or whenever terms from one language were translated into another. *Champion (champaign) land, barren land,*

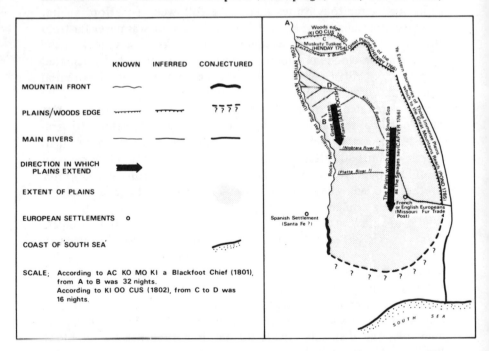

Figure 1. The Plains Region as Cognized by Late Eighteenth-Century Indians as They Are Known, Inferred, or Conjectured to Have Delimited It

meadow, prairie, savannah, desert, and *plain* were each used in printed
works, but before the last quarter of the eighteenth century only
in descriptions of specific landscapes or small areas. Thereafter, as
the frontier of exploration advanced and with increasing contacts
among frontiersmen and between frontiersmen and Indians, there
began to emerge the idea of a distinctive cis–Rocky Mountain environment. By this time French national interests in the area had
virtually ceased and those of Spain were waning. The greatest activity
was among English, Canadian, and American fur traders along the
northeastern and eastern edges of the area. Not surprisingly, therefore, an English appellation emerged as the dominant term to be
associated with the newly but as yet only dimly cognized region. The
many plains of innumerable landscapes within an area more than
fifteen hundred miles long and averaging four hundred miles in width
became fused into a single geographical image, to which the name
Great Plains was given. The expression *Immense Plains* was only
slightly less frequently used.

A manuscript map presented to Sir Guy Carleton by the Canadian fur trader Alexander Henry the Elder in 1776 marked "The
Course [edge] of the Great Plains" at the place where botanists
have since identified the boundary between the wheatgrass prairies
and parklands in south-central Saskatchewan, southern Manitoba,
and northeastern Minnesota. Nine years later, St. John de Crèvecoeur,
at the time the French consul in New York, but better known as
the author of *Letters from an American Farmer,* sent to Paris a copy
in his own hand of a map of interior and western North America by
another Canadian fur trader, Peter Pond, on which a "Prick'd Line"
parallel to and to the west of the upper Mississippi marked "ye
Eastern Boundaries of those immense Pleins which reaches to the
Great Mountains."[11] The published *Voyages* of Alexander Mackenzie, another Canadian fur trader, ends with "a geographical view
of the country," written between 1793 and 1801 either by Mackenzie
himself or by David Thompson. It describes a "narrow belt of immense plains, or meadows" to the east of the Rocky Mountains,
commencing "at about the junction of the River of the Mountain
[Liard River] with Mackenzie's River, widening as they reach the
Red River at its confluence with the Assiniboin River, from whence
they take a more Southern direction, along the Mississippi towards
Mexico."[12] Grammatically Mackenzie's "immense plains" were
many, stylistically they did not merit upper-case initial letters, but
conceptually they were clearly one.

The manuscript maps of Henry and Pond were virtually unknown
until the late nineteenth century and there can be few who read as

far as page 402 in Mackenzie's *Voyages,* even before it was virtually
forgotten after the publication of but one reprint in 1814. Together,
however, they afford conclusive evidence that Canadian fur traders
recognized and attempted to delimit a distinctive region to the east
of the Rocky Mountains and that they called it the Great or Immense Plains. It is not surprising that for them this area began to
figure distinctively against the wider background of the continent.
Its landscapes and Indians differed from those of the better-known
forests and parklands to the north and tall grass prairies to the east
and its environment compelled different modes of travel and subsistence. More specifically, much of the region contained relatively
few of those fur-bearing animals (especially the beaver) which were
the ultimate reasons for the fur traders' presence in the then remote
interior of North America. From their point of view, it was a region
of limited resources compared with the areas to the north and east,
and for a time it deflected the advance of their trading frontier
toward the Canadian northlands. Nevertheless, it was an important
concept, to which, once cognized, a name had to be given. *Great
Plains,* of which Alexander Henry's is perhaps the earliest surviving
usage, has survived the intervening two centuries as that most frequently used.

The emergence of widely communicated images of a distinctive
cis–Rocky Mountain region commenced when the United States
acquired its first part of it by means of the Louisiana Purchase of
1803. For a brief period before and after that date the United States
deliberately sought intelligence about the trans-Mississippi West; and
Saint Louis became the chief center for the exchange of information
between residents from the former French and Spanish regimes,
Canadians trading down the east-bank tributaries of the upper Mississippi, and recently arrived Americans from the East via the Ohio
country. The preparation initiated by Thomas Jefferson for what was
to become the Lewis and Clark Expedition included the assiduous
collection of printed and manuscript information, and Meriwether
Lewis deliberately acquired information in Saint Louis during the
winter of 1803–1804.[13] The publication of the official account of
the Lewis and Clark Expedition across the north-central Great Plains
was delayed until 1814, being preceded four years earlier by Pike's
report on his expedition across the south-central part of the region
during 1805. Pike's published *Account* contained a succinct appendix entitled "A dissertation on the soil, rivers, production, animal
and vegetable, with general notes on the internal parts of Louisiana . . . ," in which the "vast plains" beyond the Missouri River

were said to be treeless because "a barren soil, parched and dried up
for eight months of the year, presents neither moisture nor nutri-
tion sufficient to nourish the timber." Pike reported having seen
"in various places, tracts of many leagues, where the wind had
thrown up the sand, in all the fanciful forms of the ocean's rolling
wave, and on which not a speck of vegetable matter existed." Although he had no means of knowing it, these were the relatively
narrow but elongated zones of sandhills, deposited toward the end
of the last glacial period immediately adjacent to parts of the Arkansas and other transplains valleys by the strong winds which blew
across the sand and silt left exposed on their floodplains after the
seasonal meltwaters from the Rocky Mountains had receded. From
their general appearance and apparently great extent when seen in
parallel from a route following the valley, Pike predicted that they
might "become in time equally celebrated as the sandy deserts of
Africa."[14] Although conceding that beyond the meridian 96° 30'
west many of the valleys were potentially cultivable, his account of
the vast intervening upland plains was couched in terms of a nearly
absolute desert. It represented an extrapolation northward and
southward from observations made in late summer along one atypical
transplains route. Such an extrapolation is itself evidence that Pike
accepted the idea of a meridionally elongated cis–Rocky Mountain
region and that, like many others in later years, he endowed it with a
degree of spatial homogeneity and temporal invariance that it does
not possess. Even so, the idea of a widespread desert did not begin
to receive general acceptance for another decade until, on returning
from an expedition to the Rocky Mountains, Stephen Long restated
Pike's opinions concerning the character of the land between those
mountains and the 96th meridian. His published opinions might have
created no stronger impression than those of Pike, but in 1821 he
also supervised the construction of a map which, though never published, boldly placed the name *Great Desert* in what is now western
Oklahoma and northern Texas. Carey and Lea's widely used atlas
of the following year contained a version of that map in which the
placing of the name *Great Desert* was such as to extend the image
northward into what is now eastern Colorado and western Kansas.
In the following year a second printed version nationalized the Great
Desert into the Great American Desert.[15]

Apparently the Great Plains of the Canadian traders became the
Great American Desert farther south, and most official and supposedly informed American opinion seems to have accepted this image,
at least until the Civil War. The extent to which at midcentury a

cis–Rocky Mountain desert figured against the background of the
still only dimly cognized trans-Mississippi West varied from one social
class to another and from one part of the country to another. Martyn
Bowden has demonstrated that the Great American Desert was never
a powerful image among the less literate folk back east or among
most of those who had direct experience of the area where it was
supposed to exist.[16] It was exclusive for some, dominant for others,
recessive for yet others, and nonexistent for the remainder. Indeed,
the image of the Great American Desert had a competitor. Simultaneously, though not presumably in the minds of particular individuals, there coexisted a subdominant image (fig. 2). This can be traced
back to at least the late eighteenth century, but it was recessive until
1844, the year in which Josiah Gregg published his widely read
book *Commerce of the Prairies*.[17] His appraisal and general delimita-
tion of the prairies were similar to Long's for the Great American
Desert, deeming them to be for the most part uninhabitable because
of infertile soils and a shortage of available water. However, like his
contemporary Frémont, he envisaged that the region would afford
pasturage for domestic animals. Herein lay the essential difference

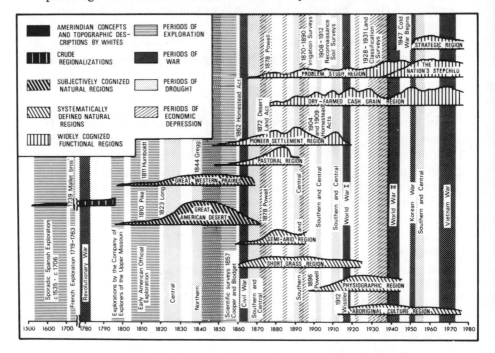

Figure 2. The Development of Regional Concepts of the Cis–Rocky
Mountain West, 1535–1977

between the still strong desert image and the hitherto weak image of the western, or short-grass, prairies. The former was associated with the concept of permanent emptiness and economic uselessness, whereas the latter heralded an economic potential. By 1870 the areas which had in the past been referred to by some as the Great American Desert and by others as the Great Western Prairies were virtually coextensive; but whereas the desert image had receded almost into oblivion and was soon to be destroyed by railroad, state, and territorial publicity, the prairie image was about to achieve a new dimension. To the pictorial imagery of bison grazing endless but otherwise empty short-grass plains, bounded by unbroken horizons and spanned by an all-pervading sky were added the cowboy, the ranch, and vast herds of beef cattle.

The strip of land to the east of the Rocky Mountains continued to generate regional images in relative profusion. Specialists in regional literature, political science, public administration, and perhaps other fields will probably recognize the waxings and wanings of other regional concepts associated with the Great Plains, but there were two prevailing sets of post–Civil War concepts: the systematically defined natural regions, recognized and delimited from without on the basis of one group of closely related characteristics as part of a continental system of regions; and widely cognized functional regions sensed by specialists and nonspecialists both from without and, to a lesser extent, from within (fig. 2). The former group reflect a stage, now passed, in the conceptual development of the earth and life sciences. It is significant, however, that in the appropriate stage in the development of their disciplines climatologists, plant ecologists, physiographers, and cultural anthropologists each recognized and cartographically delimited an area to the east of the Rocky Mountains which they felt to be both distinctive and different from elsewhere in North America. In most cases they named that region the Great Plains, doing so in complete ignorance of the fact that the name had been coined approximately one hundred years before by a Canadian fur trader after one brief trading season in the northernmost part of the region. Only John Wesley Powell, in one of his last publications, openly regretted the use of that name, pointing out that it was a region characterized not by plains but by plateaus.[18] At the same time he reluctantly conceded that the name was too well established to be replaced. Within a single discipline there was usually a high degree of agreement about the existence of a Great Plains region but considerable confusion about its geographical extent, particularly, and not surprisingly, along its eastern edge. For example, among the several physiographic subdivisions of the United

States published between 1896 and 1940, only one failed to recognize a Great Plains region. The extent of disagreement between the others as to where that region was located was such that the core area, about which they all agreed, was a mere 30 percent of the composite area of their collective Great Plains.[19]

The Widely Cognized Functional Regions of figure 2 mainly, though not entirely, represented the cognitions of those on the outside looking in and did not necessarily imply any strong sense of regional self-identity among the residents. A pastoral, pioneer, or dry-farmed region was distinctive only when seen against a wider national or continental system of agricultural systems. A problem region was distinctive only when seen against the background of a wider area having fewer, less acute, or different sets of problems. A stepchild is indeed different, but only in the nature of its relationship within a particular family. Each concept stressed distinctiveness without placing clear limits on that which was supposedly distinctive or focusing on the experience of those within. They were functional rather than existential regions.

The foregoing review of the images and concepts with which the appellation *Great Plains* has been associated essentially terminates in the early twentieth century, though figure 2 does suggest subsequent developments. In virtually ignoring the recent past it avoids a number of important questions which are of considerable social and economic significance. They are posed here because they are indeed significant and in the hope that others will accept the challenge of trying to answer them.

The appellation *Great Plains* is currently in widespread use, but is it merely an emotive name associated with a vaguely defined area no longer possessing distinctive and significant characteristics and lacking the unity with which to generate a spontaneous and dynamic image? Or does it relate to a spatial segment of North America which in the late 1970s is indeed distinctive, not merely in its landscapes and former environments, but in its function as a vital subsystem within the larger North American socio-environmental system? If the latter, then is that segment of North America sufficiently distinctive and is its population sufficiently aware of itself to be creating a true sense of regionalism? If so, can it convey to those on the outside a clearer and more up-to-date image than heretofore? If not, is there any point in perpetuating the appellation or the images that have become associated with it and should steps be taken to confine them to the past? These are some of the questions to which it is hoped others will address themselves.

Notes

The research upon which this paper is based was supported by financial assistance received at various times from the University of Sheffield Research Fund, the British Association for American Studies, the Newberry Library, and the Social Science Research Council (U.K.).

1. Martin C. Michener and Charles Walcott, "Homing of Single Pigeons: Analysis of Tracks," *Journal of Experimental Biology* 47 (1967): 114, 126; Samuel de Champlain, "The Voyages of 1604-1607," a translation from the French edition of 1613, edited by William L. Grant and published in *Voyages of Samuel de Champlain, 1604-1618* (New York: Charles Scribner's Sons, 1907), p. 65; Michener and Walcott, "Homing of Single Pigeons," pp. 112, 126.

2. Edmund S. Carpenter et al., *Eskimo* (Toronto: University of Toronto Press, 1959), unpaged.

3. Frederick W. Beechey, *Narrative of a Voyage to the Pacific and Beering's Straight . . .* , 2 vols. (London: H. Colburn and R. Bentley, 1831), 1:297; Helen E. Ross, *Behaviour and Perception in Strange Environments* (London: George Allen and Unwin, 1974), pp. 70-74.

4. Rosemary Gordon, "A Very Private World," in *The Function and Nature of Imagery,* ed. Peter W. Sheehan (New York: Academic Press, 1972), p. 63.

5. Denys Hay, *Europe: The Emergence of an Idea* (New York: Harper and Row, 1966), pp. vii-viii.

6. D. Graham Hutton, *Midwest at Noon* (London: George G. Harrap, 1946), p. 3.

7. Anthony Henday, manuscript journal for 1754-55, copied in 1792 by Andrew Graham, E.2/11, pp. 15, 20, 28-29, 31, 41, Hudson's Bay Company Archives, Winnipeg, published version edited by Lawrence J. Burpee in the *Proceedings and Transactions of the Royal Society of Canada,* ser. 3, vol. 1, sec. 2 (1907): 328, 331, 335-36, 341; Daniel W. Harmon, "A specimen of the Cree and Knisteneux tongue," *A Journal of Voyages and Travel in the Interior of North America . . .* (Andover, Mass.: Flagg and Gould, 1820), pp. 385, 403; Ki Oo Cus, untitled manuscript sketch map of the upper Missouri and upper South Saskatchewan basins drawn in 1802 and copied by Peter Fidler on 103v and 104r of a journal covering the years 1789-1804, E.3/2, Hudson's Bay Company, Winnipeg; Arapooish, "My Country," based on an undated interview reported by James H. Bradley, *Contributions to the Historical Society of Montana* 9 (1923): 306-7; "A Plan of Captain Carvers Travels in the Interior Parts of North America in 1766 and 1767," in Jonathan Carver, *Travels through the Interior Parts of North America in the Years 1766, 1767 and 1768* (London: privately printed, 1778), facing p. 181; Jonathan Carver, "Journals of travels, and the same journals put by the author into a form which he intended for publication, with several additions . . . ," Additional Manuscript 8950, British Museum, London, p. 23.

8. Arapooish, "My Country," pp. 306-7.

9. Peter Fidler, manuscript journal for 1789-1804, E.3/2, Hudson's Bay Company, Winnipeg.

10. "A Map Describing the situation of the several Nations of Indians between South Carolina and the Massisipi River was Copyed from a Draught Drawn & Printed upon a Deer Skin by an Indian Cacique and Presented to Francis Nicholson Esq., Governor of Carolina," C.O. 700 North American Colonies General no. 6(1), Public Record Office Map Room, London; "Sketch given us May 8th 1806 by the Cut Nose and the brother of the twisted hair," sketch map in the hand of William Clark, original in the Coe Collection, Beinecke Library, Yale University, reproduced in Reuben G. Thwaites, ed., *Original Journals of the Lewis and Clark Expedition, 1804-1806*, 8 vols. (New York: Dodd, Mead and Co., 1904-1905), vol. 8, map 41.

11. "A Map of the North West Parts of America. With the Utmost Respect Inscrib'd to His Excellency Sir Guy Carleton, . . . By his most Obedient Humble Servt. Alexr. Henry," manuscript map, Geography and Map Division, Library of Congress, Washington, D.C.; Peter Pond, "Copy of a Map Presented to the Congress by Peter Pond . . . Copied by St. John de Crèvecoeur for His Grace of La Rochefoucault," Additional Manuscript 15, 332C, British Museum, London.

12. John J. Bigsby, *The Shoe and Canoe; or, Pictures of Travel in the Canadas . . .*, 2 vols. (London: Chapman and Hall, 1850), 1:115; Alexander Mackenzie, *Voyages from Montreal, on the River St. Laurence, through the Continent of North America . . .* (London: T. Cadell jun. and W. Davies, 1801), pp. 402-3.

13. John L. Allen, *Passage through the Garden: Lewis and Clark and the Image of the American Northwest* (Urbana: University of Illinois Press, 1975), pp. 147-48.

14. Zebulon M. Pike, "A dissertation on the soil, rivers, productions, animal and vegetable, with general notes on the internal parts of Louisiana, . . . ," *An Account of Expeditions to the Sources of the Mississippi and through the Western Parts of Louisiana, . . .* (Philadelphia: C. and A. Conrad, and Co., 1810), appendix to pt. 2, p. 8.

15. Stephen H. Long, "Map of the Country situated between the Meridian of Washington City and the Rocky Mountains . . . ," manuscript c. 1821, National Archives, Washington, D.C.; Stephen H. Long, "Map of Arkansas and other Territories of the United States . . . ," map 35 in *A Complete Historical, Chronological, and Geographical American Atlas, . . .* (Philadelphia: H. C. Carey and I. Lea, 1822); Stephen H. Long, "Country drained by the Mississippi Western Section," in Edwin James, *Account of an Expedition from Pittsburgh to the Rocky Mountains, Performed in the Years 1819 and 1820, . . . ,"* (Philadelphia: H. C. Carey and I. Lea, 1822), atlas vol.

16. Martyn J. Bowden, "The Perception of the Western Interior of the United States, 1800-1870," *Proceedings of the Association of American Geographers* 1 (1969): 16-21.

17. Josiah Gregg, *Commerce of the Prairies . . .*, 2 vols. (New York: Henry G. Langley, 1844).

18. John W. Powell, "The physiographic regions of the United States," in National Geographic Society, *The Physiography of the United States* (New York: American Book Co., 1896), p. 86.

19. G. Malcolm Lewis, "Regional Ideas and Reality in the Cis-Rocky Mountain West," *Transactions and Papers of the Institute of British Geographers* 38 (1966), fig. 12.

Agricultural Adjustments
to Great Plains Drought
The Republican Valley, 1870–1900

Bradley H. Baltensperger

Early encounters of settlers with the Great Plains led, in the words of Walter Prescott Webb, to "a complete, though temporary, breakdown of the machinery and ways of pioneering."[1] Thousands of nineteenth-century farmers failed because of the discrepancy between their experience in humid areas and the subhumid reality of the plains, and because they began their operations in the West under the impression that they could continue to practice agriculture using midwestern crops and techniques. The adjustment of their agricultural system to the environment can be understood only with reference to their experience and their preconceptions, and to drought on the plains. The rate of that adjustment process was primarily a function of the severity of drought and the degree of aridity.

The first major surge of population onto the Great Plains began soon after the end of the Civil War. Although only 550,000 acres (222,600 hectares) of land were claimed through preemption or homestead in Kansas and Nebraska during 1868, that figure rose rapidly, reaching nearly 2 million acres annually by 1870, a level which was sustained through 1874.[2] Because of this rapid growth, the frontier of settlement reached the 98th meridian by 1870, and stretched well beyond the 100th meridian ten years later. By 1890 virtually all areas of the two states had been settled.

By far the largest proportion of new plains settlers received their agricultural experience in the Midwest. Published census figures reveal the importance of the Corn Belt states in providing plains farmers. In the five counties examined in detail in this study, approximately 28 percent of the residents born outside Kansas and Nebraska had been born in Iowa or Illinois.

Yet the place of birth of residents does not fully illustrate the importance of the Corn Belt in the development of the plains. Many nineteenth-century farmers relocated several times during their lifetime. It was somewhat unusual for a farmer to move directly to the plains from his birthplace or even from his state of birth.[3] The Corn Belt dominance is even more pronounced when the last place of residence is considered. Four Webster County, Nebraska, precincts in 1880 and four Red Willow County, Nebraska, precincts in 1885 illustrate this trend. About 60 percent of all the farmers in the two areas could be traced to previous homes in Iowa, Illinois, Indiana, or Ohio, with over 40 percent coming from Iowa or Illinois. These two states were the center of United States corn production at the time, devoting approximately 42 percent of all their tilled land to that crop in 1879.[4]

Not only were migrants to the plains accustomed to midwestern farming practices, but they expected to be able to transfer that agricultural system in unmodified form to the plains. In the last three decades of the nineteenth century the predominant image of the plains was that of an area well suited to agricultural settlement.[5] Such ideas were disseminated by a variety of means, but the sources of information which had the greatest distribution in the United States were promotional pamphlets published by railroads, state governments, and independent boosters.

The accuracy of the plains image portrayed in the promotional literature was primarily a function of the area being settled and the agricultural fortunes of the West. Through the mid-1870s much imagery was accurate, in spite of occasional literacy excesses. While possibilities for such exotic crops as tobacco, cotton, rice, and sugar cane were suggested, caution was frequently expressed. Crop production was commonly limited to eastern portions of the two states and irrigation was advocated. In the years immediately after the grasshopper invasion and drought of 1874, the literature remained generally cautious, but by the end of the decade plains settlement was booming and the promotional works reflected the expansion by limiting their discussion of irrigation and a western agricultural limit. As plains settlement moved west, so did any suggested limit to crop production.[6]

A minor drought in 1880 and 1881, accompanied by declining immigration, led to a slight revision in the accuracy of the image, but the publication of two major works on the subject of increasing rainfall led to widespread promotional use of the notion that "rain follows the plow."[7] When good crops and immigration returned, cautionary notes to potential migrants virtually disappeared.

By the time some of the most arid sections of the plains were being settled, in the mid-1880s, the prevailing image in the promotional literature was one of sufficient or increasing rainfall, unlimited westward expansion of agriculture, and no need for irrigation. Readers were led to believe that midwestern crops and practices could be transplanted without adjustments or alterations to the western portions of a homogeneous plain which stretched from Ohio to the Rocky Mountains. Only when drought struck the region in the early 1890s did significant revisions of the promotional image occur. By that time, however, migration to the area had nearly ceased and few people were able to take advantage of the newly developed promotional accuracy.[8]

How far the common people of the United States went in accepting the promoters' images of the plains will never be known with exactitude. It seems likely that potential settlers discounted many of the exaggerations of the promoters, relying instead on local newspapers and farm journals and information received from friends and relatives in the area.

The portrayal of the West in newspapers was considerably more accurate than that in the promotional literature, but there were distinct variations in the amount of information available and the content of that information. In years of retreat or limited expansion of settlement, such as 1875, 1882, and 1895, readers in most of the country received a fair amount of news about Kansas and Nebraska. In those years, when the promotional image was the most subdued and immigration was low, newspapers reported widespread drought and destitution. When crops improved and heavy migration resumed, as in 1879 and 1886, the promotional imagery became increasingly inaccurate, but the availability of conflicting information from newspapers was minimal.[9]

The opinions about the plains which prospective settlers took with them to the area were probably based upon inaccurate promotional literature, information from less biased media, and personal communications. All this was interpreted through settlers' background and agricultural experience, which was generally received in the Midwest. What the settlers expected of the plains shaped their behavior for some time after relocation. Only after their understanding of the environment had been modified by plains experience and improved information would their behavior change to take account of the recently discovered complexities of the region.

In order to examine that transformation process in detail, three areas within the Republican River basin have been selected for scrutiny: Webster County, Nebraska; Furnas and Red Willow counties, Nebraska; and Dundy County, Nebraska, and Cheyenne County, Kansas (fig. 1). The settlement of each area corresponded roughly

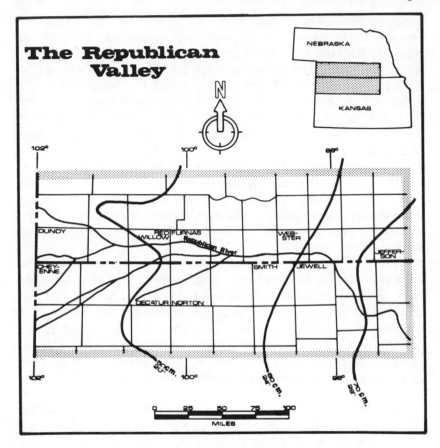

Figure 1. The Republican River Valley, Showing Counties Examined in Detail and Mean Annual Precipitation

to one of the three major surges of plains settlement (early 1870s, late 1870s, and mid-1880s, respectively). Data from neighboring counties supplement Republican Valley information.

Effective, large-scale agricultural settlement of the Republican Valley began in 1870 and moved rapidly west. As early as 1874 settlers were found at 101° west longitude. In this first boom Webster County grew rapidly. Large-scale settlement of the central counties began in 1879. The two western counties were entered in 1885.

The agricultural practices of the eastern and central study areas evolved through several well-defined stages in the first fifteen years after initial settlement.

The sod corn period. During the first few years after entry, most farmers relied upon sod corn as their principal crop. The importance of corn during these initial years of settlement is striking in both eastern and central areas (fig. 2). Just as plains migration peaked in 1874, the area experienced a severe drought, which was described by one of the first settlers of Red Willow County: "We are burning up with heat and drought. We had splendid rains through the spring, until about the first week of June and we have now had four weeks of continuous burning south wind without rain. The thermometer has marked over 100° almost every day during June, and still it grows hotter."[10] In mid-July the grasshopper invasion began and crops were totally destroyed. Almost mmediately appeals were made to the more settled areas of Kansas and Nebraska for assistance to destitute western citizens.[11]

Drought and adjustment. The difficulties of 1874, followed by poor crops for the next several years, apparently convinced many settlers that established agricultural practices would not suffice on the plains. The sod corn stage was replaced by crop diversification. Plains farmers devoted nearly as much land to wheat as to corn for the next five years.[12] They had modified their behavior in order to survive and prosper in their new homes.

Immigration overwhelms adaptation. Crop yields improved by the late 1870s, helping to stimulate a new wave of settlement in Kansas and Nebraska. Particularly heavy immigration in 1879 radically changed the composition of the population. In March 1880, at least 16 percent of all Webster County residents had been in the county less than nine months. In Furnas County fewer than half the residents had a year of local experience; in Red Willow County the figure was less than one-third. No more than one-fourth the population of the central study area had been there two years.[13]

This rapid influx of midwesterners, heavily influenced by promotional literature extolling the plains as part of the Corn Belt, had major consequences for the agricultural patterns of the Republican Valley. The sentiment of the new settlers was best expressed by the editor of the newly established *Arapahoe Pioneer,* who maintained: "There are several fields of corn in Furnas County, it is estimated will yield 100 bushels of that cereal per acre, and yet some 'know nothingites' claim this is not a corn country."[14] The overwhelming surge of population into the valley resulted in a dramatic shift in crop emphasis from diversification to concentration on corn production within three years. The ratio of corn to wheat acreage in Jewell County, Kansas, rose from approximately 1:1 in 1878 to 4:1 in 1881.

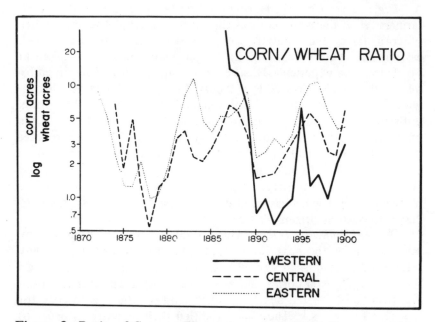

Figure 2. Ratio of Corn to Wheat Acreage in Eight Kansas and Nebraska Counties, 1872–1900. Source: Kansas State Board of Agriculture, *Annual and Biennial Reports,* 1872–1900; Nebraska State Board of Agriculture, *Annual Reports,* 1885–1900; *U.S. Census: Agriculture,* 1880, 1890, 1900; Webster County assessor's records, Nebraska State Historical Society, Lincoln; *Arapahoe* (Nebraska) *Pioneer,* January 6, 1882. No Nebraska data were available for some years.

A year later the ratio was 10:1. Other counties showed similar shifts. While wheat acreage remained nearly constant, corn acreage shot up. The crop diversification which had been carefully developed as a means of coping with environmental uncertainty during the mid-1870s was submerged by the flood of corn producers without experience with plains agriculture.[15] While drought in 1880 resulted in a slight emigration from the valley, it was not of sufficient duration or intensity to encourage the new settlers to change their farming and cropping practices. The wet years of the 1880s ensured a continuance of corn monoculture.

In the midst of these boom years of the mid-1880s the western area was entered by farmers. Within three years population density reached five persons per square mile (1.93 persons per square kilometer). In this period the boomer image of the two states was quite distorted. Increasing rainfall was a widely disseminated idea in the promotional literature, but only one of twenty pamphlets published between 1884 and 1889 suggested a western limit to crop production. Irrigation was ignored. Eastern and midwestern newspapers paid little attention to the plains during this period, producing a highly inaccurate view of the area in the minds of potential migrants.[16] The agricultural system of Dundy and Cheyenne counties moved directly from the sod corn stage to the corn monoculture stage, without any intervening period of diversification.

As of 1889 farmers throughout the Republican Valley were strongly committed to the production of corn, all but ignoring wheat and other small grains. With few exceptions irrigation was not practiced, nor were other precautions against dry weather or severe drought undertaken by the settlers.

During the last decade of the nineteenth century, severe drought afflicted the Republican Valley in four years: 1890, 1893, 1894, and 1895. Other years were only slightly better.[17] It was during this period that plains farmers began serious reevaluation of the environment. The moisture deficits upset the equilibrium of the plains agricultural system, eventually leading to differential rates of adaptation to the environments of the three areas. The most important factor affecting the rate and extent of environmental reevaluation and behavior change was the availability of moisture. A number of indicators illustrate the extent to which the rate and degree of both cognitive and behavioral change varied directly with aridity and the severity of drought.[18]

One measure of changing evaluations of the climate was the prevalence of the belief that residents of the plains could influence the environment to become more hospitable for agricultural purposes. The depth of that sentiment and the speed with which ideas about weather and climate modification were accepted varied according to the extent to which such changes were considered necessary. Where rainfall was adequate for most midwestern crops, as in eastern Nebraska, no need for additional precipitation was felt. Consequently, belief in artificial rainmaking and support for the theory of increasing rainfall did not develop in eastern counties as they did in the Republican River Valley.

Both the rate and degree of acceptance of ideas of weather and climate modification within the valley were directly related to the degree of aridity. While the strength of these beliefs within each study area is difficult to gauge, the time of first mention of various schemes can be determined from local newspaper sources (table 1).

In the most humid area the local newspaper manifested no interest in the idea that rain follows the plow during the first decade of settlement, in spite of several dry years. Discussion of the subject in the central area appeared considerably earlier. Support for the concept in the driest area was first expressed almost immediately after first effective settlement by farmers, illustrating the widespread diffusion of that concept by the mid-1880s. Inaccurate as the idea may have been, its acceptance represented a tacit admission that the area was not simply a new Corn Belt.

The first recorded effort to produce rainfall by artificial means in Dundy and Cheyenne counties occurred in 1892. Early in that year preparations were made to employ the Goodland Rain Company to furnish rain for Dundy County during the growing season. Similar action was taken in June in Cheyenne County, despite the skepticism of the local editor. In the latter case the rainmakers were paid $250, having claimed responsibility for nearly one and one-half inches of rain.[19]

The credulity of the farmers in the driest study area regarding weather modification demonstrates the differences between them and agriculturists in the other two areas. Rainmaking was not pursued in Red Willow County until 1894, and no mention of the artificial production of rainfall or the desirability of such an endeavor appeared in Webster County during the study period. Many farmers in the drier reaches of the plains were becoming aware that moisture

Table 1
Date of First Discussions of Increasing Rainfall
and of Rainmaking

Area (Counties)	First Settled	Increasing Rainfall	Rainmaking
Webster	1870	1882	None
Furnas and Red Willow	1871	1877	1894
Dundy and Cheyenne	1885	1886	1892

Source: Local newspapers, 1874–96.

was limited. Acceptance of schemes to change the climate represented a growing understanding of environmental deficiencies relative to midwestern forms of agriculture.

One behavioral alternative in coping with drought was the adjustment of relative acreages of commonly grown crops. The most popular crops of Republican Valley settlers were corn, important as a subsistence crop, and wheat, which was more resistant to drought. The changes in crop acreages during the 1890s were similar to the adjustments which had been undertaken in the 1870s along the eastern plains margin. In dry periods wheat acreage generally increased, while corn acreage remained steady or declined.

In the driest study area the ratio of corn to wheat acreage declined suddenly and stabilized near 1:1 in the two western counties. In the central area the ratio dropped to about 2:1 in the early 1890s, but after the immediate threat of drought disappeared, corn acreage increased significantly, raising the corn-wheat ratio to between 3:1 and 5:1. Similar changes occurred in the most humid counties, where corn acreage never dropped much below three times that of wheat, and rose to approximately 10:1 in 1897. Farther east, in Jefferson County, Nebraska, Martyn Bowden has found, by 1899 the tendency toward corn monoculture reached a peak with a ratio of 30:1.[20] Throughout the Republican Valley and somewhat to the east of it, the corn-wheat ratio in the period immediately after the end of the droughts of the 1890s varied directly with annual precipitation. The rate and extent of adaptation illustrated by that ratio varied directly with the degree of aridity.

During much of the late nineteenth century, farmers and local editors were often alert to the potential of new crops. Some innovative farmers experimented with seed varieties, seeking to ascertain their suitability for plains agriculture. Prominent among the new or unfamiliar crops were broom corn and sorghum. Nebraska statistics for these two crops were apparently derived from highly impressionistic estimates by local officials, but fairly accurate figures for Kansas counties were reported annually.

Only Cheyenne County farmers developed a significant interest in broom corn. By the middle of the 1890s more than 15,000 acres (6,070 hectares) were devoted to the crop. This represented 11 percent of total crop acreage in the county. Broom corn never commanded more than .5 percent of total crop acreage in the central and eastern areas (fig. 3). The proportion of land devoted to sorghum production was highest in the most arid region, but the crop

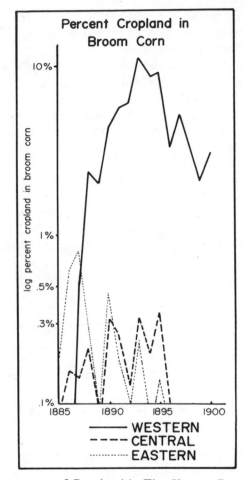

Figure 3. Percentage of Cropland in Five Kansas Counties Planted to Broom Corn, 1885–1900. Source: Kansas State Board of Agriculture, *Biennial Reports,* 1885–1900; *U.S. Census: Agriculture*, 1890, 1900.

remained relatively unimportant in the more humid counties, where its drought resistance was not recognized as a valuable property (fig. 4). On a more limited scale Cheyenne County farmers were clearly more interested in such sorghum varieties as Jerusalem corn and milo-maize, although the acreage of neither ever surpassed 1 percent of total crop acreage in Cheyenne County.

The adoption of new crops depended upon two processes. The introduction of innovations was generally made by a relatively small number of farmers who were willing and able to experiment. Small

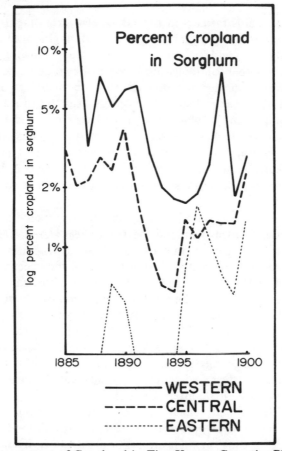

Figure 4. Percentage of Cropland in Five Kansas Counties Planted to Sorghum, 1885–1900. Source: Kansas State Board of Agriculture, *Biennial Reports,* 1885–1900; *U.S. Census: Agriculture,* 1890, 1900.

acreages of minor crops were introduced periodically by local farmers, often during years of good yields of major crops. The actual adoption of new crops depended upon acceptance by a large number of farmers. This most frequently occurred in periods of environmental stress, when solutions to immediate problems were desperately needed. The new ideas usually existed before periods of drought, but were not seriously considered or adopted by many farmers when there was no pressing need to do so. The intensity of the search for alternatives to traditional midwestern crops was strongest in the western counties. The acceptance of innovation was most pronounced in the driest counties.

Central plains farmers in the 1890s also experimented with new methods of farming which they believed might hold promise for improved crop yields. Various forms of deep plowing were introduced. A number of items appeared in newspapers of the central and western counties recommending deep planting, deep cultivation, and the use of listers to conserve soil moisture. Subsoiling, a form of plowing in which the ground was loosened to a depth as great as sixteen inches but was not turned over, was advocated for the same reason. In the most arid district, frequent cultivation to create a surface mulch was proposed.[21] This practice, later utilized in dry farming, was not discussed at the time in the two more humid areas.

Irrigation was of considerably greater importance in the adaptation process. Contrasts among the three areas were evident in degree of interest in irrigation, rate of adoption of irrigation, and relative importance of local editors in the irrigation movement. Apparently the first irrigation project in the valley was established in the western study area in 1888. By the fall of 1890 several small irrigation works were under construction in Dundy and Cheyenne counties, and the editor of the *Cheyenne County Rustler* maintained that "to produce a certain yield in all years sufficient to make farming profitable, some means of irrigation must be adopted." At the same time, editors in the eastern and central areas advocated irrigation, but local farmers expressed little interest in it.[22]

In 1891 a major canal was completed in Dundy County, and voters in the western part of the county approved bonds for the construction of a canal in their area. The South Fork Irrigation and Improvement Company ditch in Cheyenne County was completed early in 1892. Editors and local correspondents turned their attention increasingly toward the use of windmills to extend the benefits of irrigation to the numerous farmers living away from major streams. The moderate improvement in crop yields since the 1890 drought had not overwhelmed the irrigation movement in the western study area.[23]

In the central area, bonds were voted for an irrigation project in 1891, and work on a second canal began in 1892, but farmer interest in such projects appeared to be faltering by the following year. Even after the crop failures of 1893, completed projects were not operating at capacity because many farmers were unwilling to pay water fees, even when the ditches ran very near or through their property. No discussion of the potential of or need for irrigation in Webster County appeared until late in 1894, when the *Red Cloud Chief* again unsuccessfully attempted to awaken farmers to the advisability of irrigation.[24]

The amount of interest expressed in irrigation and the action taken to provide such works were closely related to the degree of aridity in the study areas (table 2). The farmers of Dundy and Cheyenne counties indicated concern with irrigation possibilities somewhat earlier than either editors or farmers in the other counties. Webster County farmers apparently saw little need to supplement natural rainfall, despite the entreaties of the local editor. The actual extent of irrigation activity in the three areas was closely related to the speed with which irrigation was adopted. By the end of the century, irrigation was significantly more important to agriculture in the driest area than it was farther east (table 3).

Available information suggests that in the humid portions of the Great Plains little adjustment of evaluation or behavior was necessary for the survival of people accustomed to areas with similar levels of moisture. Dramatic adaptations such as irrigation or new crops and practices were neither sought nor accepted. Persons from droughtless regions entering areas where drought was frequent or severe restructured their thinking about the environment and modified their agricultural practices more drastically (fig. 5).

By the end of the study period the greatest degree of cognitive and behavioral adjustment had taken place in the area most prone to aridity. Many farmers in that area had adjusted their cropping practices and their tillage techniques to their environment.

Table 2
Year of First Interest and Activity in Irrigation

	Webster County	Furnas and Red Willow Counties	Dundy and Cheyenne Counties
First farmer interest expressed	None	1889	1888
First irrigation activity	None	1889	1888
First editorial interest	1890	1890	1890
First major canal bonds	None	1891	1891
First major canal completed	None	1892	1891
First major break in interest after 1890 drought	1891	1892	None

Source: Local newspapers, 1886–96.

Table 3
Extent of Irrigation in Study Areas

	Webster County	Furnas County	Red Willow County	Cheyenne County	Dundy County
Number of Irrigators					
1889	N.A.	N.A.	3	N.A.	4
1899	N.A.	N.A.	31	N.A.	63
Number of Irrigation					
Companies, 1891	0	1	1	N.A.	3
Acres Irrigated					
1889	N.A.	N.A.	72	N.A.	41
1899	N.A.	N.A.	1,542	568[a]	4,552
Miles of Canals					
1895	0	18.08	18.58	N.A.	68.39[b]
1899	N.A.	N.A.	20	69	42[b]

Sources: Nebraska State Board of Agriculture, *Annual Report, 1891*, p. 75; ibid, *1895*, p. 150; *Twelfth Census of the U.S.: Agriculture, 1900.*

[a] On major canals only. Four irrigation wells were also reported to be irrigating 13 acres.

[b] Discrepancies between 1895 and 1899 figures for Dundy County are most likely due to different standards for data, and possibly are related to excessive optimism on the part of the State Board of Agriculture in 1895.

More than farmers in the other counties they practiced irrigation and crop diversification. Their inclination to search for alternatives to accepted agricultural practices and their willingness to believe in the efficacy of rainfall augmentation suggest that farmers in the driest counties realized more fully than those farther east that success on the plains was inextricably linked to agricultural adjustments.

Notes

1. Walter Prescott Webb, *The Great Plains* (Boston: Houghton Mifflin Co., 1931), p. 8.

2. U.S. Government Land Office, *Annual Reports*, 1868–1900 (Washington: Government Printing Office, 1869–1901).

3. James C. Malin has reported that only 30–50 percent of all native-born farm operators in Kansas had moved there directly from their states of birth. A

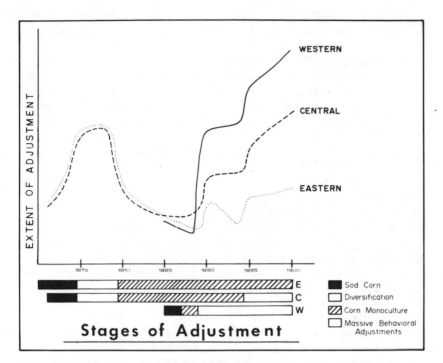

Figure 5. Changing Adaptation to the Environment and Cropping System Stages in Three Study Areas, 1871–1900

substantial proportion of those may well have lived in several locations within their states of birth before moving to Kansas (James C. Malin, *The Grassland of North America: Prolegomena to Its History with Addenda and Postscripts* [Gloucester, Mass.: Peter Smith, 1967], pp. 284–87).

    4. Enumeration Sheets, Tenth U.S. Census, 1880, and 1885 Census of Nebraska; *Tenth U.S. Census: Agriculture, 1880*. In 1889 the two states devoted about 31 percent of all improved land to corn. This was equivalent to about 38 percent of tilled land (for which no figures were published) (*Eleventh U.S. Census: Agriculture, 1890*).

    5. David M. Emmons, *Garden in the Grasslands: Boomer Literature of the Central Great Plains* (Lincoln: University of Nebraska Press, 1971).

    6. Bradley H. Baltensperger, "Plains Promoters and Plain Folk: Pre-Migration and Post-Settlement Images of the Central Great Plains" (Ph.D. diss., Clark University, 1974).

    7. Samuel Aughey, *Sketches of the Physical Geography and Geology of Nebraska* (Omaha: Daily Republican Book and Job Office, 1880); Charles Dana Wilber, *The Great Valleys and Prairies of Nebraska and the Northwest* (Omaha: Daily Republican, 1881). The concept has been analyzed by Emmons, *Garden*

in the Grasslands, and by Walter Kollmorgen and Johanna Kollmorgen, "Landscape Meteorology in the Plains Area," *Annals of the Association of American Geographers* 63 (1973): 424–41.

8. Baltensperger, "Plains Promoters," pp. 210–27.

9. Examination of daily newspapers in Massachusetts, central Illinois, and eastern Nebraska reveals that during the drought year of 1875 readers in those three areas had access to news of plains environmental conditions approximately two to four times per month. During the boom year of 1886 Massachusetts and Illinois papers carried less than one item per month about the plains. Only Nebraska readers continued to have available substantial amounts of information on the plains in good years.

10. *Nebraska State Journal* (Lincoln), July 11, 1874, p. 2, cols. 3–4, letter of Royal Buck, Red Willow, July 5, 1874.

11. Robert N. Manley, "In the Wake of the Grasshoppers: Public Relief in Nebraska, 1874–1875," *Nebraska History* 44 (1963): 255–75.

12. This is in distinct contrast to the cropping systems of the Midwest, with which most plains residents were familiar. The ratio of corn to wheat acreage in 1879 was 2.8:1 in Illinois and 2.1:1 in Iowa (Robert P. Marple, "The Corn-Wheat Ratio in Kansas, 1879 and 1959: A Study in Historical Geography," *Great Plains Journal* 8 [1969] : 79–86).

13. *The Biennial Report of the Secretary of State of the State of Nebraska* (Omaha: Omaha Republican Co., 1887) summarized population reports of county assessors for previous years. The proportion of farmers in these counties with local agricultural experience was probably even less than indicated here. The notorious mobility of frontier farmers has been well documented; see, e.g., Allan G. Bogue, *From Prairie to Corn Belt: Farming on the Illinois and Iowa Prairies in the Nineteenth Century* (Chicago: University of Chicago Press, 1963); Merle Curti et al., *The Making of an American Community: A Case Study of Democracy in a Frontier County* (Stanford, Calif.: Stanford University Press, 1959). Some residents were undoubtedly moving out at the same time that thousands were settling in the study area.

14. *Arapahoe Pioneer*, August 29, 1879, p. 5, col. 2. Corn yields during this period averaged approximately forty bushels per acre.

15. Kansas figures are from the Kansas State Board of Agriculture, *Biennial Reports*, 1877–1900 (Topeka, 1879–1901). Another factor in the rise of the corn-wheat ratio was the reliance upon corn by the frontier farmer. Paradoxically, corn was considered a highly desirable crop when yields were poor because it was needed to maintain livestock, which would have to be sold if only cash grains were produced. This subsistence-oriented emphasis on corn during the drought of 1880–81 does not explain the continued reliance on the crop after wet years returned. The surge of new settlers also increased the sod corn acreage, thus pushing the corn-wheat ratio up; but again, corn production remained high even when the population stabilized in the mid-1880s. Examination of assessment records indicates that farmers who arrived in nearby Clay County in the early 1880s were at least partially responsible for the increasing

importance of corn. These new arrivals continued to raise more corn than earlier settlers, even in the 1890s. Martyn Bowden has explored the factors which may account for the dramatic shift from diversification to corn production in the 1880s; see Martyn J. Bowden, "Desert Wheat Belt, Plains Corn Belt: Environmental Cognition and Behavior of Settlers in the Plains Margin, 1850-99," in *Images of the Plains: The Role of Human Nature in Settlement*, ed. Brian W. Blouet and Merlin P. Lawson (Lincoln: University of Nebraska Press, 1975), pp. 189-201.

16. Baltensperger, "Plains Promoters."

17. Precipitation figures for all Nebraska weather stations in operation anytime between 1854 and 1895 are reported in Nebraska State Board of Agriculture, *Annual Report, 1895* (Lincoln: Journal Co., State Printers, 1896), pp. 359-80.

18. A principal source for the study of environmental reevaluation is the massive number of local newspapers, most of which published local items and articles of interest to farmers. Nearly all available newspapers published in the three areas between 1874 and 1896 were examined for evidence of farmers' understanding of the plains environment. The termination date chosen for the study is after the end of the drought, but predates the major dry-farming adjustments. The conclusions regarding changes in the agricultural systems of the three study areas can be applied only inferentially to the adaptation of individual farming practices to the plains environment. Detailed examination of census data like that available at five-year intervals for Kansas is essential to the analysis of behavioral adjustments of individual farmers.

19. *Benkelman Republican*, February 12, 1892, p. 4, col. 2; *Cheyenne County Rustler*, June 23, 1892, p. 8, col. 3, and June 30, 1892, p. 8, cols. 2, 4; *McCook Times-Democrat*, July 15, 1892, p. 4, col. 3.

20. Bowden, "Desert Wheat Belt," p. 196. The crop adjustments in most Republican Valley counties, as in Jefferson County, were more rapid and decisive on the uplands than in bottomland precincts, where wheat production was virtually nonexistent.

21. *Cheyenne County Rustler,* June 20, 1895, p. 4, col. 1, and December 5, 1895, p. 4, cols. 1, 3.

22. *Cheyenne County Rustler*, July 24, 1890, p. 4, col. 4, and October 9, 1890, p. 4, col. 1; *Benkelman Republican*, December 5, 1890, p. 1, col. 2, December 12, 1890, p. 1, col. 2, August 14, 1891, p. 1, col. 4, and October 16, 1891, p. 1, col. 2; *McCook Tribune*, May 29, 1891, p. 5, col. 3; *Red Cloud Chief*, May 8, 1891, p. 4, col. 1, and May 15, 1891, p. 1, col. 6.

23. *Cheyenne County Rustler*, March 17, 1892, p. 4, col. 3, February 8, 1894, p. 8, col. 4, February 15, 1894, p. 8, col. 4, and March 22, 1894, p. 8, col. 2; *McCook Tribune*, July 4, 1890, p. 5, col. 3, July 18, 1890, p. 5, col. 3, September 26, 1890, p. 5, col. 3, and August 1, 1890, p. 5, col. 4. One farmer planned to use a windmill for irrigation; a second had decided to raise cranberries (*Cheyenne County Rustler*, May 25, 1894, p. 1, col. 1).

24. *Red Cloud Chief*, August 17, 1894, p. 4, cols. 2-3.

Nebraska Populism as a Response to Environmental and Political Problems

David S. Trask

Populism has long held a special fascination for historians. The multiplicity of interpretations concerning the political orientation of Populism is not just evidence of changing trends in American historiography. It is also proof of the often bewildering complexity of conflicting goals within the movement itself.[1] In contrast, the bibliography of the underlying economic and political conditions which produced Populism is less well known and less sweeping. The list of causes begins with drought and includes the grievances of the Populists themselves, which John Hicks summarized in *The Populist Revolt*. Then a highly influential generation of students argued that Populism was the result of concentrated cultivation of a single agricultural staple, either wheat or cotton, which allegedly made farmers especially vulnerable to changing market conditions. Richard Hofstadter endorsed this theory with his comment that the western advance of the diversified corn-hog economy quelled the Populist uprising on the Plains. Recent analyses have added the crop lien system and rural-urban rivalries to the list of causes.[2] In general, however, students of Populism stress underlying economic conditions as the root cause of the vigorous third-party protest, especially on the Great Plains.

The Nebraska Populist uprising is best understood as the direct result of simultaneous crises in agriculture and politics, not as the reaction to agricultural problems alone. Although the two crises were state-wide in many respects, both came to a head in 1890 in central Nebraska, along the eastern edge of the Great Plains. The Populist party probably would not have emerged as a separate political entity if the deterioration of agricultural and political conditions had not coincided. This essay examines the two crises and their relationship to Populism.

Historians have not expended enough effort analyzing the underlying causes of Populism. Scholars have frequently been content to restate the grievances of the Populists themselves, who lashed out at what they saw as oppressive mortgage rates and exorbitant rail charges. Farmers often felt they could survive drought and short crops if these other conditions were ameliorated.[3] A half century after the rise of Populism a number of writers began to explore underlying agricultural patterns and have most often reached the conclusion that Great Plains farmers in the 1890s were wheat farmers. They believe that some inherent shortcoming of wheat production caused Populism. Only in the last decade have some historians shaken this analysis with the realization that corn, not wheat, was the primary crop of the Great Plains region in 1890.[4] These conflicting analyses require examination of the Nebraska farm economy and the merits of the traditional arguments. Drought and debt, the two traditionally cited causes of Populism, fail as explanations for the political upheaval of the 1890s. These factors simply magnified deeper agricultural difficulties.

John D. Barnhart delineated the belief that drought was the source of Nebraska Populism.[5] He placed central Nebraska, the birthplace of the state's Populism, in the "Eastern Great Plains," an area of marginal rainfall. He further noted that the 98th meridian, the demarcation line of semiaridity, passed through the Populist stronghold along its eastern edge, from central Knox County in the north through eastern Nuckolls County in the south as map 1 indicates. Populism, to Barnhart, was a function of precipitation: drought caused Populism, while the return of rain cooled the political drive of agrarians.

This argument has several weaknesses. Many drought-stricken farmers remained loyal to the GOP or to the Democratic party throughout the 1890s. Furthermore, Democrats tended to become Populists at a much greater rate than did Republicans in the plains region. It stretches the imagination to believe that rainfall could be that selective.

Historians have often cited mortgage debt as a cause of Populism because they believed that this debt was accumulated as a result of economic problems such as crop failure. Census data collected in 1890 suggest, however, that mortgage debt was accumulated in the effort to enhance the value of individual farm operations.[6] High mortgage debt was not a special characteristic of either the plains strongholds of Populism or of the Populist vote in general. As table 1 shows, not one Pearsonian correlation between mortgage debt per person in 1890 and Populist or Fusion support in the 1890s is significant. On the other hand, mortgage debt per person does correlate

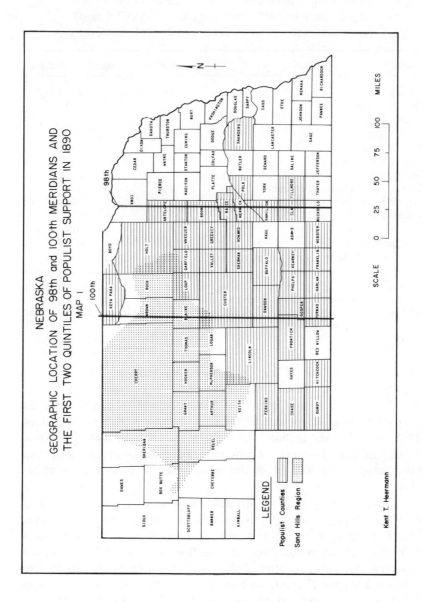

NEBRASKA

GEOGRAPHIC LOCATION OF 98th and 100th MERIDIANS AND
THE FIRST TWO QUINTILES OF POPULIST SUPPORT IN 1890

MAP I

LEGEND

Populist Counties

Sand Hills Region

Kent T. Heermann

Table 1
Pearsonian Correlation of Mortgage Debt per Person
per County in 1890 with Populist/Fusion Turnout
and with Factors Drawn from the 1890 U.S. Census

Factor	Correlation	Significance Level[a]
Populist Vote, 1890	.144	.179
Populist Vote, 1892	-.052	.628
Fusion Vote, 1894	.185	.082
Fusion Vote, 1896	.018	.870
Fusion Vote, 1898	.080	.458
Fusion Vote, 1900	.014	.894
Percentage of Population Foreign-Born	.438	.0001
Percentage of Cropland in Corn	-.341	.001
Percentage of Improved Acres	.298	.005
Percentage of Cropland in Oats	.268	.011
Number of Hogs per Farm	.249	.019
Average Value of Farm	.229	.031
Percentage of Farms Owner-Operated	-.228	.032

[a]In general, the higher the numerical value of a correlation, the greater its significance. For correlations found in this essay, any numerical value above .267 is considered significant at the .01 level or higher; a numerical value above .205 is considered significant at the .05 level or higher.

with the percentage of improved acres per farm at .298, and with hogs per farm at .249.[7] Both of these factors suggest that farmers were borrowing in anticipation of future growth. Measures of a low level of farm development correlate negatively with mortgage debt. These correlations include the percentage of cropland in corn at - .341, and owner-operated farms at - .228. The highest values of these two factors were located in the most recently settled parts of Nebraska.

The foregoing analysis of debt does not include the role of chattel mortgages, which often carried extremely high interest rates. This type of mortgage is presumably a direct indicator of personal financial distress because the collateral is personal rather than real property. Although records of this type of mortgage are incomplete, it seems apparent that a farmer would not seek this type of mortgage unless he had exhausted all sources of traditional real estate mortgages. Therefore, chattel mortgages, although they would correlate significantly with Populist voting, still underscore the basic problem in Nebraska: agricultural practices inappropriate to the region.[8]

Most characterizations of the farm economy and its relationship to Populist success revolve around the presumed shortcomings of the pioneer farming methods thought to have been practiced in Populist strongholds. Although the assumptions underlying this model do not reflect Nebraska conditions, the concept has strongly influenced scholars. According to the hypothesis, pioneers planted wheat as their initial crop. The economic success of these persons was thus totally dependent upon the market price of their one crop. After a period of time, "pioneer" farming was supplanted by a diversified corn-hog operation, which provided the farmer with additional marketing options.

The theoretical superiority of a corn-hog operation lies in the corn-hog cycle. It is axiomatic, according to Fred Shannon, that ten bushels of corn will put one hundred pounds of meat on a hog.[9] In the years when the price per hundredweight of pork is more than ten times the market price of a bushel of corn, the farmer fattens his hogs with his corn and sends them to market. In those years when the price ratio is less than ten to one, the farmer sells his hogs before fattening them and places his corn directly on the market. In theory the prices of corn and hogs fluctuate in a generally predictable manner so that one of the two options is always profitable. In practice, according to Shannon, there were only three years from the close of the Civil War to 1897 when the theory did not hold true.

The relationship of this model to Populism is clear: the Populist was a staple wheat farmer whose market vulnerability made him susceptible to agrarian radicalism. Conversely, the farmer who had developed a corn-hog operation was insulated from radicalism by his superior market position. In the lexicon of the historian, the corn-hog economy is more "mature" than a staple wheat operation. Thus the "maturation" of the farm economy in effect precluded agrarian radicalism; the model explains both the failure of Populism in eastern Nebraska and its success farther west.

Data located in the 1890 Census of Agriculture demonstrate that Nebraska Populism was not wheat radicalism. In only one county in the state did the wheat acreage exceed corn acreage. The highest percentage of cropland in wheat was 40.4 in Sheridan County, while Kearney County was second with 33.1 percent. The cropland of every other county was less than 28.0 percent in wheat. The counties with the higher wheat concentrations were Populist, but this crop was not the primary endeavor in those counties. As map 2 indicates, there was no staple wheat belt in Nebraska in 1890.

During the Populist era the principal crop of Nebraska farmers in

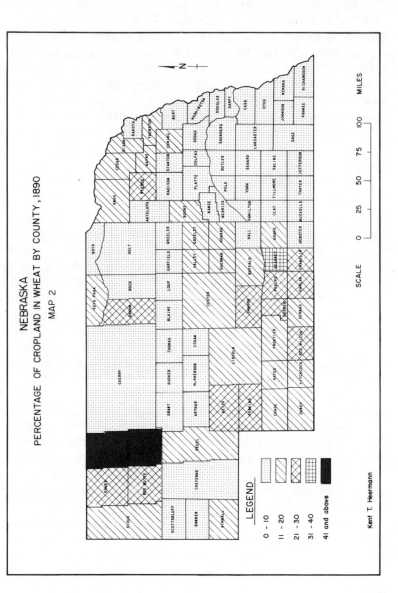

NEBRASKA
PERCENTAGE OF CROPLAND IN WHEAT BY COUNTY, 1890
MAP 2

LEGEND

0 - 10
11 - 20
21 - 30
31 - 40
41 and above

Kent T. Heermann

SCALE

0   25   50   75   100

MILES

all parts of the state was corn. In terms of acres raised, every county except three devoted at least 50 percent of its cropland to corn, as is apparent from map 3. There is an explanation for this deviation from the staple wheat theory. According to the model, the farmer started in wheat, the "pioneer" crop, and then converted to a corn-hog operation. In practice, however, the pioneer crop was corn, planted with a hoe or spade before the sod had been broken. Nebraska farmers also probably raised the same crops that had characterized their operations "back home." The tendency to maintain the old familiar patterns in a new situation has been noted in Kansas. Robert Marple discovered that the variation in crops raised from county to county in that state was a function of the point of origin of the farmers.[10]

It might be argued that the reliance on acreage statistics is misleading. Did Populist farmers receive more cash from their wheat acres than they did for their more numerous corn acres, and were they therefore more dependent financially on wheat than corn? An examination of crop yields and prices undercuts this hypothesis.[11] The 1890 census report of the 1889 crop year demonstrates the relative importance of corn. Although the price for a bushel of corn in 1889 was 17 cents, compared to 52 cents for wheat, the difference was almost totally offset by the higher yield in bushels per acre for corn. On a state-wide basis, an acre of wheat yielded an average of 13.23 bushels, which had a market value of $6.87. Corn, on the other hand, returned $6.70 per acre with an average yield of 39.4 bushels. This analysis also holds true on a county-by-county basis. In only six counties did the value of the wheat produced either equal or exceed the value of corn. Just one of these counties, Perkins, returned a large vote for the Populists. The rest of these counties were located in the Panhandle, an area of general resistance to Populism. Farmers in thirteen of the seventeen counties which comprise the first quintile of Populist support in 1890 produced a corn crop worth at least 2.9 times as much as the wheat crop.

If central Nebraska's farm economy were oriented toward crop production alone, then the traditional explanations of Populism might hold true. Any grain production would, of course, be subject to the same shortcomings as concentrated wheat production, i.e., a lack of marketing options. But the old theory, even with this modification, does not characterize the Nebraska situation, because that state's farmers were undoubtedly intent on duplicating the corn-hog pattern of older settlements.

Map 4 demonstrates that farmers across much of the state had introduced numerous swine to their farms prior to 1890. Counties

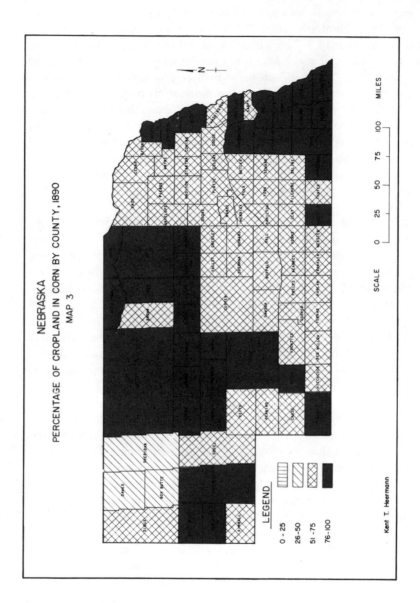

NEBRASKA

PERCENTAGE OF CROPLAND IN CORN BY COUNTY, 1890

MAP 3

LEGEND

0 - 25
26 - 50
51 - 75
76 - 100

SCALE

0   25   50   75   100

MILES

Kent T. Heermann

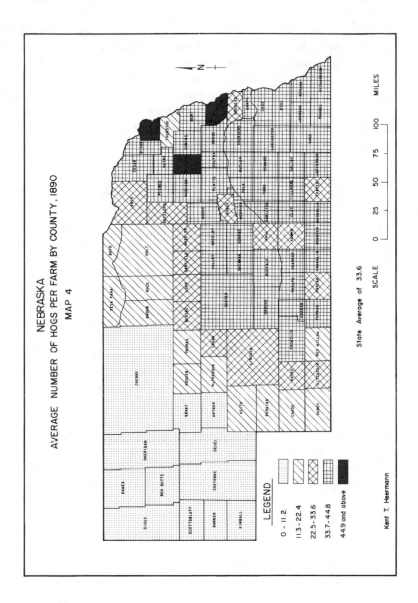

NEBRASKA

AVERAGE NUMBER OF HOGS PER FARM BY COUNTY, 1890

MAP 4

State Average of 33.6

SCALE

0   25   50   75   100   MILES

LEGEND

0 - 11.2

11.3 - 22.4

22.5 - 33.6

33.7 - 44.8

44.9 and above

Kent T. Heermann

with marked Populist success generally had as many hogs per farm as the state average. Those counties which greatly exceeded the state's hogs-per-farm average were usually located in the eastern portion of Nebraska. However, that section was not characterized on the whole by extremely high hog populations. Census evidence thus suggests that there were more similarities than differences in the farm economies of the various sections of Nebraska in 1890, with the exception of the Panhandle and parts of the Sandhills, which together make up northwestern Nebraska. Consequently, efforts to explain Populism as the product of a particular type of farm economy or stage of development lack supporting evidence for this state. Differences required to document those theories did not exist.

The significant connection between economic factors and the Independent movement lies in the attempt by farmers to create a corn-hog operation in parts of Nebraska where the climate rendered it unsuitable. Thus, in the days before the perfection of dryland farming methods, men were attempting to raise corn with the same techniques that prevailed in wetter regions. The abnormally high rainfall of the 1880s helped promote this trend in Great Plains agriculture by encouraging settlement where "normal" weather might have discouraged migration. When moisture declined, these people faced disaster.

This development was fostered by the high price of hogs relative to corn, a condition which rewarded feeder operations. When the rainfall amounts declined and the corn yields diminished, farmers in some sections of Nebraska had no feasible way to fatten their swine. Consequently, drought-stricken farmers found themselves with the exact opposite of the presumably ideal situation; instead of multiple marketing options, they possessed a double economic liability.

The real economic problem of many Nebraska farmers along the edge of the Great Plains was the misguided attempt to develop a corn-hog farming pattern in an area unsuited to it. This is not to say that drought is not devastating and that mortgage debt did not have to be paid. But a key point in this hypothesis is that as the agricultural crisis impelled many farmers to seek relief politically, they found a highly unresponsive two-party system. This situation channeled economic discontent into the third-party movement.

When Nebraska farmers turned to politics for redress of their grievances, they confronted two established parties prepared to carry out yet another conventional canvass of the electorate. The winning formula for the GOP was emphasis on the accomplishment of unprecedented economic growth, coupled with the promise that expansion would continue under Republican guidance. This formula was compatible to the core of Republican leadership, which was drawn from Nebraska's many small towns. These men sought to employ the political process to facilitate the growth of their home towns into bustling commercial and industrial centers. Most farmers were excluded from the inner circle of the party but accepted that situation during the 1880s, a decade which seemed to fulfill the exaggerated promises dispensed by land developers.[12] Prosperity had always undercut the claims of critics such as the antimonopoly Republicans that railroads and other corporations dominated the GOP while ignoring the needs of the people.

The only real threat to continued GOP political domination had always been the prohibitionist leaning of many Republicans. Party leaders had apparently dodged this threat when the state legislature submitted a prohibition amendment to the voters for the 1890 general election. This action allowed the electorate to back the Republicans for prosperity and the amendment for prohibition. Consequently, Republicans were decidedly reluctant to recalculate the political equations to figure in the weight of agrarian protest.

Attempts by some members of the GOP to address the issues raised by many farmers were short-lived. An antimonopoly Republican convention, designed to tap the energy of the agrarian revolt, attracted little support from the majority of rank-and-file Republicans. Reform Republicanism died when Governor Thayer rescinded his call for a special session of the state legislature scheduled for June 5, 1890. The agenda of the extra session included the examination of the Australian ballot, the free coinage of silver and railroad rate regulation.[13]

The presence of the prohibition amendment on the November ballot so preoccupied the Democratic leadership that they had no time for other concerns. The 1880s had been laced with issues which threatened the "personal liberty" of some voters, most notably the Germans.[14] The Democrats had devoted all of their efforts to defeating these challenges. Woman suffrage had appeared on the ballot in 1882 but had been defeated. Still, constant vigilance was needed because prohibition legislation consistently seemed no farther away than the next legislative session. The placing of the liquor question on the 1890 ballot eliminated any thoughts most Democratic leaders may have had about championing the agrarian cause. Therefore in 1890 the farmers were forced to establish their own party.

Charges and countercharges highlighted the 1890 campaign. Populists characterized Republicans as the pawns of large corporations, while the GOP branded the adherents of the new party as a splinter group of lazy farmers. Populists were denounced for blackening the state's reputation as well as its credit rating with their allegation that prosperity was on the wane. The Democrats regarded both opposing parties as essentially prohibitionist in orientation and exhorted Nebraskans to vote for the Democrats and against the liquor amendment.[15]

Although the 1890 election returns suggest the presence of three relatively equal political parties, this condition would not extend to subsequent elections. The Republicans, winners of all the state offices below that of governor, would continue as a powerful if not always dominant force in Nebraska politics in the 1890s. The Populists, swept into control of the legislature, would not be able to attain complete control of all facets of state government simultaneously. This failure, frustrating for Populists, would lead them to establish an alliance with the Democrats in 1894. Nebraska's Democrats, vanquishers of prohibition and the supporters of the newly elected governor, represented a mercurial coalition which was drastically weaker two years later.

The most significant development of the years following the 1890 election was the disintegration of the Democratic party, which had fought consistently for "personal liberty." In 1890 many Democrats in the plains region voted Populist, demonstrating that a broadening of the Democratic platform to include Populist concerns would have yielded immense political gains in that region. However in both 1890 and 1892 the established "Bourbon" leaders of the Democratic party held exclusively to the "personal liberty" issues, which had never yielded them control of Nebraska's government. These men, economic conservatives, opposed the Populists as strongly as the Republicans did. Consequently, many Democratic voters switched to the Populist column, leaving the Bourbon leaders in charge of the party machinery but without electoral support.

Populism's appeal for many Democratic voters is proved by the tendency of the 1888 Democratic supporters to defect to Populism at a greater rate than Republicans did in both 1890 and 1892. This trend occurred in 1890 in the strongest Populist counties, especially in the plains region, while in 1892 the tendency became statewide. This trait of the electorate, presented through an index of defection, is shown in table 2 by quintiles of Populist support.[16] In brief, an index of defection of zero for a county means that the composition of the Populist party was identical to the composition of that county's electorate in 1888. A positive index means that the Populist party contained a higher proportion of Democrats than did

Table 2
Index of Defection of Republicans and Democrats
to Populism as Measured by Gubernatorial Returns

Quintile of Populist Support	1890 Index of Defection	1892 Index of Defection
1	8.2	12.3
2	7.3	12.0
3	1.7	15.0
4	-9.1	16.0
5	-16.2	13.5

the 1888 electorate of that county; a negative index means Populism proved relatively more appealing to Republicans than Democrats in that election.

Fusion of Populists and Democrats behind a common slate of candidates occurred in 1894 at the state level. Many of Populism's key leaders were disaffected Democrats. At the same time, a group of Democrats receptive to agrarian concerns wrested control of their party's machinery from the Bourbon hierarchy. Fusion was the natural outcome of this situation. A splinter group of Democrats, the hard core of the Bourbons' "personal liberty" following, offered a separate "Straight Democrat" ticket, which received 3.4 percent of the gubernatorial vote.

The collapse of the Democratic party under the crush of agrarian issues is underscored by Pearsonian correlations. Table 3 shows that support received by the Democrats in 1890 correlates significantly only with the Democratic vote of 1892 and the "Straight Democrat" ballot of 1894. For other elections and other parties the 1890 Democratic vote is not a significant predictor of electoral behavior. This indicates that the coalition which helped defeat prohibition and place Democrat James Boyd in the statehouse was short-lived. The widening division between Democratic voters and Bourbon leaders was responsible for the instability of the Democratic following. Conversely, both Republicans and Populists enjoyed a relatively high level of group cohesiveness throughout the decade. Their 1890 returns were significant predictors of support accorded all parties in most subsequent elections.

Patterns of party support stabilized after the 1894 canvass. Correlations among the election results of 1894, 1896, 1898, and 1900

Table 3
Intercorrelations of Election Returns for the Years 1890–1900

	1890			1892		
	Populist	Republican	Democratic	Populist	Republican	Democratic
1890						
Populist	1.0	- .542	- .806	.757	- .277	- .605
Republican		1.0	- .054	- .286	.629	- .164
Democratic			1.0	- .690	- .129	.343
1892						
Populist				1.0	- .430	- .737
Republican					1.0	- .278
Democratic						1.0
1894						
Fusion	.277	- .275	- .101	.416	- .471	.075
Republican	- .164	.334	- .069	- .276	.556	- .122
Straight						
Democratic	- .343	- .051	.446	- .235	- .291	.488
1896						
Fusion	.377	- .571	- .027	.443	- .649	.043
1898						
Fusion	.469	- .576	- .140	.461	- .589	- .010
1900						
Fusion	.383	- .647	.012	.253	- .561	.182

	1894			1896	1898	1900
	Fusion	Republican	Straight Democratic	Fusion	Fusion	Fusion
1894						
Fusion	1.0	- .831	- .174	.572	.539	.530
Republican		1.0	.036	- .631	- .527	- .513
Straight						
Democratic			1.0	.131	.105	.096
1896						
Fusion				1.0	.787	.751
1898						
Fusion					1.0	.740
1900						
Fusion						1.0

are consistently high, indicating that the pattern of votes for the two parties fluctuated little.

With the advent of the twentieth century, there were again only two political parties in Nebraska. One was the Republican and the other, although called Fusion and officially labeled Democratic-People's Independent, would drop its "Populist" designation during World War I. With the exception of active local organizations in a few scattered counties, Populism as a separate entity was dead. The demise of the agrarian revolt happened in part because the two-party system had been reoriented by Nebraska politicians to include a voice for the previously excluded farmers. The political conditions of 1890 which had seemed to necessitate a third-party movement had faded.

The waning of the agricultural crisis of the early 1890s paralleled the reorientation of the Nebraska political system. It is erroneous to assert simply that the return of prosperity spelled the death of Populism. The problems encountered by the farmer in central Nebraska were resolved by changes in farming patterns and by alterations in agricultural practices.

The traditional hypothesis about wheat and Populism can be turned upside down: the increase in wheat production rather than the spreading of corn-hog agriculture accompanied the decline of Populism. Data found in the 1900 census reveal that many farmers began to stress wheat during the 1890s as part of their accommodation to the environment.[17] Whereas the portion of cropland in wheat of only two Nebraska counties exceeded 28 percent of total cropland in 1890, there were thirty-six counties in this category in 1900. Many of them were concentrated in the central Nebraska stronghold of Populism. Map 5 shows the emergence of a wheat belt in Nebraska in 1900.

Corn-hog farming declined in most sections of Nebraska during the 1890s. The percentage of cropland in corn in 1900 was generally lower than the 1890 level throughout Nebraska. Map 6 shows that in 1900 fifteen counties devoted less than 50 percent of their cropland to corn, compared to three in 1890. At the same time, Nebraska swine herds declined in size in all parts of the state except the northeast and some counties south of the Platte River. Map 7 documents the general reduction in swine herds which shows the reordering of farming priorities by many agrarians.

Another aspect of the changes in agriculture during the 1890s was a revolution in farming practices. Using Kansas data, James C. Malin points to the selective recovery from the economic crisis by those farmers who adopted dryland farming techniques.[18]

Nebraska Populism developed as a response to simultaneous crises in agriculture and politics. Difficulties arising from farming practices incompatible with the plains environment propelled many

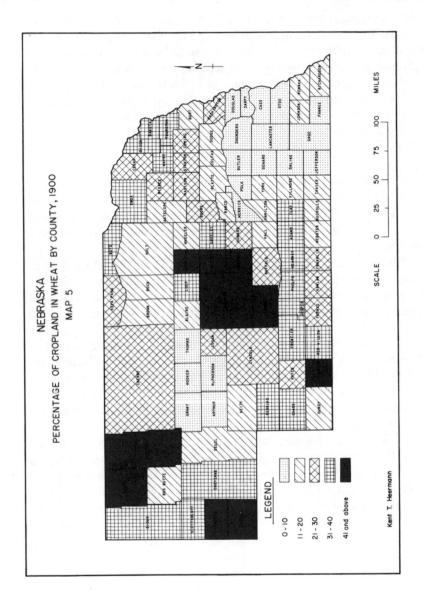

NEBRASKA

PERCENTAGE OF CROPLAND IN WHEAT BY COUNTY, 1900

MAP 5

LEGEND

0 - 10
11 - 20
21 - 30
31 - 40
41 and above

Kent T. Heermann

SCALE

0   25   50   75   100

MILES

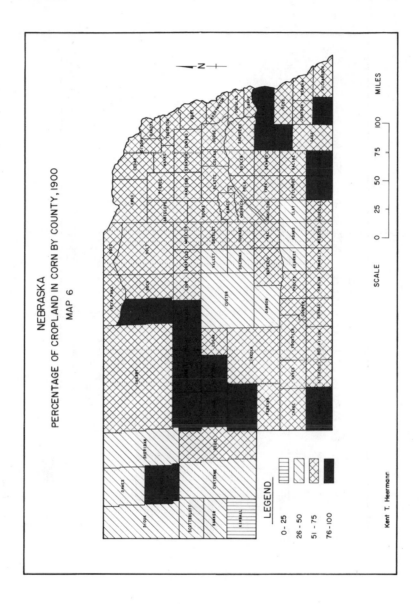

NEBRASKA
PERCENTAGE OF CROPLAND IN CORN BY COUNTY, 1900
MAP 6

LEGEND

0 - 25
26 - 50
51 - 75
76 - 100

SCALE

0   25   50   75   100   MILES

Kent T. Heermann

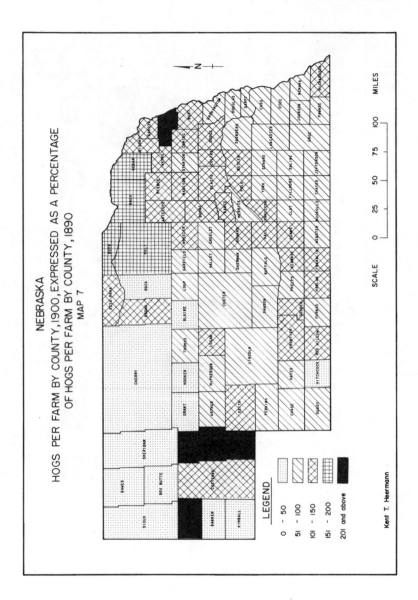

NEBRASKA

HOGS PER FARM BY COUNTY, 1900, EXPRESSED AS A PERCENTAGE
OF HOGS PER FARM BY COUNTY, 1890

MAP 7

LEGEND

0 - 50
51 - 100
101 - 150
151 - 200
201 and above

Kent T. Heermann

farmers to seek relief through politics. The disinclination of both political parties to accommodate the agrarians led to the formation of the People's Independent Party in 1890. Concomitantly, the decline of Populism during the 1890s was accompanied by modifications of both agricultural and political conditions. These changes represent the adaptation of many farmers to the plains as well as the willingness of the Republican and, to an even greater extent, the Democratic leaders to listen to, if not act on, the complaints of the farmer. Nebraska Populism was thus both a product of the Great Plains and a by-product of the state's political party system.

Notes

1. The bibliography of Populism has been reviewed many times. See, e.g., David Trask, "The Nebraska Populist Party" (Ph.D. diss., University of Nebraska, 1971), pp. 2–8.

2. John D. Hicks, *The Populist Revolt* (Minneapolis: University of Minnesota Press, 1931), chap. 1; Richard Hofstadter, *The Age of Reform* (New York: Vintage Books, 1955), p. 100. See Lawrence Goodwyn, *Democratic Promise: The Populist Movement in America* (New York: Oxford University Press, 1976) for the importance of the crop lien system. Rural-urban tensions are stressed by Stanley Parsons, Jr., *The Populist Context: Rural versus Urban Power on a Great Plains Frontier* (Westport, Conn.: Greenwood Press, 1973).

3. Hicks, *The Populist Revolt*, chap. 1.

4. Walter T. K. Nugent, "Some Parameters of Populism," *Agricultural History* 11 (October 1966): 255–70. Hofstadter, *The Age of Reform*, p. 100, summarizes the development of the wheat farmer theory.

5. John D. Barnhart, "Rainfall and the Populist Party in Nebraska," *American Political Science Review* 19 (August 1925): 527–40.

6. A review of the role of mortgages appears in Parsons, *The Populist Context*, pp. 27–30. Census Office, *Report on Real Estate Mortgages in the United States at the Eleventh Census, 1890* (Washington, D.C.: Government Printing Office, 1895), 739–40.

7. All election returns analyzed in this paper were drawn from Nebraska Legislative Reference Bureau, *Nebraska Bluebook and Historical Register for 1918*. All data on the Nebraska farm economy for 1890 were drawn from U.S. Census Office, *Report on the Statistics of Agriculture in the United States at the Eleventh Census, 1890* (Washington, D.C.: Government Printing Office, 1894).

8. Parsons, *The Populist Context*, pp. 29–30.

9. Fred Shannon, *The Farmers' Last Frontier: Agriculture, 1860–1897* (New York: Rinehart and Co., 1945), pp. 165–68.

10. Robert Marple, "The Corn-Wheat Ratio in Kansas, 1879 and 1959: A Study in Historical Geography," *Great Plains Journal* 8/2 (Spring 1969): 79–86.

11. Information on crop yields for 1889 on a state-wide as well as a county-by-county basis is located in U.S. Census Office, *Statistics of Agriculture*, pp. 375-76. For prices, see Nebraska Department of Agriculture and Inspection and United States Department of Agriculture, *Nebraska Agriculture Statistics: Historical Record, 1866-1954*, pp. 12, 18.

12. This portrait of Nebraska Republicanism is based on Parsons, *The Populist Context*, pp. 35-59.

13. *Omaha Daily Bee*, May 1, May 21, and June 2, 1890.

14. Frederick C. Luebke, *Immigrants and Politics: The Germans of Nebraska, 1880-1900* (Lincoln: University of Nebraska Press, 1969), pp. 122-50.

15. Charges against the Populists were reprinted in *Farmers' Alliance* (Lincoln), October 11, 1890. *Blair Courier*, August 23, 1890.

16. The index of defection was derived by a mathematical calculation. First, the Republican vote of 1890 was subtracted from the 1888 Republican vote. The difference was regarded as the portion of the electorate which transferred political allegiance from the Republican to the Populist party. This figure was divided by the percentage of the 1890 vote won by the Populists. The dividend (D) was then compared to the 1888 GOP percentage to determine if the 1890 Populist following was more Republican or less Republican than the pre-Populist electorate. The index of defection itself was derived by subtracting D from the 1888 GOP percentage. If the remainder was zero, then the Populist party was believed to contain as many Republicans as the pre-Populist electorate. If a positive number resulted, then the Populist party was believed to contain fewer Republicans (and therefore more Democrats) than the pre-Populist electorate. A negative result indicated that the Populist party contained more Republicans than the 1888 electorate, meaning that in these instances pre-1890 Republicans tended to find Populism more attractive than Democrats did. This explanation of the index of defection along with a fuller description of the political events related to the defection of voters is located in David S. Trask, "A Natural Partnership: Nebraska's Populists and Democrats and the Development of Fusion," *Nebraska History* 56 (Fall 1975): 419-38. For a somewhat fuller treatment of the index of defection, see Trask, "The Nebraska Populist Party," pp. 99-101.

17. All data on the Nebraska farm economy for 1900 were drawn from U.S. Census Office, *Twelfth Decennial Census of the United States, 1900* (Washington, D.C.: Government Printing Office, 1902).

18. James C. Malin, *A Concern about Humanity: Notes on Reform, 1872-1912, at the National and Kansas Levels of Thought* (Lawrence, Kans.: James C. Malin, 1964), pp. 221-22. For a comprehensive study of dryland farming techniques, see Mary W. M. Hargreaves, *Dry Land Farming in the Northern Great Plains, 1900-1925* (Cambridge, Mass.: Harvard University Press, 1957).

The Great Plains
as Part of an Irrigated
Western Empire, 1890–1914

Timothy J. Rickard

It is a historical truism that the cultural and economic institutions of the Great Plains have derived from the East with modifications in the plains environment. As regards land use systems, two notable exceptions to this empirical model are ranching, which despite Spanish roots may be considered indigenous to the Great Plains, and irrigation, another plains institution that is truly western. Otherwise, settlers and capital came from the East, farm products have always gone to eastern markets, social institutions derive from the East, and national political decisions are made in the East. What of the plains culture and economy derives from the West? Have plainsmen ever looked to the West for their social and economic institutions? Once they did, certainly. In the early 1890s, eastern farmers were beaten back from the western Great Plains. At the same time, westerners seeking the agricultural development of their section of the country turned to irrigation as the panacea for aridity. Concerned plainsmen created local irrigation movements and joined the western crusade of government officials, businessmen, politicians, and even some leading irrigators. They hoped to create an irrigated "Western Empire" with social and economic institutions quite different from those in the East. The Great Plains were to become an important part of that empire. This paper will present the irrigationist arguments for annexing the Great Plains to the irrigated western empire, analyze the irrigationist imagery of the new western civilization, and explain the demise of these ideas in the late 1890s and early 1900s.

Irrigationist images of the Great Plains environment were always deliberate and purposeful. Even before 1890, it was well established that the desert core of the western states would not support agriculture without irrigation, but there was no cohesive movement to promote regional development through irrigation. The drought, population retreat, and political turmoil of the years 1888–90 in the plains created numerous converts to the cause of irrigation and led directly to the first National Irrigation Congress at Salt Lake City in 1891. The evidence that the westward population movement of the frontier had overextended itself with disastrous results provided vivid imagery for those who wished to establish the necessity for irrigation in arid America.

The irrigationists found it necessary to define the eastern margin of the semiarid part of the Great Plains, since this line would be the eastern boundary of irrigation. Many subsequent views were influenced by John Wesley Powell's ideas. In 1879 he placed the eastern boundary of the arid region at the twenty-inch isohyet, which he estimated to coincide roughly with 100° west longitude. Eastward from this meridian to the twenty-eight-inch isohyet, Powell found a transition zone which he predicted would be "subject, more or less, to disastrous droughts, the frequency of which will diminish from west to east." In the western part of this "sub-humid region," he predicted, the agriculturalist would soon irrigate to secure immunity from drought. Toward the east irrigation would be adopted more slowly until "at a time not far distant irrigation [would] be practiced to a greater or lesser extent throughout this sub-humid region." By 1890, Powell had moved this zone west to become "along the hundredth meridian." He placed no eastern or western limits on it and only reluctantly accepted the term *semiarid* over his personally coined "sub-arid" and "sub-humid."[1]

Initially William E. Smythe, the leader of the irrigation movement from 1890 to 1895 and perhaps the most influential image manipulator of all, grasped the 100th meridian as a worthy boundary. This limit to arid America was "less imaginary than most boundaries," being "not merely a line on a map but a vivid mark on the face of the earth." "East of that line," he said, "agriculture is a fairly safe pursuit by dependence upon the rainfall. West of that line nothing is so certain about the fate of the crops as uncertainty." He identified "a semi-arid belt, where the region of assured humidity fades imperceptibly into the region of assured aridity." This region was, however, west of, not astride, the 100th meridian. In 1895, Smythe again defined the eastern boundary of arid America and the semiarid plains as the 100th meridian, but in 1905 he found a "plain mark on the face of the earth" at 97° west longitude. In remarking that "there have formerly been some costly doubts about the precise location of the line, but these have been dispelled by experience," he implied that settlers on the plains had come to accept the existence of a clearly defined barrier to nonirrigated agriculture. Certainly they had not. His own inconsistent attempts to locate a distinct boundary between humid and semiarid areas indicate that the irrigationists were practicing simplification for propaganda purposes.[2]

In general, irrigationists wishing to annex as much land as possible to arid America increasingly cited 97° west longitude as its eastern margin. The meridian received early official support in 1889 when Congress awarded twenty thousand dollars to the United States Department of Agriculture "to investigate the proper location of artesian wells and their use in irrigation in the arid region lying between the ninety-seventh degree of west longitude from Greenwich and the eastern foothills of the Rocky Mountains." In 1893, however, Col. Richard J. Hinton, who led this investigation, identified the 98th meridian as the boundary. Few, however, placed any significance in this line, which Walter Prescott Webb considered so significant later.[3] For irrigationist purposes it was more important that this limit be established at all than it be established accurately. In Congress, Irrigation Congress, and irrigation literature, the 97th meridian was most favored and excellently served irrigationist purposes.[4]

The western boundary of the semiarid region was even more elusive to irrigationists, to most of whom it was much less important than the eastern boundary. To Edmund G. Ross, former governor of New Mexico, the semiarid region "extended indefinitely westward" from the "one hundredth degree of longitude." Others, such as E. V. Smalley, identified a pastoral zone "of unquestioned aridity . . . , great grass plains, covered for the most part with bunch-grass or grama, spangled with wild sunflowers, larkspurs and lupines . . . the home of the range-cattle and sheep industries," stretching east of the Rocky Mountains an indeterminate width. Frederick H. Newell, a United States Geological Survey engineer who later became director of the Reclamation Service, was more precise when he located the semiarid region between the 97th and 101st meridians. More commonly, however, irrigationists found the eastern foot of the Rocky Mountains a convenient boundary to semiaridity. This to Newell was the boundary of the Great Plains physiographic region, which he perceived as distinct from the climatic region of semiaridity.[5]

Most irrigationists recognized the transitional nature of the zone of semiaridity in the Great Plains. Powell, in 1889, described vividly the "wonderful transformation" that occurred as "passing westward, species after species of luxuriant grass and brilliant flowering plants disappear; the ground gradually becomes naked, with 'bunch' grasses here and there; now and then a thorny cactus is seen, and the yucca thrusts out its sharp bayonets. At the western margin of the zone the arid lands proper are reached." In this transition lay treachery, as Smalley recognized in writing, "The rainfall decreases steadily as you go west across this plain but no stakes can be set to warn the settler he shall go thus far and no farther." He acknowledged that the region was "by no means inhospitable in appearance," a common perception. Few irrigationists derived "the appalling sense of a vast, barren desert" that D. H. Anderson, editor of *Irrigation Age*, chose to emphasize in promoting the necessity for irrigation.[6]

Most irrigationists defined the semiarid region in terms of its utility as well as its physical characteristics and realized that this utility varied from year to year with the vagaries of the climate. Powell noted that "in seasons of plenteous rain rich crops can be raised without irrigation. In seasons of drought the fields are desert." Fortunately, said Powell, the people were now "turning their industries" toward irrigation, and none too soon, for he had himself seen "in different portions two or three tides of emigration from the east, each ultimately disastrous," which took place "in seasons of maximum of rain."[7]

Newell, in 1902, produced a map showing all the localities where crops had been raised by dry farming, noting that in all the areas west of the 97th meridian, recurring droughts had compelled abandonment and had ruined homes. "The only people left in the country," he said, were "those who had secured a water supply through wells."[8] Previously, in 1897, Newell had described the enticing treachery of the Great Plains, which he "characterized as a region of periodic famine." Typically, he wrote, such regions "are not those of sterility, but rather those of excessive fertility and of salubrious climate inviting a dense population" where drought comes "almost imperceptibly" until "the settlers depart with such of their household furniture as can be drawn away by the enfeebled draft animals, the herds disappear, and this beautiful land, once so fruitful, is now dry and brown, given over to the prairie wolf."[9]

In particular, western Kansas was the core area of these irrigationist images of the treacherous Great Plains. Settlement had advanced farthest there with the most notably disastrous consequences. Furthermore, many Kansans were not reluctant to appraise their state and publicize its problems in the 1890s. Charles M. Harger, the prominent Kansas journalist, deplored the widespread presence of unsalable real estate in Kansas cities which should never have been established and unsalable abandoned farmsteads "where some family tried to make a home and failed." In 1897, Judge J. S.

Emery of Lawrence, Kansas, national lecturer for the Irrigation Congress, wrote that "the advancing wave of civilization has dashed up against these arid lands and then receded," creating great discontent. Thus, Kansas and Nebraska became "political storm centers, the starting points of new parties."[10] Indeed, the birth and success of the Populist party in Kansas was substantially a response to widespread crop failure and consequent rural mortgage debt.

Irrigationists resented any suggestion that dryland farming could be successful in western Kansas. Smythe, in 1894, attacked the claims of the Rock Island Railroad, the only one disputing the value of irrigation at that time, to the effect that "any part of Kansas is suitable for farming without the artificial application of water." He called Kansas west of the 97th meridian a "starvation belt for non-irrigators" and proclaimed, "It is little short of criminality to impose upon innocent purchasers a sort of land that will be paid for in children's hunger and woman's tears."[11]

Many Kansans were quite happy to tell the Irrigation Congresses that irrigation was the only solution to the economic problems of the western part of their state. Emery proclaimed in 1891 that the western half of Kansas "wants a few more drops of water . . . year in and year out than what nature gives it." At the 1893 Irrigation Congress, Judge J. W. Gregory of Garden City presented a detailed analysis of climatic statistics which concluded that the annual average of 18.89 inches of rainfall was enough to support dry farming between the 99th and 104th meridians. More than offsetting the favorable seasonality of this rainfall, however, was its capricious distribution, in which Gregory discerned a cyclical series of good and bad years. For the gambling dry farmer, Emery concluded in 1896, "the chances are he won't get the crop of wheat west of the 100th meridian." In western Kansas, he said, "we fail oftener than we succeed." Irrigation guaranteed prosperity, however, said I. L. Diesem, who proclaimed himself to be living on the first irrigation ditch in Kansas and the state's first pumper of water for irrigation. George W. Watson, a Kansan who dry farmed land in thirty counties, then told the same congress that despite improved results with deep plowing, which virtually assured a crop, his yields from dry farming frequently did not pay his taxes. Consequently, he was experimenting, most successfully, with irrigated alfalfa in the Arkansas Valley.[12]

The irrigationists, while making the case that the semiarid plains were naturally unsuitable for dryland farming, were not prepared to concede that the climate could be made more humid by human intervention. Smythe called rainmaking a "brief but exciting" and futile interlude, and Newell dismissed both dryland farmers and "rain belters" who believed in environmental modification in writing that "temporary or trivial expedients will not suffice. The heavens have been bombarded in vain, both with supplication and with dynamite."[13] A theory that irrigation would lead to increased evaporation, a saturated atmosphere, more rainfall, and an end to drought received some attention but failed to excite the general interest of irrigationists.[14] It was not in their interest to advocate turning the semiarid plains into a humid region even if irrigation were the means.

Another potent irrigationist argument for the annexation of the semiarid plains was the success already achieved by irrigation. Inventories of the success of irrigation in the arid West did not fail to mention the oases of the semiarid plains. The Greeley colony of Colorado ranked with Salt Lake City and Riverside-Anaheim as one of the three pioneer efforts immortalized in the irrigationist legendry.[15] If Greeley was "simply Colorado at its best" to Smythe, Kansas was "the mother of irrigation on the plains" and Garden City the "Mecca of students of irrigation." "Nowhere," he wrote, "are there sharper contrasts than that which is presented by these green and fruitful farms gleaming like islands of verdure upon the brown bosom of the far-stretching plains which have been seared by the hot breath of rainless winds."[16] Final testimony that the semiarid plains had been annexed to the irrigated western empire came from the United States Congress when the 1902 Reclamation Act specified that the United States Reclamation Service use the reclamation fund in all the states of the arid and semiarid West except Texas.

The irrigationists argued that widespread use of irrigation in the West would mean far more than the adoption of a suitable agricultural system. Great social changes would inevitably occur. Ranching and dryland farming promoted large landholdings and sparse settlement. Irrigation, on the other hand, led to small farms and high rural population densities. The irrigationists believed that the social institutions of the East were already established, and being Jeffersonian in perspective, they considered cities to be evil places. In the densely populated irrigated farming areas to be created in the virgin land of the West, however, they thought that Americans could create a new culture. The semiarid Great Plains would naturally partake of this culture when the area embraced irrigation.

Irrigationists expected that the size of an irrigated farm would be small. In 1891, Smythe noted, "The tendency of the man who tills the ground in the rainbelt is to spread out" and farm large areas "promiscuously and carelessly," while the irrigating farmer "farms a few acres and farms them well." The tendency toward larger farms in the Midwest, he observed in 1896, was "in order to reduce the chances of complete failure," whereas on irrigated farms the crops were "not only absolutely sure, but from two to four times as large per acre as where the dependence is on rainfall." Thus, he said, experience was constantly diminishing the size of farms in the arid region, where intensive cultivation was rewarded by large crops. Evidence from Utah, where the average farm size in 1890 was 27 acres, and from California supported these theories. William Hammond Hall, the state engineer of California, wrote, for example, that in Fresno and San Bernardino counties large tracts of land, frequently 10,000 or 20,000 acres in area, had been subdivided into 20- and 40-acre irrigated tracts. Irrigationists not only vigorously pursued the repeal of the Desert Land Act, which provided for 640-acre units, but also asserted that the basic 160-acre unit of the Reclamation Act would "be in the coming years subdivided into 80, 40 and in some favored sections into 20 and 10 acres upon which a man will live with his family in plenty."[17]

The experience of irrigators on the Great Plains was also cited to demonstrate the small size of irrigated farms. Newell talked in 1896 of the dry farmers' scorn at the idea that a farmer should confine his attention to forty acres or even ten acres in the Great Plains. He wrote, "The idea that any man on the boundless plains would concentrate his energies on 10 acres has seemed ridiculous. Yet this is what stern necessity is compelling the farmer to do, and is making him unlearn his old habits and methods, relentlessly forcing him to abandon the cultivation of great areas, turning them over perhaps to grazing, and giving his main attention to the few acres almost within a stone's throw of his door." Judge J. W. Gregory insisted that the most satisfactory size for an irrigated farm was from five to twenty acres and he claimed from experience that "in western Kansas it has been found that as low as three and a half acres, although the people are new to the business, will support a family. I know a family of nine who have made a good comfortable living on four acres, 216 miles from a city of any size and 419 from one that would be a central market for produce." Smythe outdid even this improbable story in asserting that an industrious family could get from one acre of irrigated land an income in excess of the $490.95, which represented the average income for American wage earners, and therefore "make a better living than half the people of the United States."[18]

Dry farming was attacked by irrigationists on social and economic

grounds other than the sometimes disastrous results of its dependence on rainfall. Newell, anticipating that experiments with "new
and valuable plants" and tillage methods would encourage the
resurgence of agriculture without irrigation, concluded that dry farming would never "add greatly to the population and wealth of the
arid region; it will rather tend to perpetuate the condition of sparse
settlement and careless tilling of large areas." I. W. Hart attacked the
bonanza wheat farmer of typical "rain-belt" carelessness in "skim-
ming the fertility from hundreds of square miles with successive
crops and then throwing "the land aside like a squeezed orange."
To replace dry farming with irrigation, according to Gregory, would
be to replace "desolation" and "comparative nothingness" with a
dense population and "multitudes of home-desiring, home-deserving
people."[19]

Irrigationists also branded ranching as inherently wasteful of
natural resources and as antisocial. To Governor George C. Pardee of
California, the worst insult for the West was that it "was fit only for
occupation by cattlemen." Newell called it "unquestionably a duty
of the highest citizenship to enable a hundred homes of independent
farmers to exist, rather than one or two great stock ranches, controlled by non-residents, furnishing employment only to nomadic
herders." In Franklin E. Brooks's opinion, sixteen families would
replace the two or four on each square mile as the ranch changed to
the farm. Calling the cowboy "more picturesque but less stable"
than the farmer, he predicted that "association, civilizing companionship, intercourse of man with his fellow man will follow the
isolation, crime-breeding loneliness and remoteness of the ranges."[20]

The irrigationists were convinced that their assault would mean
the end of the domain of the cattlemen. Frank W. Blackmar, a
historian who preached the irrigationist cause, praised "man's ration-
al selection directing the selection of nature," so that the cowboy,
"an essential creation of Western conditions," was "rapidly passing
away," having had, like the buffalo, "his place in the drama of
civilization." Opinion in Washington was sometimes no kinder to
ranching. The 1889 report of the secretary of agriculture to Congress
stated that "the patriotic citizen" did not "regret the decadence of
the old idea of ranching," which could neither sustain population nor
advance civilization. The report rejoiced in the progress of irrigation
and affirmed that "America can give no permanent adhesion to the
Arab or any other nomad." Smythe later picked up on this sentiment
and the range wars of Wyoming to brand the conflict one between
the "civilization of irrigated America and the barbarism of cattle

raising Uraguay [*sic*]." There could be "but one outcome," he proclaimed, as land "hitherto fit only for cattle" would be irrigated,
with consequent population growth and economic development.
"Whatever stands in the way of this development must go down,"
he trumpeted, continuing, "whoever defies the spirit of progress,
the march of civilization, will be destroyed"—by legal means, of
course.[21]

The idea that a dense population would result from irrigation
was fundamental to irrigationist dreams. The high population density
of the estimated 60 to 125 million irrigable acres scattered throughout the West would mean an effective conquest of rainfall deficiency.
Indeed, the irrigated western empire would be able, according to the
1895 Irrigation Congress, to sustain "a population at least as large
as the present total number of inhabitants of the United States."
This idea was endorsed in virtually the same words by President
Theodore Roosevelt in his inaugural address. George H. Maxwell,
the major congressional lobbyist for irrigation, boasted that home-
building opportunities in the arid West would be "on so broad a
scale that no matter how many [occupied] it, there [would] always
[be] an open gateway for them to march out of poverty and priva-
tion in the East to comfort and independence in the West."[22]

Much of the irrigationist propaganda was based on the idea that
people would leave eastern farms and cities for the superior way of
life that was to be found west of the 97th meridian. Thomas F.
Walsh, president of the 1902 Irrigation Congress, told his audience
that the small farm meant plenty of neighbors, a social advantage
for which people were leaving the isolated, lonely farms in humid
America to acquire in the city. Smythe, profoundly disturbed by the
rural-to-urban movement in America, wrote, "The bane of country
life is its loneliness, since not only the young folks, but the old as
well, keenly feel the dearth of human sympathy and companionship." This was not "purely sentimental," he said, since towns offered "many literary, social and religious advantages only to be
enjoyed at rare intervals by those who live in a region of large
farms." Irrigationist opinion was that only life in irrigating rural
communities was sufficiently tempting to stem and reverse the tide
of migration. In southern California, for example, said Newell, "the
irrigated tracts in orchards and vineyards" were so small that the
farming region took on the appearance of suburban communities,
with houses "within a few rods of one another" instead of "being a
mile apart, as on the prairies and plains of the central part of the
country." Consequently, he asserted, "cultivation of arid lands by

means of irrigation results in a far higher type of civilization than is possible on isolated and lonely farms." "The small farm and suburban life," Newell concluded, "alone make it possible for . . . people to leave the city environment and become tillers of the soil." When life on an irrigation scheme became known to be so idyllic, said Alexander H. Revell of Chicago, "life in the squalid quarters in crime and disease ridden districts of great cities will not be so alluring." The West therefore represented, said Revell, "the new land of promise."[23]

The irrigated western empire would surrender none of the "peculiar blessings" of rural life while approaching "most nearly to the realization of the best features of town life."[24] Rural virtues, argued the irrigationists, were essential to the health of the nation. Owning a farmhouse and the soil that sustained him made a farmer independent, contented, and patriotic, while life in the pure country air created a healthy mind and body. On the other hand, cities, while crime-ridden, squalid, and unhealthy, provided important cultural amenities, including ready access to public libraries, schools, churches, and public entertainment. Fortunately, said Elwood Mead, "the agricultural society of the future in the Western valleys will realize a happy combination of town and country life—the independence which springs from the proprietorship of the soil and the satisfaction of the social instinct which comes only with community association." Such conditions, he said, were "favorable to the growth of the best forms of civilization and the noblest institutions."[25]

The view that irrigating communities would be able to enjoy the most advanced amenities of urban life brought forth powerful and optimistic imagery. Franklin Brooks emphasized advanced communications media in predicting: "Through areas so thickly settled will run multitudinous telephone lines, affording instant communication; daily mail delivery will keep the individual in touch with the world, and rapid transit by suburban railway will annihilate space and free the inhabitant from the thralldom of locality." He, Frank Blackmar, and James J. Hill eulogized the "ideal democracy" created by "cooperation and associative enterprise" on the "one continuous village" of the reclamation project and endowed the community with all conceivable material and intellectual opportunities, from gas and electric lights to public libraries, theater, and opera.[26]

The most idealistic visions were of a new civilization, produced by irrigation in the arid West, that would be even beyond the comprehension of the irrigationists' own imaginations. It would involve more than the best of the current American way of life and institutions, more than "the highest degree of industrial independence and social equality yet realized by mankind," more than the most modern technology and cultural emporiums. All these would blend into the best civilization yet known, and it would happen in the desert, the best environment for mankind and in a virgin area where there were no past mistakes to erase. Smythe wrote that the character of New England, the South, and the Middle West was fully developed and the arid West was "where the genius and energy of man will win its victories in the next decade and next quarter century." Furthermore, "our agriculture being sure, our industries diversified like our resources, our climate suited to the robust physique and active temperament of the Anglo-Saxon race, we shall work out here in western America the highest forms of civilization that have been seen beneath the sun."[27]

For a variety of reasons, the arid West never achieved a utopian civilization based on irrigation. The acreage reclaimed by irrigation was inadequate as a base for a new economic system. Only 14 million acres were irrigated by 1910 and 18.6 million acres by 1920 in the whole West. Failure rates among irrigators were high and crop marketing proved uncertain. Engineering problems and administrative difficulties frequently meant an erratic water supply on irrigation schemes. In social terms, too, there were difficulties as bona fide settlers proved much harder to attract than speculators. The euphoria after the passage of the 1902 Reclamation Act gave way progressively to disillusionment until the movement ceased in 1914. Enthusiasts never doubted the economic and social potential of irrigation: failure was attributed to Americans' inability to grasp the opportunities presented.[28]

The irrigationists never disowned the Great Plains. Congressmen from the plains states fought as vigorously as anyone for the passage of the 1902 Reclamation Act, which recognized the plains states as meriting federal investment in irrigation. The line between humid America and arid America was never moved westward at any irrigation convention. After 1902, however, when images of the retreat of the frontier and the treacherous temptation of plains settlement for easterners had been used again, irrigationists drew less and less on events in the Great Plains for their propaganda.

Irrigationist propaganda about ranching and dry farming, both institutions associated primarily with the Great Plains, changed as the years passed. Irrigation enthusiasts always believed irrigation socially and economically superior but had to concede that there was not enough water to irrigate the whole West and that substantial areas would have to be ranched or dry farmed. In the Great Plains, for example, irrigationists believed that dry farmers should have an irrigated core to their farms so that they could have a pleasantly green setting for the farmhouse and a small guaranteed income in drought years. Mead, while chief of irrigation and drainage investigations for the United States Department of Agriculture, advocated that dry farmers pump underground water or store storm water on their farms in order to irrigate a few acres. He felt sure that there were few localities in arid America where enough water could not be had "for the irrigation of 1 to 10 acres on each section." Where this happened, of course, dry farming absorbed irrigation socially and economically.[29]

Irrigationists insisted after 1900 that where irrigation would replace ranching, the rangeland would be divided among the farms of the irrigating community and stock farms would result. Cattle raising would become only an appendage of irrigation. In reality, much of the irrigated land in the West came to be used to supply winter fodder to the ranchers. Alfalfa became the staple crop of the federal reclamation projects, occupying 42 percent of their area in 1911 and being the leading crop on most. In the United States in 1909, alfalfa was grown on 30.6 percent of the irrigated cropland and, altogether, fodder crops occupied three-quarters of the irrigated area. Certainly, fruit and sugar beets were important crops in favored locations, but in many arid and semiarid areas, ranching absorbed irrigation.[30]

The major problem facing the growth of irrigation in the Great Plains was the lack of an easily obtainable water supply. From the start, irrigationists realized that in the arid West as a whole, irrigation would be almost exclusively from rivers but that in the plains, where Newell branded stream waters as "exceptional in occurrence," underground supplies could play the major role. Initially, great significance was attached to the artesian properties of this underground water. Smythe noted an artesian well on a farm near Huron, South Dakota, from which a two-and-one-half-inch stream of water rose 125–140 feet in the air—more than enough "to furnish every man, woman and child in South Dakota with at least four gallons of water every twenty-four hours." W. W. Barrett, the state superintendent of irrigation and forestry for North Dakota, told the 1896 Irrigation Congress that "the largest artesian deposit in the world" existed in North and South Dakota. In the two states, he added, there were two thousand artesian wells which were "flowing continually" and had "never yet ceased to flow." He added, however, that should the artesian property be lost, the vast deposits of water would still be available because "we can put windmills throughout the entire state."[31]

It soon became obvious that the "immense accumulation of the underwater" would have to be pumped to the surface.[32] Attention, not least by state and federal investigators, then turned to ascertaining the depth and volume of groundwater and experimenting to modify windmill design. The 1909 Census recorded, however, that Texas led the plains states with 65,643 acres irrigated by pumped water, but Kansas was second with only 1,979 acres and in the Dakotas, Nebraska, and Oklahoma, underground water was even less important. The windmill was simply inadequate to pump up sufficient water to support an irrigated farm. Mead observed that at Garden City, for example, seventy-two windmills irrigated "from a quarter of an acre to 7 acres each." This volume was supplemental to dry farming only. He foresaw that gasoline or steam engines had a bright future but reported widespread experience to the effect that such devices were not currently profitable.[33]

At the same time as the problems of obtaining a water supply for irrigation became appreciated in the Great Plains, the drought passed and the gospel of dry farming gained support.[34] Many irrigationists remained faithful, but others embraced scientific dry farming or, like James J. Hill, supported both causes. The transcontinental railroads which bankrolled the Irrigation Congresses now sponsored the Dry Farming Congresses as a means of developing the arid West. On the plains, however, irrigation fervor died well before the first Dry Farming Congress in 1907. In Kansas, Garden City remained a hotbed of enthusiasm and agitation for surveys and experiments, but interest in the state legislature virtually ceased after 1897. In Texas, there was no state irrigation movement until the drought of 1907–10: the High Plains remained the domain of the cattleman, and pump irrigation was for the benefit of livestock. Response to this drought was predictably, as elsewhere on the Great Plains, irrigation; but by 1916, Texas High Plains farmers had rejected irrigation as unprofitable and their pumps lay idle. In North and South Dakota, also, irrigation interest evaporated in the late 1890s. Wet years returned, skepticism arose regarding artesian water, and many farmers ceased to irrigate. According to Mary Hargreaves, however, "irrigation remained the major consideration of those who planned for agricultural expansion in Montana."[35] So it was for the truly arid West, where irrigation was vital for crop production. In the semiarid plains between 1900 and 1920, irrigation agitation revived temporarily in drought years but declined in wetter periods.

For social, economic, and environmental reasons the national irrigation movement ended with very limited success in 1914. Ideas of an irrigated western empire then also expired. In the Great Plains, where wet periods followed dry ones, where water supplies could not be economically exploited, and where there was great reluctance to admit that traditional humid-area methods could not be adopted or at least adapted, the utopian connotations of irrigation were even sooner rejected.

Notes

1. John Wesley Powell, *Report on the Lands of the Arid Region of the United States with a more Detailed Account of the Lands of Utah* (Washington, D.C.: Government Printing Office, 1879), p. 3; idem, "The Irrigable Lands of the Arid Region," *Century Magazine* 39 (November 1889–April 1890): 770.

2. William E. Smythe, "The Irrigation Idea and Its Coming Congress," *Review of Reviews* 8 (October, 1893): 396; idem, "The Conquest of Arid America," *Century Magazine* 50 (May 1895): 85; idem, *The Conquest of Arid America* (New York: Macmillan, 1905), p. 21.

3. *Report of the Secretary of Agriculture, 1890* (Washington, D.C.: Government Printing Office, 1890), p. 39; Richard J. Hinton, "A Continental Issue," *Arena* 47 (October 1893): 618; Walter Prescott Webb, *The Great Plains* (Boston: Ginn, 1931).

4. This meridian was adopted by, for example, Congressman Omar M. Kem of Nebraska in 1894, J. S. Emery in 1897, W. V. Doyle in 1898, and F. H. Newell in 1902; *Congressional Record*, 53d Cong., 2d sess., August 10, 1894, 26:8395; J. S. Emery, "Our Arid Lands," *Arena* 17 (February 1897): 389; W. V. Doyle in *Proceedings of the Seventh Annual Session of the National Irrigation Congress Held at Cheyenne, Wyoming, September 1, 2 and 3, 1898* (Cheyenne: S. A. Bristol and Co., 1899), pp. 131–32; F. H. Newell, "Irrigation," *Annual Report of the Board of Regents of the Smithsonian Institution, 1901* (Washington, D.C.: Government Printing Office, 1902), p. 417.

5. Edmund G. Ross, "The Future of the Arid West," *North American Review* 161 (October 1895): 439; E. V. Smalley, "The Future of the Great Arid West," *Forum* 19 (June 1895): 469; F. H. Newell, *Irrigation in the United States* (New York: Thomas Y. Crowell, 1902), p. 370.

6. Powell, "The Irrigable Lands of the Arid Region," pp. 775–76; Smalley, "The Future of the Great Arid West," pp. 446–48; D. H. Anderson, extract from chap. 3, "The Semi-Arid Lands—Their Origin and Peculiarities," of his book *The Primer on Irrigation*, quoted in *Irrigation Age* 18 (June 1903): 243.

7. Powell, "The Irrigable Lands of the Arid West," p. 776.

8. Newell, "Irrigation," p. 417. Newell also wrote that "in western Kansas and Nebraska there are comparatively few places where crops are successful more than three years out of five."

9. F. H. Newell, "Irrigation on the Great Plains," *Yearbook of the United States Department of Agriculture, 1896* (Washington, D.C.: Government Printing Office, 1897), pp. 168–69.

10. C. M. Harger, "A Problem of Aridity," *North American Review* 163 (December 1896): 711-15; Emery, "Our Arid Lands," pp. 390-91.

11. William E. Smythe, editorial, *Irrigation Age* 6 (January 1894): 8.

12. J. S. Emery in *Official Report of the Irrigation Congress Held in Exposition Building, City of Salt Lake, Utah, September 15, 16, 17, 1891* (Salt Lake City: George Q. Cannon and Sons Co., 1891), p. 107; J. W. Gregory in *Official Report of the International Irrigation Congress Held at Los Angeles, California, October 1893* (Los Angeles: Los Angeles Chamber of Commerce, 1893), p. 43; J. S. Emery in *Official Report of the Fifth National Irrigation Congress, Held at Phoenix, Arizona, December 15, 16, and 17, 1896* (Phoenix: Local Committee Publishers, 1897), pp. 83-84; I. L. Diesem, ibid., p. 82; George W. Watson, ibid., pp. 85-86.

13. Smythe, *The Conquest of Arid America*, p. 108; Newell, "Irrigation on the Great Plains," p. 172. See also F. H. Newell, "The Reclamation of the West," *Annual Report of the Board of Regents of the Smithsonian Institution for the Year Ending June 30, 1903* (Washington, D.C.: Government Printing Office, 1904), p. 834, and idem, *Irrigation in the United States*, pp. 366-67.

14. John Hay, "Irrigation: Prevention of Hot Winds, Salutary Change in Atmospheric Conditions—Actual Increase in Rainfall, and Occurring at the Time When Most Needed by the Growing Crops within the Sub Arid Regions on the Eastern Slope of the Rocky Mountains," *Mid-Continental Review* 3 (May 1891): 109-28; idem, "Atmospheric Absorption and Its Effect upon Agriculture," *Mid-Continental Review* 3 (March 1891): 55-128; B. A. McAllester, "Irrigation by the Use of Windmills," *Irrigation Age* 6 (January 1894): 20; Congressman Wesley L. Jones of Washington, speech in *Congressional Record*, 57th Cong., 1st sess., June 13, 1902, XXV, 6754.

15. Smythe, *The Conquest of Arid America*, pt. 2, chap. 1, "The Mormon Commonwealth," pp. 51-76; chap. 2, "The Greeley Colony of California," pp. 77-91; chap. 3, "The Evolution of Southern California," pp. 92-105; idem, "The Conquest of Arid America," pp. 86-96; idem, "The Irrigation Idea and Its Coming Congress," pp. 402-3; Elwood Mead, *Irrigation Institutions* (New York: Macmillan, 1903), pp. 41-56; idem, "Rise and Future of Irrigation in the United States," *Yearbook of the United States Department of Agriculture, 1899* (Washington, D.C.: Government Printing Office, 1900), pp. 591-94; A. C. Blount, "Soil, Water and Crops," *Proceedings, Fifth National Irrigation Congress*, p. 65.

16. William E. Smythe, editorial, "Riverside and Greeley—Two Types," *Irrigation Age* 5 (May 1893): 8; idem, *The Conquest of Arid America*, p. 110; idem, "Ways and Means in Arid America," *Century Magazine* 51 (March 1896): 745.

17. William E. Smythe, editorial, *Irrigation Age* 1 (March 1891): 27; idem, "Ways and Means in Arid America," p. 751; United States Department of the Interior, Bureau of the Census, *Report on Agriculture by Irrigation in the Western Part of the United States at the Eleventh Census, 1890*, by F. H. Newell, Special Agent (Washington, D.C.: Government Printing Office, 1894), pp. 1-4; William Hammond Hall, "Irrigation in California," *National Geographic* 1 (April

1889): 289; Department of the Interior, United States Geological Survey, *Second Annual Report of the Reclamation Service, 1902-1903,* House Document 44, 58th Cong., 2d sess. (Washington, D.C.: Government Printing Office, 1904), p. 28; Guy Elliot Mitchell, "Small Farms for the West; They Constitute the Communities of Greatest Prosperity and Highest Social Success," *The Official Proceedings of the Twelfth National Irrigation Congress Held at El Paso, Texas, November 15, 16, 17, 18, 1904* (Galveston: Clark and Courts, 1905), p. 391.

18. Newell, "Irrigation on the Great Plains," p. 173; J. W. Gregory, "The Size of the Farm Unit under Irrigation," *Official Proceedings of the Fourth National Irrigation Congress Held at Albuquerque, New Mexico, September 16-19, 1895* (Santa Fe: New Mexico Printing Co., 1896), p. 36; Smythe, "The New Gospel: A *Little Land* and a Living," *Official Proceedings of the Eighteenth National Irrigation Congress Held at Pueblo, Colorado, September 26-30, 1910* (Pueblo: Franklin Press, 1911), p. 117.

19. Newell, *Irrigation in the United States,* pp. 51-2; I. W. Hart, "Exhaustion of our Soil," *Irrigation Age* 2 (November 1891): 291; Gregory in *Official Report . . . International Irrigation Congress . . . Los Angeles,* p. 44.

20. George C. Pardee, "Governor Pardee's Address," *Official Proceedings of the Thirteenth National Irrigation Congress Held at Portland, Oregon, August 21-24, 1905* (Portland: Bushong and Co., 1905), p. 13; Newell, *Irrigation in the United States,* p. 3; Franklin E. Brooks, "The Future of Colorado under Irrigation," *Official Proceedings of the Tenth National Irrigation Congress Held at Colorado Springs, Colorado, October 6-9, 1902* (Colorado Springs: Consolidated Publishing Co., 1902), p. 130.

21. Walter M. Kollmorgen, "The Woodsman's Assault on the Domain of the Cattlemen," *Annals of the Association of American Geographers* 109 (June 1969): 215-39; Frank W. Blackmar, "The Mastery of the Desert," *North American Review* 182 (May 1906): 688; United States Department of Agriculture, *Report of the Secretary of Agriculture, 1889* (Washington, D.C.: Government Printing Office, 1889), 266; William E. Smythe, editorial, "The Lesson of Wyoming," *Irrigation Age* 3 (May 1892): 30.

22. "An Address to the American People," *Proceedings, Fourth National Irrigation Congress,* p. 66; *Congressional Record,* 57th Cong., 1st sess., December 3, 1901, XXV, 85; George H. Maxwell, "Labor, Land and Water," *Proceedings of the Ninth National Irrigation Congress Held at Chicago, November 21-24, 1900* (Saint Louis: Interstate Manufacturer, 1901), p. 315.

23. Thomas F. Walsh, "The Humanitarian Aspect of National Irrigation," *Proceedings, Tenth National Irrigation Congress,* pp. 24, 26; Smythe, "The Irrigation Idea and Its Coming Congress," p. 401; Newell, "Irrigation," pp. 422-23; Alexander H. Revell, "A Nation's Opportunity," *Proceedings, Ninth National Irrigation Congress,* p. 224.

24. Smythe, "The Irrigation Idea and Its Coming Congress," p. 401.

25. Mead, "Rise and Future of Irrigation in the United States," p. 611.

26. Brooks, "The Future of Colorado under Irrigation," p. 130; Frank W.

Blackmar, "Economics of the Reclamation Service," *Forum* 38 (July 1906): 138; James J. Hill, *Highways of Progress* (New York: Doubleday, Page and Co., 1910), p. 202.

27. "An Address to the American People," *Proceedings, Fourth National Irrigation Congress*, p. 66; William E. Smythe, "A Plain Talk with My Readers," *Irrigation Age* 3 (April 1892): 1.

28. Timothy J. Rickard, "Perceptions and Results of the Irrigation Movement in the Western United States, 1891-1914" (Ph.D. diss., University of Kansas, 1974).

29. F. D. Coburn, "All Kansas Not to be Irrigated," *Irrigation Age* 8 (December 1895): 234; Elwood Mead, "The Relation of Irrigation to Dry Farming," *Yearbook of the United States Department of Agriculture, 1905* (Washington, D.C.: Government Printing Office, 1906), p. 437; Samuel Fortier, "The Use of Small Water Supplies for Irrigation," *Yearbook of the United States Department of Agriculture, 1907* (Washington, D.C.: Government Printing Office, 1908), p. 409.

30. "Report of the Secretary," *Yearbook of the United States Department of Agriculture, 1901* (Washington, D.C.: Government Printing Office, 1902), p. 94; Congressman Ashton C. Schallenberger of Nebraska in *Congressional Record*, 57th Cong., 1st sess., June 12, 1902, XXV, 6705; Carl S. Scofield, "The Present Outlook for Irrigation Farming," *Yearbook of the United States Department of Agriculture, 1911* (Washington, D.C.: Government Printing Office, 1912), p. 375; United States Department of the Interior, *Thirteenth Annual Report of the Reclamation Service, 1913-1914* (Washington, D.C.: Government Printing Office, 1914), pp. 10-14; United States Department of Commerce and Labor, Bureau of the Census, *Thirteenth Census of the United States Taken in the Year 1910*, vol. 5, *Agriculture: General Report and Analysis*, pt. 2, "Irrigation" (Washington, D.C.: Government Printing Office, 1913), pp. 856-57.

31. Newell, "Irrigation on the Great Plains," p. 174; William E. Smythe, editorial, "Anecdotes from the Irrigation Empire," *Irrigation Age* 1 (May 1891): 48; W. W. Barrett in *Proceedings, Fifth National Irrigation Congress*, p. 86.

32. J. W. Gregory, "Significance of Irrigation with Respect to the Great Plains Region of the United States," *Proceedings, Second National Irrigation Congress*, p. 42; Newell, "Irrigation on the Great Plains," pp. 174, 178, 183.

33. B. A. McAllester, "Irrigation by the Use of Windmills," pp. 18-20; *Report of the Board of Irrigation Survey and Experiment for 1895 and 1896 to the Legislature of Kansas* (Topeka: Kansas State Printing Co., 1897); Erwin H. Barbour, *Wells and Windmills in Nebraska*, Water Supply and Irrigation Papers of the United States Geological Survey, no. 29, House Document 299, 55th Cong., 3d sess., serial 3815 (Washington, D.C.: Government Printing Office, 1899); *Thirteenth Census of the United States Taken in the Year 1910*, vol. 5, *Agriculture: General Report and Analysis*, pt. 2, "Irrigation," p. 847; Elwood Mead, ed., *Annual Report of the Irrigation and Drainage Investigations, 1904*, Bulletin 158 of the Office of Experiment Stations of the U.S.D.A. (Washington, D.C.:

Government Printing Office, 1905), pp. 62-63; Mead, "The Relation of Irrigation to Dry Farming," p. 431.

34. Kollmorgen, "Woodsman's Assault," pp. 234-36.

35. Conner Sorensen, "A History of Irrigation in the Arkansas River Valley in Western Kansas, 1880-1910" (M.A. thesis, University of Kansas, 1968), pp. 92-112; A. Bower Sageser, *Joseph L. Bristow: Kansas Progressive* (Lawrence: University of Kansas Press, 1968), p. 25; idem, "Editor Bristow and the Great Plains Irrigation Revival of the 1890's," *Journal of the West* 3 (January 1964): 87-88; Donald E. Green, *Land of the Underground Rain: Irrigation on the Texas High Plains, 1910-1970* (Austin: University of Texas Press, 1973), pp. 14, 26-29, 62-118; Mary Wilma Hargreaves, *Dry Farming in the Northern Great Plains, 1900-1925* (Cambridge, Mass.: Harvard University Press, 1957), pp. 65-66, 126-31, 208-9, 453-67.

The Plains Country Town

John C. Hudson

What is a plains town? Cattle towns like Caldwell, Abilene, and Belle Fourche are one type that comes to mind. Dust, noise, longhorns, and Texans here met iron rails, stockyards, and the poker-faced merchants and bankers who had come from back east. There were mining towns like Galena, Crook City, and Whitewood Gulch in the Black Hills, but they passed the way of most towns born amid gold fever. Although cattle and precious minerals still form an important part of the region's wealth, the old-style cattle and mining towns all but vanished from the plains before 1910. By far the most representative type of plains town is the elevator town. Hundreds of places like Cando, Kulm, Woonsocket, and Beresford were links to the outside world for thousands of American, German, and Scandinavian farmers who populated the Northern Plains, and the list continues on down through Nebraska, Kansas, and the Texas Panhandle. Class conflicts, ethnic divisions, entrepreneurial cunning, fortunes made, and fortunes lost all were a part of life in these country towns that dotted the western grasslands.

Functionally, plains towns were first links between a staple-exporting region and a world market that could fluctuate enough to cause an advance or retreat of wheat farming over thousands of square miles. Up close, the picture was one of false fronts, boards and batten, boardwalks, mud, and hitching rails. Elevators—two, three, four, or more per town—were both symbol and function. Northern Pacific, St. Anthony and Dakota, and other giants in transportation and grain loomed in contrast with the local businesses.

Although the towns show certain adaptations to the Great Plains environment, differences between them and communities in the Middle West and East are related also to the timing of settlement. The later the settlement, the larger the accumulated stock of material and nonmaterial culture traits that are of potential importance. Thus, the institutions and circumstances of economic life upon which

99

Dakota towns were founded are different from those upon which the first Missouri towns were based, because Dakota towns had a greater stock of innovations surrounding their origins.

Towns can be considered part of the cultural heritage of the plains in the sense that inheritance implies the receipt of something from an earlier generation. Today's open-country plains village is not just the product of a peculiar pattern of adaptations begun within the region one hundred years ago. The influences reach far back into the past, they are only partially related to the natural environment, and they involve general factors of town formation as much as they reflect how those factors operated in a particular region. There are, then, two basic questions: From what previous developments did plains towns emerge? and What was different about plains towns?

Western towns have been criticized for the lack of imagination shown in their planning.[1] The grid pattern of countless towns along the tracks, ranging from Chicago down to places of fewer than a dozen inhabitants, was a logical outcome of the township and range survey system. A quarter-, half-, or full-section town plat had to fit into a system which provided no special places for towns, and it is not surprising that many western towns were microcosms of the grid of townships and ranges in which they were placed. The grid-pattern town came to North America with the French and the Spanish and was also implanted early in New England, the Middle Colonies, and the Tidewater plantation country. With minor exceptions, the agricultural villages of Central Europe did not come to North America. The dispersed pattern of farmsteads encouraged by the survey system after 1796 and various laws which opened the public domain to settlement did not promote agricultural villages along medieval European lines. There was, of course, no need for peasant villages under the dominant mode of land tenure in the plains.

If one examines many of the town plats for plains villages, it soon becomes apparent that they were not all alike, even though virtually all of them followed some sort of rectangular grid arrangement. The original plats for many towns laid out along railroad lines were oriented to the railroad's direction, which, in turn, was seldom, except by chance, in one of the cardinal directions. Many original plats were tilted with respect to the rectangular survey system for this reason. When additions were made, there was often an attempt to abandon the geometry dictated by the railroad line, and hence diagonal streets, wedge-shaped intersections, and other oddities occurred along what have been called the "breaks" in the street pattern.[2] For most towns, these departures from a uniform grid were simple, utilitarian attempts to fit village form into the land division system.

Town plans changed little in the two hundred years it took urban settlements to spread from the eastern seaboard to the plains, but town functions underwent a number of changes. It is useful to review the developments which preceded town building in the late nineteenth century in order to understand why plains towns contained the combination of businesses and business buildings found in their early years of existence.

How did the fund of knowledge, concepts, and institutions available to a prospective village businessman in the Red River Valley in the 1880s compare to what was available to, say, a Mississippi cotton country merchant in the 1840s? For one thing, the Northern Plains merchant had available to him a national banking and currency system which permitted long-distance business transactions without traveling to conduct those transactions personally. By the 1880s, also, there was a uniform, nation-wide transportation system which linked staple crop–exporting regions to warehouse and terminal facilities in the major markets. Thus it was far easier for the pioneer plains merchant to "plug in" to the national system without leaving his place of business. With the exception of early plains river towns, the sutlers who operated around military posts, and factors in the fur trade, the phase of general merchants who were buyers, sellers, and overseers of the transport of goods was omitted in the plains. Unlike that in the country to the east, most pioneer agricultural settlement in the plains occurred after those important advances in banking, transport, and warehousing functions had been made.[3]

Specialization in terms of wholesaling and retailing as well as within various retail lines was an accepted fact before most plains towns were built. Many country towns in the Dakotas could count general mercantile establishments among their earliest businesses, but specialized grocers, hardware dealers, and lumberyards were also common. This situation created more business establishments, but of smaller size each, than would have been the case if specialized retailing had not yet emerged by 1880. The imposing general mercantile company at the crossroads of the country town was less common in the plains than was a collection of smaller buildings scattered along Main Street.

These many small-town businesses carried a greater variety of items in 1880 than had been available even to the sophisticated urbanite when the first general stores were built in country towns of the Middle West and South. The decades after the Civil War also saw the emergence of name brands. Frontier newspapers carried advertisements for name brands in many items by the 1890s. Canned goods, for example, were advertised widely and there can be no doubt that western plains pioneers brought their preferences for certain brands with them. Such delicacies as canned tomatoes and canned salmon were a boon to the isolated country store owner. His stock turned over slowly in many instances and canned goods provided an excellent way of offering something beyond sugar, flour, and coffee to the isolated homesteader.

To these examples of standardization and specialization in business practices must be added the architectural standardization in business buildings that was well established by the late nineteenth century. Small frame buildings, built in roughly similar sizes and shapes, were the rule in early plains towns. It was not uncommon, for example, for the same building to serve as a hotel, then grocery store, then cafe, then perhaps a granary on a farm. A single building, small enough to be moved easily, was shuttled from one function to another, accompanying the ups and downs of business and the arrival and departure of settlers. Railroad depots probably were the highest form of architectural standardization. Styles varied from one company to another, but a single set of easily modifiable plans was used over and over again by railroad companies as they pushed their tracks westward.[4]

Three important developments had not occurred by the time most plains towns were built, and these three changes foreshortened the life span of many of the smaller trade centers. Capital intensification and labor deintensification in agriculture were occurring as plains towns were springing up, but a continued shift in the balance of capital and labor inputs reduced the farming population and hence curtailed the economic base of smaller trade centers. A second development was the automobile, which made it possible for the farmer to bypass the small town to trade in the county seat or even larger regional center. A third development, though of lesser importance, was the rise of the mail order house. The importance of Sears and Roebuck for the plains farmer may have been even greater than it was for his middle western counterpart because so many plains trade centers were small, farther from distribution centers, and offered a narrower variety of goods. If the frontier had been thirty years later in its sweep across the plains, it seems likely that the number of trade centers would have been smaller and the spacing greater.

The villages of the Great Plains were just about the last true trade center towns built in the United States. Their heritage consists of the total stock of traits and innovations in existence at the time of their founding. Plains towns skipped certain phases of frontier mercantile activity because of their timing. For the same reason, the life span of many such towns was very short; they became obsolete for their intended purpose in some cases within a decade after their founding. That condition is not unique to towns of the Great Plains, but this region undoubtedly contained more "surplus" towns than any other agricultural region of the country.

Of all the factors which differentiate the form and function of towns between East and West in the United States, I believe that the railroad is the most important. The rail network lagged behind the frontier over most of the South, catching up finally in the Mississippi Valley. Rails followed settlement across the eastern Middle West, and then pioneer farmers got into phase with the iron horse in central Illinois. The rails led the way from there to the Rockies, outdistancing the spread of the farming frontier only on the dry margins of the plains. Towns built with a railroad in mind seldom have the same form as those laid out before the railroad was anticipated.

The principal importance of the railroad in influencing town form lies, in turn, in the form of the railroad: a line. Railroad towns (i.e., places laid out around a railroad) have a linear focus. While there are other examples of towns with linear foci, namely, river towns and seacoast towns, the railroad affected the form of a far larger number of places, especially those towns built west of Chicago. Up until the 1850s, it had been common to plat towns that had at least modest aspirations around a central square. This was especially true of county seat towns, but a central green, park, or square was the focus of many other places as well. Central courthouse squares dot the eastern states and much of the upper South, but they are comparatively rare in the trans-Mississippi West.[5]

The difficulty of creating a single, central focus in a town with a railroad bisecting it gave rise to a new form in the Middle West and plains. For lack of a better term, I call it the "T-town." In its purest form, the T-town follows a basically rectangular grid oriented according to the railroad (fig. 1). The plat is lopsided, with most of the business district located on one side of the tracks. The principal avenue is a perpendicular beginning near the centrally located depot and terminating in a square or park which may contain a school, courthouse, or other public building. Two state capitals, Bismarck and Cheyenne, follow this plan, and both Lincoln and Topeka contain elements of it. The design reflects an accommodation to the linear focus dictated by the railroad, but does not sacrifice the

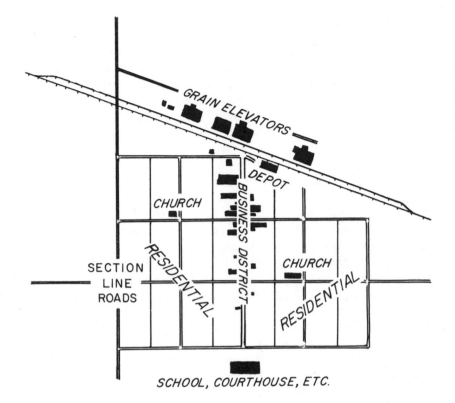

Figure 1. The "T-town." The sketch shows typical features of a type of town plat used commonly in the Great Plains, especially after the late 1880s. The basic characteristic is a main business street that joins the railroad at the depot. The T-town grew to be more popular than the symmetrical railroad town with businesses on a main street facing the railroad.

time-honored custom of locating a significant building at the end of a major avenue. The difference is that the railroad depot, rather than the courthouse, is the most centrally located building in town.

The symbolic value of a major avenue linking the railroad and the government need not be elaborated upon. The message is not subtle, but neither was the reality of corporate railroad influence. On a more practical side, the most expensive lots on a townsite were those near the center; and if the railroad donated lands to state and local governments, they did not wish to give away those parcels which could command the highest price. A tract on the edge of town was a less expensive gift. In many cases, plains towns acquired their county seat status after bitter confrontations with other aspirants for the honor. By the time the courthouse was built, the only land remaining lay at the edge of town. For these several reasons, then, railroad-focused towns with off-center public buildings became a hallmark of the West.[6]

The prototype of the railroad town probably was the standard plat used by the Illinois Central Associates. The several dozen town-sites platted by this railroad-affiliated group of promoters in the 1850s on Illinois' prairie peninsula were among the first railroad towns.[7] The plat was symmetrical, with business lots on both sides of the tracks. Standardization extended even to naming the streets identically in each town. Similarly, a number of North Dakota towns located along lines of the Northern Pacific had an N.P. Avenue, just like Fargo.

While it would have been possible to plat every single town on the flat to gently rolling Great Plains with the same kind of sym-metrical, railroad-oriented grid, that did not happen. The plat that finally came into widest use made a good deal of sense in terms of organizing and separating business and residential activities. This was the lopsided, depot-centered T-town. The focus of heavy wagon traffic was the string of grain elevators and warehouses often located on the opposite side of the tracks from the rest of the town. The "T" plan reduced wagon traffic in the business district by as much as three-fourths, compared with the symmetrical plat, which made it necessary for all farm-to-town moves to pass through the business district. Placing all of the retail businesses on the same side of the tracks with the residential area also reduced the amount of "town" traffic that had to cross the tracks, thus making a safer design with less restricted accessibility.

Geographers are in the habit of calling the trade center towns just described central places. A central place is a place that performs central functions, i.e., a small area set within farming country that is devoted to the sale of goods and services to the surrounding farm population and also buys the agricultural produce of the area imme-diately surrounding the central place. The number of central func-tions performed in a central place depends on the size of the trading area the town dominates; the larger the tributary area, the more and the greater the variety of central functions performed by the town (fig. 2). An elaborate theory has been deduced from these relation-ships and the Middle West-Great Plains has been a favorite area for testing it.[8] The characterization of a town as a place which performs

Figure 2. Market Day at Scranton, North Dakota, 1922. (Photo courtesy of Agnes Potter, Bowman, N.D.)

central functions for a surrounding farm population turns out to be almost uncannily accurate for early plains towns.

An agricultural village is a different type of settlement, although it resembles a central place in that both are clusters of buildings amid the open expanse of fields. An agricultural village is a place where farmers (owner, tenants, or laborers) live. Such villages may perform central functions for the farming population, but that population lives in the village instead of on the land. Agricultural villages were found in colonial New England and were used in the civic pueblo form of Spanish agricultural colonization. They are also found in other scattered areas where settlement was planned from the outset. This type of village, which has ancient origins and still is dominant in parts of Europe and much of Africa and Asia, was eclipsed by the central place very early in the westward movement of the American frontier.

The idea of a "place" in open country which performed a function but was not necessarily a place of residence was first represented in America by the isolated courthouses, churches, and country stores of the South. The practice of collecting these scattered central functions into a central place inhabited only by those performing central functions may have its origins in the fortress towns of Europe. Whatever the origins, the idea definitely predates white settlement in

North America, but on this side of the Atlantic it gained dominance because it was in favor during the initial settlement phase when decisions about such things were made.

By the time agricultural settlement reached the plains, the central place was nearing its ultimate state of development. The neophyte from back east was startled to find towns that contained streets, schools, business buildings, and churches but only a handful of dwellings—just the bare minimum to house those who felt they had to live in the town to run their businesses. Great Plains towns, then, were central places par excellence: they performed central functions for the surrounding rural population, but often they contained few inhabitants.

In the one-hundred years since their founding, many central places on the plains have gone through changes completely reversing the initial balance between people and functions. Today, the old stores are boarded up or are sometimes used as residences. When farmers in the surrounding country retire, they move into town. The towns have acquired inhabitants while they have lost central functions.

I will use what is perhaps an extreme example to illustrate the nature of early central places on the plains. Fredonia, in Logan County, North Dakota, was founded in 1904, consisting of a grain elevator and nothing else. George Gackle, a businessman from nearby Kulm, enticed the local farmers to build a railroad siding at the soon-to-be Fredonia so that Gackle's firm, which owned the surrounding land, could put an elevator there. This country elevator was sought by the local farmers because up until then they had had to haul their grain a much longer distance. The Salzer Lumber Company of Minneapolis sent out quite a bit of lumber to build Gackle's elevator, and instead of letting what was left over go begging, they opened a lumberyard; now the town had two central functions. A local farmer, Gottlieb Gieser, was hired to manage Gackle's elevator, and in his spare time he sold lumber for Salzer. Meanwhile, Gackle's firm acquired another business partner, and the new partner's son, Daniel Flaig, was sent to Fredonia to open up a general mercantile business. When a post office was acquired, it was housed in Flaig's store and he was made postmaster. During 1904 and 1905, Gieser and Flaig were the only two inhabitants of Fredonia; Flaig lived in the store-post office, but Gieser finally moved his family to Fredonia, building the first house. The town grew, adding a central function each time a new inhabitant arrived, until by 1915 it contained an additional general store, a livery stable, two banks, a depot, a hardware store, a school, three more elevators, a meat market, hotel, novelty store, and a church, but not more than a few dozen inhabitants.[9] The population grew to more than four hundred, even at the end of the Depression, but the role of Fredonia as a central place kept shrinking. It contains fewer than one hundred inhabitants today and has all but lost its role as a central place, save for grain marketing, the basis upon which it was founded.

Too many towns were built on the Great Plains. If any generalization about plains towns has been documented adequately, it would have to be this one.[10] Since the early town builders did not have our advantage of hindsight, it must be asked if they acted in bad faith, or if they acted simply out of ignorance of the changes to come which made so many of the towns obsolete. I think it is unlikely that most town promoters would have acted as they did had they anticipated what was to come once the Model-T gained acceptance. There were "paper" towns, of course, but the number was small compared with that of towns actually built. Many town promoters were also businessmen, bankers, or merchants whose fortunes depended on the economic growth of their town. I doubt that many of these small-town banker-promoters were in the business because they anticipated making foreclosures in later years.

Plains towns were based on a transportation technology consisting of railroads, teams, and wagons just as surely as today's gargantuan shopping centers are based on the family automobile. When transportation shifted from horse power to reliance on the internal combustion engine, the settlement pattern of the plains (and other areas) was antiquated.

Railroads dictated not only the internal form of most plains towns but also their spacing along the line. Railroad townsite promoters might have become so greedy at the prospect of selling business and residential lots that they created more towns than could survive. Any tendency in this direction had to be tempered by the realization that the railroad faced certain fixed costs in terminal and handling facilities in every town constructed. There were instances in North Dakota (such as Fredonia) where the railroad planned too few towns and farmers petitioned for additional central places.

If any group or class can be blamed for encouraging the overbuilding of towns, it would have to be the farmers themselves. Having a conveniently located trade center meant much to the homesteader, who often arrived with nothing except his draft animals to get him to town. A twenty-mile trip meant an overnight stay in town for such a person. Many a pioneer farmer spent the cold months of winter making trip after trip hauling his grain to the nearest elevator. It is little wonder that grain farmers were seldom found in the larger interstices not yet served by railroads, and it seems only natural that even the hint of a new railroad branch with new towns nearby was welcomed with great enthusiasm by the farmers.

Another piece of technology that influenced the spacing of elevator towns was the elevator itself. An economical size for a country elevator in the late nineteenth century was a storage capacity of about thirty thousand bushels; this was a standard size in which dozens of identical-looking elevators were built by the line elevator companies operating out of Minneapolis and elsewhere. Assuming (somewhat conservatively) that 20 percent of the land area was sown to wheat, that yields varied in the range of fifteen to twenty bushels per acre, and that a single elevator could turn over between three and five times its storage capacity per harvest, then it would require between thirty-five and seventy-eight square miles to support a single elevator. The lower estimate would be about one elevator per township, the upper estimate about one elevator for every two townships. An optimal pattern of elevators from the farmers' viewpoint would have been one elevator in each township, a pattern in which no one would have been more than six miles from an elevator.

Nothing close to this density of uniform spacing occurred, even in the best wheat country, because not that many miles of railroad track seemed warranted. Instead, each town along the railroad contained a number of separate elevators, usually constructed by competing grain companies. There might well have been more elevator towns had not the railroad actually concentrated elevators into fewer locations than a uniform spacing optimal for the farmers would have produced.

There was a remarkable uniformity in the types of central functions performed by early trade centers in the Great Plains. Everyone knew that any up-and-coming town had to have a bank, and when town lot auctions were held, it behooved the aspiring banker to bid on one of the high-priced corner lots on the townsite. Banks, after all, belong at the principal intersection in the heart of town. If there was more than one banker, and there often was, he was engaged in fierce competition with his stronger rival right up to the day he was forced to sell out, or to the day the "state men" found certain irregularities in his books, or to the Depression, whichever came first.

One of the first buildings constructed in many plains towns was a hotel. Prospective land buyers had to have a place to stay, as did the drummers out from the big city with their sample cases brimming full of the goods that everybody needed. Transients needed transportation, so dray lines and livery stables were other early additions. Restaurants came early, too, catering especially to the large transient labor force that was putting up the buildings in town. Most of these businesses, along with general mercantile establishments, butcher shops, hardware stores, and others, were owned locally and occupied the original, central portion of the townsite (figs. 3 and 4).

Down at the tracks were the three enterprises that were seldom owned by local folks: the railroad itself, the grain elevator, and the lumberyard. In later years, especially, farmers formed cooperatives and went into the elevator business themselves. Many lumberyards controlled from afar were eventually sold to local people, but initially they were usually owned by outsiders and managed by a local citizen.

It is difficult to imagine how anyone could have lost money in the lumber business in a plains frontier town. Virtually the whole town was built of sawed lumber and practically all of it had to come from outside (fig. 5). A lumberyard in one of these budding communities was not often anything fancy: it consisted of stacks of usually green lumber sawed in standard dimensions, sometimes a

Figure 3. Flasher, North Dakota, ca. 1907. (William H. Brown Co. photo.)

Figure 4. Social gathering in the general store at Rock Lake, North Dakota. (Harrison Collection, State Historical Society of North Dakota.)

Figure 5. Lumber being freighted into Mott, North Dakota, from Richardton, in 1910, before the railroad reached Mott. (William H. Brown Co. photo.)

shed to protect the merchandise from the elements, but often nothing more than a few pieces of canvas for cover. The yard man was
there to protect the supply from thieves, to unload carload shipments, and to sell. Many line elevator companies operated lumberyards as a sideline, and eventually added coal and feed as other
sidelines once the farming population reached sufficient numbers.

Regional patterns of urban influence are revealed in a map of
lumberyards for North and South Dakota in 1905 (fig. 6). Minneapolis lumbermen (and, coincidentally, grain buyers) ran strings of line
lumberyards in both Dakotas. Agreements between lumber, grain,
and railroad people resulted in certain companies dominating the
lumber business along the tracks owned by specific railroad companies. Lumbermen from Winona, Minnesota, operated quite a few
yards in central South Dakota, and in southeastern South Dakota,
Iowa lumbermen set themselves up in business. The local urban
centers, such as Grand Forks, Fargo, Aberdeen, and Sioux Falls,
were headquarters for line yards that were not quite as far-flung. The
arrangement of market areas is a familiar one, with smaller markets
nesting within the area of dominance of larger places.

When the railroad was pushed on west, there was commonly an
exodus of transient laborers not quite matched by the continued
influx of new business persons. The use of standardized—one might
even say modular—business buildings allowed new merchants to take
over from those who left. It is difficult to piece together the sequence and locations of business activities of plains frontier towns
because the turnover was so rapid. The same individuals often engaged in a sequence of sometimes quite unrelated businesses; separate
individuals often moved the same business (including the building)
from one site to another, because even though the town lots were
sold rapidly, comparatively few lots actually had buildings on them;
and a single individual often operated more than one business at a
time. This fluidity characterized locally owned businesses more than
those owned by line elevator and lumberyard companies, but there
was a turnover among the latter as well. It took ten years for this
phase of trial-and-error moving about to be replaced by a more
stable pattern. By that time, nearly all plains towns were marked for
either growth or stagnation, whether by the circumstances of geography or by the entrepreneurial skills of their business people.

Even to most landlubbers the term *inland town* suggests a community located away from navigable water. This was not, nor is it
today, the meaning understood on the Great Plains: an inland town is
a town not on a railroad. In fact, it is a category whose numbers are

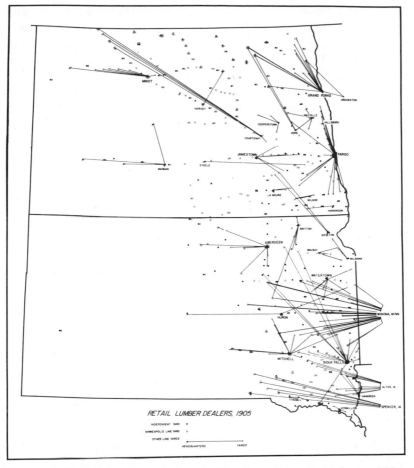

Figure 6. Retail lumber dealers in North and South Dakota, 1905. All the dealers in towns containing at least one member of the Northwestern Lumbermen's Association are shown. This Minneapolis-based association had more than 2,600 members in 1905, in Minnesota, Iowa, North Dakota, South Dakota, and northeastern Nebraska. Source: *Directory of Regular Retail Lumber Dealers* (Northwestern Lumbermen's Association, Minneapolis, 1905).

growing each year as railroad branch lines are abandoned, leaving country elevator towns high and dry (to continue the nautical terminology). During the pioneer settlement phase, inland towns frequently did not survive when a railroad passed them by; their central functions were transferred to the new railroad town. The only inland towns which survived this dislocation with honor were those located some distance from the railroad, and their determined inhabitants stayed put in hopes that the promised branch line one day would be built.[11]

No accurate count of the number of these proto-central places has been made, but in some areas there were as many as five inland towns for each railroad town eventually built.[12] Some of them contained a dozen or more businesses, but usually there was nothing more than a combination store and post office. Inland towns often did a good business in the relatively brief period after settlers arrived and before the railroad was put through, but their location out ahead of the railroad put them at a competitive disadvantage with the railhead town.

The disadvantage to the inland merchant came in the much higher per-mile costs of overland drayage compared with the relatively cheaper per-mile costs of rail transport. The inland merchant usually purchased his stock at the railhead, either from a local merchant or from urban wholesalers who shipped by rail. If his business was large enough to sustain contact with a wholesaler, or if he was able to buy from the railhead merchant below the retail price, then he could dominate his market by taking a smaller markup (fig. 7). If he had to buy at retail himself, then the farmer located

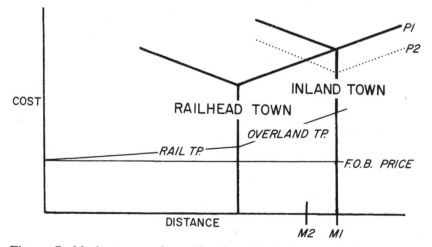

Figure 7. Market areas for railhead and inland towns. The inland town was at a disadvantage because all supplies had to come by wagon from the railhead. If the inland merchant took the same profit per item as the railhead merchant, the inland merchant could not dominate a market. If he reduced his profit margin from *P1* to *P2*, then his market boundary was at *M2*.

near an inland town would be indifferent between a longer trip to the railhead and a shorter trip to the inland merchant, assuming that the inland merchant included his own transport costs in the selling price of the goods in his store.

Hence the isolated homesteader had a choice between a short trip to a nearby inland town and a longer trip to the railhead town. Since he commonly went to town with a wagon and thus had a large carrying capacity, and because nearly all the goods available were nonperishables, he often preferred to do his trading in the railhead town, but he made fewer trips than if he traded closer to home. His infrequent visits to the railhead town combined trips to market crops and livestock with trips to absorb some of the exciting life in a place actually connected to the outside world he had left behind. Another problem that worked against the success of the inland merchant was his inability to maintain a sufficient stock of goods. His business was not large enough to justify the inventory carried by his counterpart in the railhead town.

There was one "perishable" that the inland merchant could acquire: if he got enough local signers on a petition, he could become a postmaster. His trips to the railroad to pick up mail then paid for his transportation, and, more important, he had the advantage that local folks stopped at his place anyway in order to get their mail. The institution of rural free delivery (1896) was the final blow to many inland towns which thereby lost their one advantage.

The railhead merchant had a competitive advantage over the inland merchant, but he, too, faced hard times when the railroad moved on. I believe that accounts of town abandonment caused by the railroad when it pushed ahead have been exaggerated. Railhead towns did command much larger market areas because farmers (usually to the west of the railhead) had no alternative market, no matter how far ahead of the rails they chose to locate. Some merchants chose to move each time the railroad moved ahead, but that did not produce outright abandonment of former railhead towns in most cases, although it did mean that the marketing or tributary area of the town contracted in the direction in which the railroad was built.

The scattered central functions found in areas not yet reached by the railroad were collected into central places largely by the activity of platting a townsite along the railroad. Few inland merchants were willing to absorb the transportation cost disadvantage that they faced by remaining isolated. Like grain elevators, railroads probably did more to concentrate central functions into fewer central places than they did to proliferate the number of such places.

The plains country town, like all towns in America, has its origins in building, planning, and business traditions brought from Europe. In addition, plains towns were the product of two hundred years of economic, social, and geographical changes in America. In their internal geography, the functions they performed, and their number and spacing, plains towns also grew out of the peculiar circumstances of rapid settlement of the western grasslands in the late nineteenth century. In the past one hundred years, the villages of the Great Plains have suffered from innovations that were still unknown at the time of their founding.

I have not touched on many aspects of the plains town, concentrating mainly on the traditional themes of form and function, and in closing I would like to suggest briefly one other theme that ought to attract scholars to this subject. There is growing evidence of strong rural-urban frictions which may have been implanted in plains towns from their founding.[13] Businessmen were far more likely to be native-born Americans, born to American parents, than were the farmers. The kind of life these businessmen and their wives favored resembled the society they left behind in more established towns of the Middle West and East. The proliferation of town businesses was matched by the proliferation of social clubs, lodges, church groups, and other organized activities. The social life of the pioneer homesteader was something else entirely; socials and dances held at neighbors' homes, ball games, picnics, and the like were more typical for the rural dweller in the early days. When rural social neighborhoods collapsed after the consolidation of rural schools and the abandonment of country churches, social life for rural and urban people tended to come together, especially since the automobile permitted the farmer to get to town. Whether or not the division in social life was caused by isolation in the early days, or whether it was inevitable given the different backgrounds of townspeople and farmers, probably is less important than the fact that the division came with the arrival of the settlement frontier itself.

The cultural heritage of the plains is most often approached from the point of view of the farmer-homesteader. This is logical, considering the overwhelming importance of agriculture, but some of the more distinctive institutions of the region could not have emerged without the contrasting way of life in the towns. Political radicalism is perhaps the most notable of these traits which grew at least partly out of the different interests represented by town and rural folk. The town contained both the aspects of life that the farmer longed for and those he detested. Given what might have been strong predispositions to distrust or disrespect one another, I can think of no settlement arrangement that could more effectively have segregated farmers and merchants than the compact central places and dispersed farm residences which blanketed the Great Plains.

Notes

1. John W. Reps, *The Making of Urban America* (Princeton, N.J.: Princeton University Press, 1965), chap. 11.

2. Grady Clay, *CLOSEUP: How to Read the American City* (New York: Praeger, 1973), pp. 42–50.

3. Lewis Atherton, *The Frontier Merchant in Mid-America* (Columbia: University of Missouri Press, 1971); idem, *The Southern Country Store* (Baton Rouge: Louisiana State University Press, 1949).

4. Frank E. Vyzralek, H. Roger Grant, and Charles Bohi, "North Dakota's Railroad Depots: Standardization on the Soo Line," *North Dakota History* 42 (1975): 5–25.

5. Edward T. Price, "The Central Courthouse Square in the American County Seat," *Geographical Review* 58 (1968): 29–60.

6. Central squares did appear in some plains towns. Several townsites platted along branches of the Great Northern Railroad contained central squares. The rarity of this design for the plains is indicated by a recent proposal to nominate the square of Antler, North Dakota, for inclusion in the National Register of Historic Places. See Dawn Maddox, "The National Register in North Dakota," *Plains Talk* 8 (1977): 1–2.

7. Paul W. Gates, *The Illinois Central Railroad and Its Colonization Work* (Cambridge, Mass.: Harvard University Press, 1934), pp. 126–27.

8. Brian J. L. Berry, *Market Centers and Retail Distribution* (Englewood Cliffs, N.J.: Prentice-Hall, 1967).

9. "Historical Survey of Fredonia, North Dakota," MS, State Historical Society of North Dakota, Bismarck, North Dakota.

10. Towns platted after the boom of the 1880s, and especially those platted after 1900, were of more modest aspirations than those platted earlier. There does not seem to have been any tendency to increase the spacing in later years, however.

11. New railroad construction more or less halted on the plains by World War I. Some areas of agricultural settlement never were reached by the railroads. For example, homesteaders poured into Harding County, South Dakota, between 1907 and 1914, and several attempts were made to get a railroad, the last one in 1921. See *Building an Empire: A Historical Booklet on Harding County, South Dakota* (Buffalo, S.D.: Buffalo Times-Herald, 1959), p. 33. The "Jordan Country" of Garfield County, Montana, was settled by farmers between 1913 and 1919. The dry-farming country around Jordan was seventy-five miles from the nearest railroad, and there was much interest in getting either the Great Northern or Northern Pacific to build through the area. Despite assurances and

expressions of interest by both companies, no railroad was built. The local newspaper editor continued to state his belief that the railroad was coming, even
through the early 1920s, but in 1931 he wrote that "what Jordan needs most is
a first-class drug store and a first-class bank"*(Jordan Tribune*, April 16, 1931).

12. For example, Sanborn County, South Dakota, contained at one time or
another approximately twenty-five places performing some type of central function. Twenty were abandoned and the remaining five were on the railroad. See
S. S. Judy and W. G. Robinson, "Sanborn County History," *South Dakota
Historical Collections* 26 (1952): 1-180. A manuscript history of Medford
Township, Walsh County, North Dakota, indicates that this township had a
general store, a blacksmith shop, a post office, a doctor, three schools, and a
church, all in scattered locations. When the village of Medford (now Fordville)
was platted in the township, all the scattered facilities except the rural schools
and church were replaced by the village. See "Medford Township (155-56),"
MS, State Historical Society of North Dakota, Bismarck, North Dakota.

13. The most thorough study of this theme is Robert Dykstra, *The Cattle
Towns* (New York: Knopf, 1968). See also idem, "Town-Country Conflict: A
Hidden Dimension in American Social History," *Agricultural History* 38 (Octo-
ber 1964): 195-204, and Stanley B. Parsons, Jr., *The Populist Context: Rural
versus Urban Power on a Great Plains Frontier* (Westport, Conn.: Greenwood
Press, 1973).

The Standardized Railroad Station on the Great Plains, 1870–1920

H. Roger Grant

Not so long ago the American railroad station served as a vital community focal point. From the bustling eastern metropolis to the sleepy prairie village, train time meant much to the local citizenry. "The depot," observed an Iowa real estate broker in 1903, "is always a beehive of activity. The hustle-bustle, which is America, can be found there."[1] The depot held special significance in towns and villages before the automobile, truck, and bus gained their present dominance in intercity travel. Unquestionably, it served as the community's gateway to the world.

Thus, it is understandable that communities continually sought to obtain and to improve depot service. The records of state railroad commissions are full of complaints about carriers' neglect of depot matters. Citizens, whether living in Vermont or Nebraska, eagerly labored to make the local railroad station a "first-class" facility.

While the role the railroad station played in the daily lives of Americans did not differ regionally, depot architecture did. When the country is viewed by geographic sections during the late nineteenth and early twentieth centuries, the hundreds of railroad stations that dotted the Great Plains shared characteristics that made them distinct from those constructed elsewhere. Depots on the plains were adapted to meet special geographic and business conditions. The results were evident to the discerning traveler. Writing in the 1890s to a Burlington Route official, a perceptive Boston, Massachusetts, businessman and stockholder remarked, "After spending months traveling through Dakota, Wyoming Terr., Colorado, and Nebraska, I am struck by the poor quality of most buildings. . . . Small stations especially are often of the dullest and most despicable types. I saw few elegant and commodious stations while in this rather unpleasing part of the Republic. Yet there are wonderful ones east of the Missouri R., out in California and throughout the Southlands." He concluded, "I suppose a railway company like ours [Chicago,

Burlington and Quincy] cannot afford to spend large sums for such accommodations and the absence or rather reduction in this item of expenditure is one of the causes why railroads out there have such poor buildings for the public."[2]

While there are exceptions, the gentleman's view of the typical Great Plains railroad station was correct. Depots built there tended to be cheap, wooden, often architecturally sterile structures fashioned from standardized plans. Moreover, some initial stations were flimsy portable or temporary ones. If the carrier replaced them, it likely built a carbon copy combination-style depot, often with living quarters.

Why stations of standard design predominated on the plains is subject to several explanations. For one, the construction of trackage in the trans-Missouri West coincided with national trends toward standardization in both life-styles and architecture during the late nineteenth century. Railroad building boomed on the prairies during the 1880s and 1890s. Dakota claimed only 1,225 miles of rail lines in 1880, but by 1900 the states of North and South Dakota had a collective total of 5,581 miles; Nebraska's mileage was 1,953 in 1880; twenty years later it reached 5,685; Kansas trackage rose from 3,400 miles in 1880 to 8,719 at century's end; while the combined railroad mileage of Indian and Oklahoma territories and Texas soared from 3,533 to 12,037 during this same period. Comparable increases occurred in the High Plains regions of Montana, Wyoming, Colorado, and New Mexico. Of course, with this vast railroad construction, numerous station buildings were needed at trackside to serve the public's needs.[3]

These years, 1880–1900, witnessed the triumph of standardization in American life. While the average citizen likely expressed an abiding belief in individualism as it supposedly sprang from the frontier experience, he quickly accepted a homogenized way of living. Standardized brand-name consumer products, for instance, became commonplace by the turn of the century. In *Main Street on the Middle Border* historian Lewis Atherton demonstrates how the "Battle of the Brands" shortly after the Civil War revolutionized the country's merchandising and buying habits. "Once Singer Sewing Machines had been widely advertised," Atherton writes by way of illustration, "women demanded to see them before making a final choice, and retailers had to carry Singer models or lose trade to stores which did."[4] Standardization came in other diverse forms as well: in a uniform railroad gauge (4'8½"), standard time zones, and even the regularization of playing rules for the national pastime.

Standardization similarly invaded American architecture. During the latter part of the century decorative building parts for both internal and external use could easily be ordered from scores of mill-work factories; one had only to choose from their profusely illustrated catalogs. Perhaps architectural standardization reached its zenith when prefabricated houses, churches, and even hotels and privies could be ordered by mail for shipment to virtually any location. These trends showed up particularly in the West. Hamlin Garland, for one, noted those "flimsy little wooden towns" on the South Dakota prairie where elevators, stores, and houses shared a depressing sameness.[5]

The cost factor, however, was the principal determinant of standardized architectural styles on the Great Plains, whether for grain elevators or railroad depots. In the East, especially, most towns existed before the coming of the rails. Therefore, companies could predict the traffic potential of each community. A college town, a county seat, or an important trading center deserved a station that reflected its standing. But this was generally not the case in the trans-Missouri West, where railroads often preceded settlement. Railway carriers were regularly in the townsite business and frequently planned communities every five to fifteen miles along their lines. The economic prospects of such new towns were uncertain. While railroads might paint glowing pictures of these "New Edens" through their townsite operators and in close conjunction with local boosters, the harsh reality dictated that a sizable number of these raw villages were destined to remain whistle stops. Town promotion was risky. Great Plains roads, often hard pressed for funds because of high construction costs and related expenses, did not want to invest in a depot for a new settlement that might not last. Similarly, they did not desire a station that would be too large for local needs.

Closely related to cost considerations in explaining the popularity of standardized stations on the Great Plains was convenience. A railroad's central or divisional offices could have a set of station drawings suitable for various community sizes, real or anticipated. The building engineer merely selected the necessary blueprint and made any necessary modifications, a procedure that proved extremely useful when a company faced massive new depot construction as lines were built. The structures engineer of the Pierre, Rapid City and North-Western Railway commented on this subject shortly after completion of that western South Dakota road: "It became a simple task for us to use either the standard Chicago & North Western [the

PRC&NW was a wholly owned subsidiary of the C&NW] combination passenger and freight station with living rooms for agent on the second floor for the more important sites or the Standard No. 3 depots without living quarters at the other station locations."[6]

The history of standardized Great Plains railroad stations is seen more clearly when the specific design plans of various carriers are examined. These ranged from primitive shelters to attractive county seat depots. When roads penetrated the virgin territory of the plains, they were more likely to employ portable or temporary buildings. While retired passenger or freight car bodies were used in all sections of the country, only carriers serving the Great Plains specially designed portable stations. These short, often narrow standardized structures were easily moved by flatcar from location to location. They could be assembled rapidly so that an agent might be at work soon after a line opened, in fact, in some cases while the road was still under construction. The design philosophy was simple. "If the townsite makes it," observed an official of the Burlington and Missouri River Railroad in Nebraska, "residents will get [a regular] depot."[7]

While the spartan portable was indeed practical, those residents whose town had such a structure often complained that it was wholly unsuitable. Perhaps the settlement's growth produced enough traffic to warrant a better building. City fathers, too, likely thought an attractive station would symbolize the importance and unlimited future of the community.

La Bolt, South Dakota, had a portable depot. But the several hundred residents of this bustling village on the Great Northern Railway's Benson, Minnesota, to Huron, South Dakota, line thought they deserved better. As the local lumber dealer said in 1902, "The depot accommodations are a disgrace to the railroad company and an insult to this community." Understandably, La Bolt began agitation for needed changes. Early complaints to both the carrier and the South Dakota Board of Railroad Commissioners went unheeded. Great Northern officials argued, "We already have an agent [but only part-time] at that point, also a small building for the handling of freight, which we consider adequate for the business offered in the past." Soon tempers flared. One resident, who led the local crusade to final victory, succinctly explained La Bolt's unwillingness to agree with the Great Northern's position: "In regard to the depot: the building is 10 x 22 [feet] and in the poorest shape. I would not have it for a dog house. Whenever any freight comes to amount to anything it has to remain outside; and as for accommodations for passengers is [*sic*] concerned, there isn't any." Finally, pressure from the state railroad commission caused the Great Northern to relent in September 1905. A replacement depot measuring 30 by 60 feet, albeit of standard design, was speedily constructed. La Bolt's triumph produced a joyful community farewell to the old portable when it rode out of town on a rail flatcar in 1906.[8]

The La Bolt example illustrates how designs for small-town depots on the Great Plains evolved. Although economic necessity dictated a less elaborate station than most boosters thought appropriate, the erection of a shacklike shelter would bring howls of protest. Records of various plains roads reveal that civil pressures often influenced small-station design. Frequently, as seen in the case of the La Bolt squabble, the carrier responded to public unhappiness with another but larger standardized depot. The Great Northern already had plans for inexpensive stations that met both its own requirements and demands for structures that would be objects of community pride.

Vastly more abundant than portables on the Great Plains were the standardized combination freight and passenger stations. Although

Figure 1. The portability of the Great Northern "temporary" station is obvious in this early-twentieth-century view of the "old depot" leaving La Bolt, South Dakota. (Courtesy of the South Dakota Historical Society.)

this depot style was found elsewhere in the United States, particularly in the Middle West and the Far West after the 1870s, combination stations on plains lines frequently shared one distinguishing feature: they contained living quarters for the agent and his family. A dominant but secondary distinction was that these stations were nearly always of wooden construction with a standard paint scheme, while brick, brick veneer, and stucco commonly adorned combination depots outside the Great Plains. Finally, combination stations of the Northern Plains might contain a "warm room" for perishable freight and express—a rare feature outside this area.

The origins of the combination type of railroad station are obscure. Likely it first appeared after the Civil War when the nation's railway net rapidly expanded west of the Appalachians. (Combination depots built in the early 1870s are still in service along lines in Ohio, Indiana, and Michigan.) These compact and functional stations provided the carrier with a convenient place to offer its multiple services. Generally they were divided into three sections: waiting room, central office, and freight-baggage house. The freight area usually had a wooden platform attached to either the front or rear for the transfer of shipments. At one point, mostly in the 1880s and 1890s, the combination depot, especially in the Middle West, contained separate rooms for men and women ("Ladies" and "Gents"). The fairer sex and children, railroad officials thought, required protection from "coarse and vile" males. Cost considerations later reduced the practice.[9]

As with portables, the function of the combination station was to provide adequate yet inexpensive facilities to the communities served. These buildings later might be replaced or upgraded. Noted one railroad spokesman shortly before World War I, "Roads . . . have had their engineering departments design a cheap, wooden standard station. If business justifies, they improve it."[10]

The richness in standard combination styles is a function of both the time period and varying internal railroad architectural policies. In the last quarter of the nineteenth century the combinations reflected the general themes of late Victorian American architecture: they commonly had long roof overhangs and elaborate gingerbread trim. But with the advent of the early-modern style around the turn of the century, the overhang was often shortened and the gingerbread, if it still remained, was usually made with beveled corners instead of the earlier turned and carved pieces. By World War I the overhang and the gingerbread trim disappeared and floors and walls up to the window sills were made of concrete rather than wood. Stucco and brick veneer became widespread.

Railroad companies varied in how they designed stations. Some Great Plains carriers at times had a highly decentralized method of originating depot plans. Each operating division functioned like a railroad within itself, with a general manager, general superintendent, and superintendent of bridges and buildings. With such a corporate structure, styles often differed along sections of the same railroad. Even when a company, like the Minneapolis, St. Paul, and Sault Ste. Marie (Soo Line), had a central engineering office, designs for combination and other stations might vary. For example, roads absorbed other ones. Depots of the present Soo branch from Fairmount, North Dakota, south into northeastern South Dakota are standard combination ones, yet they are unlike the dominant but comparable Soo Line stations. The reason is simple: the branch was originally an independent shortline, the Fairmount and Veblen Railway Company, built in 1912 but not acquired by the Soo until 1915. The reverse process could also work. The Midland Continental Railroad built its Clementsville and Nortonville, North Dakota, depots using plans of a "second-class" Soo station, and the depots of the Missouri, Oklahoma and Gulf followed the specifications of a standard St. Louis and San Francisco combination station. Clearly, if a plan was practical, it might well be pirated![11]

Other railroads continually altered their standard designs for the combination station. The Northern Pacific is a premier example. Pressures from employees, civic groups, and even state railroad commissions collectively contributed to the diversity of Northern Pacific styles. For example, agents asked the company to redesign the freight room so that it would help block winter winds and thus keep the waiting room and especially the office warmer. The Northern Pacific, too, seems to have had a series of building engineers who sought to refine the road's set of standard small-station plans. In nearly every decade from the 1880s through the 1920s major architectural modifications occurred, indeed at a much more rapid pace than national architectural changes.[12]

The inclusion of living quarters in Great Plains combination stations is a fine example of architectural adaptation to a new environment. Generally speaking, if a railroad station was built in an area with a sparse population, the likelihood that it would have living accommodations was great. High Plains stations, in particular, had living sections, at least for the first combination types. Replacement depots built after World War I, however, might omit such accommodations. When rail lines pushed ahead of population in the Middle West, as in western Minnesota and Iowa in the 1870s and early 1880s, companies regularly built depots with apartment space. This also occurred in the Rocky Mountain and desert West; however, the total number of stations there was much smaller than on the plains and many served solely as train-control centers (where agents reported train movements past their depots to regional dispatchers and then relayed orders from dispatchers to train crews).

The building design policy followed by the Union Pacific Railroad for its Nebraska stations is a good case study. The company provided depots with living quarters east of North Platte primarily in towns located on branch lines rather than on the main line. (Some mainline stations, e.g., Duncan and Maxwell, did contain apartments.) Parts of this section of Nebraska boasted established communities prior to railroad construction and village populations grew rapidly along the Union Pacific's main stem. On the other hand, communities served by branch lines were often smaller and hence offered less chance of adequate housing for agents. In the less populated western section of the state, the railroad customarily provided living facilities on both main and branch lines. "Beyond North Platte," recalled a Union Pacific employee, "agents would not have much hope of finding a decent place to live for years after lines opened." He added, "In some spots . . . not until mobile trailers came into use was the housing problem solved."[13]

Railroads on the Great Plains varied in how they might shelter an agent. The Union Pacific, Frisco, Great Northern, Northern Pacific, and Fremont, Elkhorn and Missouri Valley, for instance, frequently used depots of one-story design. For example, the Fremont, Elkhorn and Missouri Valley's standard 22-by-80-foot station contained the common arrangement for living space—kitchen, sitting room, and two bedrooms—all attached to the writing room end. Like the vast majority of plains depots before the 1920s, the Fremont, Elkhorn and Missouri Valley made no provision for indoor plumbing. The Soo Line, Chicago and North Western, and Burlington, to note leading examples, often opted for the two-story structure. While these stations were more costly, the second-floor location for the agent's apartment had two distinct advantages over the single-floor arrangement: it kept family members away from business operations, and it allowed for building expansion with a minimum of disturbance.[14]

A few railroads operating on the plains—the Minneapolis and St. Louis and the Atchison, Topeka and Santa Fe, for instance—either experimented with or regularly used cottages to house agents. Located near the depot, these boxlike structures were often prefabricated. The practice of supplying houses for agents disappeared

Figure 2. Rather than providing living space for agents in depots, the Minneapolis and St. Louis early in the century designed double section houses for use along its pioneer trackage on the South Dakota prairie. These two-story affairs appeared every five to fifteen miles along the road's newly opened Watertown–Le Beau and Conde-Leola lines. Maintenance-of-way employees also occupied these structures. This photograph, taken about 1920, shows the double section house at Wetonka, South Dakota. (H. Roger Grant Collection.)

largely for financial reasons. (Some roads built similar buildings for other railroad employees—section foremen, water-supply supervisors, and signalmen.) The Santa Fe largely abandoned the cottage concept by 1900. In fact, the company in 1906 began to test a new depot design for its routes through arid and semiarid regions. The idea was not only to use concrete rather than wood or brick for the exterior walls but to have a second story for living quarters. Twenty-one of these two-story concrete depots were later completed for the Santa Fe's subsidiary, the Eastern Railway of New Mexico. Concerning living accommodations in these stations, *Railway Age* remarked, "[They are] a consideration of some moment in the small New Mexico towns."[15]

The popularity of stations with living quarters is not explained solely by the need for those facilities. Companies discovered that they benefited from having live-in agents. Employees would be on call twenty-four hours a day, and occupied stations would discourage burglars—a widespread concern because of the cash receipts kept in depot offices. This arrangement also meant that companies, if they carried fire insurance, could expect significantly reduced rates.

Figure 3. The Santa Fe station at Fowler, Colorado, is one example of that company's widely used second-generation "county seat" design. (H. Roger Grant Collection.)

Finally, companies came to consider the extra investment in living quarters worthwhile, since they viewed married agents as more stable and responsible than single ones.

Residents of the Great Plains did see railroad stations designed by private architectural firms. These were the urban stations and division office buildings that also accommodated the traveling public. Occasionally a small-town station might be built in this fashion. At the turn of the century, Minneapolis architect William J. Keith, for example, designed the 20-by-68-foot Wilton, North Dakota, station for the Bismarck, Washburn and Great Falls Railway. The structure was of a traditional, though nonstandard, design to the apex of the roofline, but a stubby Japanese-like pagoda tower then rose above it. (The second floor and tower provided living quarters for the short-line's founder, William Washburn, who conducted extensive lignite mining operations in the vicinity.)[16]

At various times architectural firms or building engineers employed by Great Plains carriers sketched plans for standardized replacement depots. For the lucky community that had outgrown its portable or combination station, a replacement meant more space, and possibly a lunchroom. Certainly the structure would be more visually pleasing. By World War I the Santa Fe often used a standard "county seat" depot of handsome Spanish mission style with brick walls and a slate roof. Even a poured concrete logo adorned each of the building's four gables. As in other sections of the country, some replacement or special-purpose stations on the Great Plains were constructed in unique designs. In 1908 the Milwaukee Road, for example, needed more than a standard station at the village of Marmarth, North Dakota, on its newly opened line to the Pacific Northwest: the community had been selected as the junction of the Trans-Missouri and Musselshell divisions. Therefore, the railroad's Bridge and Building Department drew an appropriate plan, which included a kitchen and lunch and dining rooms. Even then, apart from the eating facilities, the Marmarth station, especially its end elevations, closely resembled other, standard depots.[17]

The complexities of standardized railroad design are illustrated by the building policies of two railroads that served the Northern Plains, the Soo Line and the Milwaukee Road. The Soo employed a rich variety of standard and nonstandard styles for its small-town stations in upper Michigan, Wisconsin, and eastern Minnesota. But when the road left the forest and entered the prairies of western Minnesota, Dakota, and eastern Montana during the late nineteenth century, it relied heavily on a limited number of economical, convenient, and highly functional depot plans. The hallmark was flexibility. Individual stations could easily be expanded to suit local needs, usually by merely extending the freight section.

The Soo Line utilized almost exclusively five easily replicable designs on its "west end." The simplest was the portable. Prefabricated in Minneapolis and hauled in sections on flatcars to the desired location, the building was twelve feet wide, but of varying length. The Soo stretched some portables to more than one hundred feet! So flexible was this plan that even living quarters could be provided at one end while the necessary freight house, office, and waiting room occupied the remaining space.[18]

For communities that seemed destined to remain hamlets and where acceptable housing existed, Soo Line personnel developed an appropriate depot plan. Although a nonportable, this 24-by-24-foot structure was little more than a shelter. Typical of the combination station, it contained waiting room and freight house sections, but it lacked a separate office. The agent, often part-time, placed his desk, tariff case, and other equipment in a corner of the waiting room.[19]

A somewhat larger depot, designated as a "third-class" station, closely resembled the 24-foot boxlike structure. This 24-by-56 foot building, however, contained a bay window and separate office space. The Soo regularly used it as the replacement design for stations, often larger ones, that had been destroyed.[20]

By far the most popular Soo Line prairie style was the "second-class" depot. The company constructed this station in such numbers that for Northern Plains residents it became the visual symbol of the road—a type of architectural logo! More than two hundred of these adaptable depots were built in North Dakota alone between 1891 and the end of World War I.[21]

The design origins of the "second-class" station are uncertain. It seems plausible that the Soo borrowed it from the Canadian Pacific, a railroad that controlled the company for much of its corporate life. Yet, the basic lines of the depot resemble the two-story stations built by the Burlington Route, Chicago and North Western, and other lines on the plains.

The "second-class" Soo depot was stark in appearance. Covered by a gable roof unbroken by dormers, it had attached to the office section a rectangular bay with three large windows. The interior floor plan provided only the most basic facilities. Railroad business was conducted in an 18-by-23-foot waiting room, an office 12½ feet by 19 feet 2 inches, and a 23-by-24-foot freight house. A 12-by-12-foot warm room was regularly included. A few depots even had an extra waiting room for women and children. The most common variation, however, was to expand the length of the freight house when increased local traffic warranted it. The freight section of the Carrington, North Dakota, depot, for instance, was twice extended to make the original 80-foot structure 136 feet in length. In the upstairs over the office and waiting room, the second-story section contained a 12-by-17 foot living room, a 12-by-14-foot kitchen, and two bedrooms, one 6½ by 13½ feet and the other 10 by 13 feet. No doubt agents and their families found these quarters cramped, but they compare favorably with living facilities provided by other railroads.[22]

In 1903 the Soo introduced a combination depot design that it classified as "first-class." This particular style did not emerge as a refinement of the highly successful "second-class" station, but rather as a direct response to demands by larger communities for a more esthetically pleasing structure. However, this new blueprint met Soo requirements that its prairie stations be inexpensive and functional.

The most ornate of the five Soo plans, the "first-class" design was characterized by a double-pitched hip roof with wide overhangs supported by decorative brackets. For esthetic reasons the road also

Figure 4. The Soo Line erected one of its ubiquitous "second-class" depots at Westby, Montana. (Charles W. Bohi photograph.)

Figure 5. The flexibility of the Soo Line's "second-class" plan is evident in this view of its station at Carrington, North Dakota. Because the town was an important shipping point, the railroad expanded the freight office to an unusually long length. (Frank E. Vyzralek photograph.)

rounded the office bay windows. Inside the 24-by-96-foot structure, the office and the two sexually segregated waiting rooms occupied half the building: the remainder contained a 23-by-48-foot freight house, which, like the "second-class" ones, could be expanded to any desired length. Since the company used this design in towns that had ample housing, it omitted living quarters. It became, in fact, the Soo's "county seat" depot. As the company itself said, "It is the capstone design to our logical and highly efficient Western depot construction program. Any community should be pleased with this station; it is as fine as most court houses. . . . Many [towns] long for this depot."[23]

Unlike the Soo Line, which utilized only a few architectural styles for its nonurban Great Plains depots, the Chicago, Milwaukee and St. Paul (Milwaukee Road) employed a hodgepodge of standard designs for small-town stations along its seven-thousand-mile system in Illinois, Michigan, Wisconsin, Minnesota, Iowa, Missouri, and the Dakotas. It made no distinction between depots constructed east and west of the Mississippi River, except that prairie ones were more likely to have living quarters. Only when the road pushed west from South Dakota to the Pacific Northwest early in the century did it adopt a rigid policy of standardization.

Multiple reasons explain the Milwaukee's more complicated station design policies. For one, the road embarked on its standardized depot building program at least twenty years earlier than the Soo; thus, its depots of the 1870s have a Victorian look rather than the modern flavor of the Soo's prairie designs. Furthermore, the company's Chicago-based Bridge and Building Department regularly redrew designs. Like the Northern Pacific, the Milwaukee never seemed satisfied with any set of basic country-station drawings. Matters of overall style, interior layout, and cost, especially during the catastrophic depression of the mid-1890s, prompted continued rethinking of station designs. For the county seat type of depot, the Milwaukee failed to develop a single plan comparable to the Soo's "first-class" one. Rather, more than a dozen standardized large-town styles emerged. "We could never seem to get our act together on the standard county seat depot," recently remarked a company architect.[24] Moreover, the Milwaukee encompassed a larger number of predecessor lines than did the Soo. Roads like the Dakota Southern, Fargo and Southern, and Sioux City and Pembina all had their own notions about small-station design.

Thus, styles for the Milwaukee Road's Great Plains depots varied dramatically. For example, Ellendale, North Dakota, claimed a standard 26-by-108½-foot Spanish mission depot; Ortley, South Dakota, had one of the seventeen semiportable 16-by-24-foot structures; and Lake Andes, South Dakota, boasted a fairly common 24-by-60-foot two-story station. All of these plans, however, were also used outside the Dakotas, usually in Minnesota and Iowa. But the plan selected for the depot at Garden City, South Dakota, became the most popular one system-wide and the design was ideally suited for prairie usage.[25]

Introduced in 1902, this single-story 24-by-60-foot station resembled scores of combination depots built earlier by the Milwaukee and other Granger roads, except that it contained living quarters. Patrons saw a 20-by-24-foot waiting room, a 16-by-24-foot freight house, and a cozy 10-by-10-foot office. The agent's private section consisted of a 10-by-12½-foot bedroom, a 10-by-11½-foot sitting room, and an 11½-by-12½-foot kitchen. There were also a tiny closet and a pantry, all of which made the Soo "second-class" depot seem spacious by comparison. Common lapboard siding covered the exterior. Desiring to improve the building's overall appearance and

Figure 6. The Milwaukee Road extensively used this 24-by-60-foot combination station with living space on its lines in the Northern Plains. This is the depot at Garden City, South Dakota, built in 1902. (Charles W. Bohi photograph.)

reflecting popular architectural tastes, the Milwaukee later added decorative wood filigree along the roof ridge and at the top of the front and rear walls. Gingerbread also appeared under the eaves and on the end elevations.

So successful was the Garden City type of depot (agents' complaints about cramped living quarters notwithstanding) that when the Milwaukee Road faced massive new depot construction in 1906 and 1907 on its sparsely populated Pacific extension between Evarts, South Dakota, and Butte, Montana, it modified the design into a "Standard Class A Passenger Station Plan." A no-frills drawing, this revised plan abandoned every decorative detail except the necessary roof-support brackets. Totally utilitarian, the building represented the quintessence of Great Plains standardized railroad station architecture.[26]

Walter Prescott Webb's notion that the arid and semiarid Great Plains modified institutions of the humid eastern United States remains debatable.[27] Nevertheless, one might conclude that the

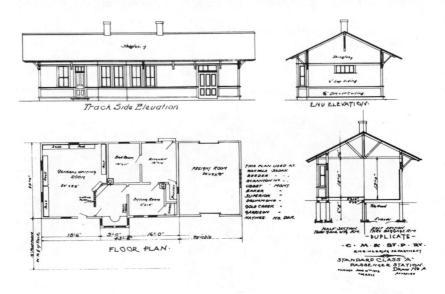

Figure 7. A simplified version of the Garden City, South Dakota, structure is the Milwaukee's "Standard Class A Passenger Station" used on the Pacific Coast extension in the Dakotas and Montana. The variable length of the freight house is a common characteristic of plains stations. (Courtesy of the Chicago, Milwaukee, St. Paul and Pacific Railroad Company.)

plains environment greatly influenced small-town railroad station design. Only plains carriers perfected the portable depot and used in large numbers combination stations with living quarters; they learned that sterile, inexpensive standardized plans worked best in this region. Moreover, depots on the Great Plains appeared different to visitors—they were "often of the dullest and most despicable types."

Features that once distinguished the country stations on the Great Plains from those in other sections of the United States have now disappeared. Today's railroad firms, when replacing older depots, are likely to use buildings of a carbon copy style just as present-day highway commercial architecture is characterized by highly standardized structures, excellently represented by modular gas stations with their clip-on mansard roofs. Solutions that proved expedient on the plains remain usable. For example, some depots recently constructed by the National Railroad Passenger Corporation (Amtrak) are truly portable, often being modifications of mobile homes. When the new Amtrak station opened in Cleveland, Ohio, in 1977, the former structure (commonly dubbed an "Amshack") was moved to another stop.[28]

The standardized railroad stations on the Great Plains have largely disappeared since the early 1960s. Of those remaining in service, most are used as storage buildings for section crews. A few have been donated to municipalities, park boards, and historical societies, while others have been turned into grain sheds, machine shops, and even private dwellings. Whatever their present usage, these depots should be viewed not necessarily as symbols of a decaying or rapidly changing industry, but as structures of architectural significance adapted to fit environmental and business conditions.

Notes

I wish to thank the Faculty Research Committee of the University of Akron for aid in preparing this study.

1. William Hexter to E. Y. Mitchell, August 26, 1903, E. Y. Mitchell Papers, Western Historical Manuscripts Collection, University of Missouri, Columbia, Missouri.

2. John MacMaster to Charles W. Perkins, September 2, 1894, Chicago, Burlington and Quincy Papers, Newberry Library, Chicago, Illinois.

3. John F. Stover, *American Railroads* (Chicago: University of Chicago Press, 1961), pp. 223-24.

4. Lewis Atherton, *Main Street on the Middle Border* (Bloomington: Indiana University Press, 1954), pp. 222-29.

5. See Arthur M. Hart, "M. A. Disbrow & Company: Catalogue Architecture," *Palimpsest* 56 (July-August 1975): 98-119, and Daniel J. Boorstin, *The Americans: The National Experience* (New York: Random House, 1965), pp. 148-52; Hamlin Garland, *A Son of the Middle Border* (1917; rpt. New York: Macmillan, 1962), p. 312.

6. Quoted in letter to the author from William Armstrong, Structures Engineer, Chicago and North Western Transportation Company, Chicago, Illinois, December 14, 1976.

7. George W. Holdrege to Charles W. Perkins, n.d., Chicago, Burlington and Quincy Papers, Newberry Library, Chicago, Illinois.

8. Noah Adams to Board of Railroad Commissioners, April 11, 1902, South Dakota State Railroad Commission Papers, State Historical Society of South Dakota, Pierre, South Dakota; *Seventeenth Annual Report of the Board of Railroad Commissioners of the State of South Dakota* (Huron, S.D.: Huronite Printing Co., 1906), p. 79; caption on back of La Bolt depot photograph, State Historical Society of South Dakota, Pierre, South Dakota (the "1913" on front is incorrect).

9. Letter to the author from W. P. Beesley, Regional Engineer, Norfolk and Western Railway Company, Saint Louis, Missouri, January 14, 1977.

10. Quotation from *Farms in Iowa* (Chicago: Chicago, Burlington and Quincy Railroad, 1907), pp. 6-7.

11. John A. Gjevre, *Saga of the Soo: West from Shoreham* (La Crosse, Wis.: published by the author, 1973), pp. 54-56; James M. Hall to Frank A. Seiberling, March 27, 1917, Frank A. Seiberling Papers, Ohio Historical Society, Columbus, Ohio; *Railway Age* 40 (December 15, 1905): 752.

12. Letter to the author from B. G. Anderson, Engineering Department, Burlington Northern Railroad Company, Saint Paul, Minnesota, January 3, 1975.

13. Various drawings supplied by the Union Pacific Railroad Company, Omaha, Nebraska; letters to the author from R. M. Brown, Chief Engineer, Union Pacific Railroad Company, Omaha, Nebraska, January 20 and February 28, 1977.

14. See "Standard Depot Plan, No. 3," Fremont, Elkhorn and Missouri Valley Railroad Company, March 20, 1902, copy supplied by William Armstrong, Structures Engineer, Chicago and North Western Transportation Company, Chicago, Illinois.

15. Letter to the author from C. L. Holman, Assistant General Manager-Engineering, Atchison, Topeka and Santa Fe Railway Company, Topeka, Kansas, February 25, 1977; "Santa Fe Standard Concrete Depots," *Railway Age* 41 (March 23, 1906): 438-40.

16. See *Bismarck Daily Tribune*, July 10, 1900; *Washburn Leader*, November 2, 1901 and September 26, 1903.

17. Letter to the author from C. L. Holman, February 25, 1977; "Album of Depot Plans—1919," Office of the Architect, Chicago, Milwaukee, St. Paul and Pacific Railroad Company, Chicago, Illinois.

18. See Frank E. Vyzralek, H. Roger Grant, and Charles Bohi, "North Dakota's Railroad Depots: Standardization on the Soo Line," *North Dakota History* 42 (Winter 1975): 5–25.

19. Ibid., p. 12.

20. Ibid.

21. Ibid., pp. 8–9.

22. Various drawings supplied by the Soo Line Railroad Company, Minneapolis, Minnesota, letter to the author from E. G. Creelman, Engineering Department, Soo Line Railroad Company, Minneapolis, Minnesota, February 23, 1977.

23. Vyzralek et al., "North Dakota's Railroad Depots," p. 10; quoted in letter to the author from B. E. Pearson, Chief Engineer, Soo Line Railroad Company, Minneapolis, Minnesota, February 2, 1977.

24. Interview with Lou Bolwahnn, Assistant Architect, Chicago, Milwaukee, St. Paul and Pacific Railroad Company, Chicago, Illinois, October 20, 1976. For the standard history of the Milwaukee Road, see August Derleth, *The Milwaukee Road: Its First Hundred Years* (New York: Creative Age Press, 1948).

25. "Album of Depot Plans—1919."

26. Ibid.

27. See Kenneth R. Philp and Elliott West, eds., *The Walter Prescott Webb Memorial Lectures: Essays on Walter Prescott Webb* (Austin: University of Texas Press, 1976); and Necah Stewart Furman, *Walter Prescott Webb: His Life and Impact* (Albuquerque: University of New Mexico Press, 1976).

28. *Cleveland Plain-Dealer*, December 2, 1976.

Agricultural Technology
in the Dust Bowl, 1932–40

R. Douglas Hurt

Before 1930 the American farmer commonly regarded soil erosion as a "spasmodic phenomenon" largely confined to lands subject to washing. Many farmers believed moderate blowing was beneficial because it mixed the soil and thereby helped maintain fertility. The average agriculturist seldom did more to contend with the problems of erosion than haphazardly place brush in gullies. Urbanites understood the problems of erosion even less than farmers did. The fourth decade of the twentieth century quickly challenged such carelessness. The drought which began in the summer of 1931 lasted seven years and made plainsmen acutely aware that they had to change drastically their agricultural methods.[1]

Shortly before World War I, Great Plains farmers became particularly negligent in their conservation practices as they increasingly used tractors, gang plows, and headers to expand their wheat acreage. High wartime prices and American participation in the conflict stimulated plains farmers to break new lands, and rainfall was sufficient to allow, if not encourage, this expansion. Wheat acreage in the Great Plains increased almost 17,000,000 acres between 1909 and 1924. When wheat prices collapsed in the early 1920s, plainsmen broke about 15,000,000 acres of sod (largely with the newly adopted one-way disk plow) between 1924 and 1929 and planted more wheat to offset the economic loss. Much of the expansion occurred in the Southern Plains, where wheat acreage increased 200 percent between 1925 and 1931; in many counties this expansion ranged from 400 to 1,000 percent.[2]

At that time Great Plains farmers gave little thought to plowing under crop residues to increase soil humus. Mechanical difficulties and labor and equipment shortages and costs often prevented them from working wheat stubble into the ground. The common practice of burning off the stubble hindered the return of crop residue to the soil; as its organic content decreased, the soil became less productive.

Farmers also hesitated to work wheat stubble into the soil because it caused a temporary decrease in fertility. During a period of drought, though, plowing under the stubble more than offset the fertility loss because it increased the ability of the soil to absorb water. Farmers all too often left their herds in the stubble fields until they consumed every bit of vegetation, leaving the ground unprotected from the wind. And, finally, continued cultivation pulverized the soil so that from five to seven years after the sod had been broken, it was in excellent condition for blowing.[3]

Ordinarily, the Southern Plains receive approximately eighteen inches of precipitation annually. This amount is adequate for a satisfactory crop yield only when it is carefully conserved. Southern Plains farmers seldom tried to preserve moisture in the subsoil prior to 1935, however, so the drought of the 1930s proved devastating. The Springfield, Colorado, area averaged over three inches below normal between 1931 and 1935; the Meade, Kansas, area over five inches below normal from 1931 to 1933; the Goodwell, Oklahoma, area over nine inches below normal from 1932 to 1933; and the Amarillo, Texas, area over seven inches below normal from 1933 to 1935. Snows were insufficient to protect the soil, and winter contributed to erosion by loosening the ground with alternate freezing and thawing. The lack of precipitation and the harsh winters aided the prevailing winds of the Southern Plains, which averaged ten to twelve miles per hour or more throughout most of the region, in bringing the dust storms in January 1932.[4]

By spring 1935, the wind erosion hazard was the worst in a 97,000,000-acre section of the Southern Plains which an Associated Press reporter writing for the *Washington* (D.C.) *Evening Star* appropriately termed the Dust Bowl. This area encompassed eastern Colorado and New Mexico, western Kansas, and the panhandles of Texas and Oklahoma, and extended nearly four hundred miles from north to south and three hundred miles from east to west. The approximate center of the Dust Bowl was Liberal in the southwestern corner of Kansas, and the wind erosion problem was the most severe within a hundred-mile radius of that town. Of the nearly 34,000,000 acres in the Dust Bowl which suffered serious wind erosion, the Soil Conservation Service considered over 6,000,000 acres destroyed. Clearly, something had to be done to save Southern Plains agriculture from complete ruin.[5]

The wind erosion problem of the Great Plains occurred not because farmers grew too much wheat, but because the drought prevented them from growing much wheat at all from 1932 to 1940.

During the years of normal rainfall, wheat offered excellent protection against wind erosion. At that time, however, an inadequate moisture supply prevented a suitable growth of ground cover in the early spring "blow season" of February, March, and April. The drought was the first in a chain of events, leading next to crop failure. The abandonment of lands without a protective soil cover in turn allowed the nearly constant winds to begin erosion. The dust storms that followed drifted soil, ruined additional land, and contributed to more crop failure. Even though erosion worsened during 1933, when insufficient and poorly distributed rainfall together with winds of above-average velocity brought widespread damage to the southern Great Plains, most farmers were still more concerned with crop failure, low prices, and the depression. By August 10, Goodwell, Oklahoma, had experienced more than thirty dust storms. In May 1934, the drought was the most severe on record and the erosion problem steadily worsened as the wind stripped the topsoil to the depth of the plow in many parts of the Great Plains.[6]

Dust storms and drifting soil were by no means new experiences for Dust Bowl farmers. Neither was the technology they used to bring the soil under control unique. At the turn of the century, farmers in the Oklahoma Territory used the lister and the disk harrow to check soil blowing. Farmers in western Kansas also used the lister to control blowing dust in 1913. The lister was essentially a double moldboard plow that split the furrow and turned the slice each way. It left the soil deeply furrowed and in a cloddy condition that retarded the wind velocity over the surface of the ground and caught blowing soil. Farmers succeeded in checking wind erosion when they listed five rows contrary to the prevailing winds and left unbroken strips of fifty to sixty feet in between. They then planted cane or kafir corn in the furrows; by the time the listed furrows were drifted full, the crop was tall enough to retard further soil movement. Farmers also left stubble on the land when blowing was a problem, or, if it had already been turned under, they spread straw across the fields.[7]

During the great plow-up of the 1920s, though, Great Plains farmers largely ignored the lister and turned to the one-way disk plow because it plowed faster, handled heavy stubble without clogging, efficiently broke hard, sun-baked soil, and destroyed weeds. However, if used continuously on fallowed ground, the one-way pulverized the soil and subjected it to the wind. Some Dust Bowl farmers were reluctant to use the lister when their fields began to

Figure 1. Furrows like these, photographed near Dalhart, Texas, in June 1938, helped check soil blowing. (Photograph from the Library of Congress.)

blow because they believed any further tillage would stir the soil and intensify the problem.[8]

By spring 1934, wind erosion in the Dust Bowl was so serious that most farmers and ranchers were willing to adopt the appropriate measures to bring their soil under control, and the lister became one of the standard implements used for such purposes. Some farmers preferred a modified lister which incorporated a shovel attachment that built small earthen dams in the furrows. This "basin," or "damming," lister enabled twice as much moisture penetration as land treated with the standard lister, but unfortunately, it did not work well on dry soil. Some farmers obtained a similar effect by shearing off a portion of a one-way's disk so that it pocked the soil instead of making a clean cut across a field. Other farmers modified their one-ways by removing all but four evenly spaced disks; this adjustment furrowed the soil less deeply and enabled the farmers to level their fields more easily after the blow season. Dust Bowl farmers also used a combined lister-seeder for planting row crops. Even though its plantings started more slowly and produced less, it was the cheapest planting method and greatly reduced the wind erosion hazard.[9]

The lister was not the only useful implement for controlling soil blowing. Virtually any tillage machine that roughened the ground was effective. The duckfoot cultivator and the rotary rod weeder

Figure 2. A "basin listed" field in the Texas Panhandle, June 1938. (Photograph from the Library of Congress.)

were particularly good on summer fallow. The duckfoot cultivator not only killed weeds but also ridged the soil and kept the trash on the surface. The shovels cut beneath the surface and did not pulverize the soil. The edges dulled quickly, but this problem could be overcome by treating them with a hardening material. The rotary rod weeder consisted of a square rod that ran approximately two inches beneath the ground surface and rotated backward. In so doing it cut weed roots, kept trash on the surface, and left the soil intact. It was especially effective for preparing the seed bed because it leveled the ground and permitted greater uniformity in planting depth.[10]

The spring-tooth harrow was useful in controlling wind erosion, but it gathered trash badly and was more effective when subsurface shovels replaced the harrow teeth. Some farmers used the subsurface packer equipped with a series of narrow, wedge-shaped discs that

Figure 3. Prowers County, Colorado, dust storm, March 1937. (Photograph from the Western History Collections, University of Oklahoma Library.)

broke crusted soil and created deep crevices which caught wind-blown soil and retarded further soil movement. All lands subject to blowing needed periodic treatment with these implements. Listing, for example, held the soil during the blow months for about one week, then the work had to be repeated.[11]

Limited use of these implements could not markedly improve the wind erosion conditions in the Dust Bowl; they had to be used widely and properly. If one farmer, for example, listed his fields while his neighbors did not, the listed fields would have little or no effect on soil blowing. In addition, the implements had to be used in such a fashion as to ensure maximum benefit from every drop of rain that fell. This was particularly important when approximately three-fourths of the annual precipitation fell between April and September. The Southern Plains farmers failed to conserve this moisture properly in 1934 and, as a result, harvested Russian thistles for cattle feed; in 1935, when the thistles had dried up, they cut soapweed.[12]

The semiarid, dusty conditions prompted the Soil Erosion Service and the Department of Agriculture to stress the benefits of contour plowing and terracing. Hugh Hammond Bennett, director of the Soil Erosion and Moisture Conservation Investigations, recognized that technical supervision of such a program would be necessary; and Harold Ickes, secretary of the interior and head of the Public Works Administration, made that support possible on August 25, 1933, when he allotted five million dollars of emergency funds to the Department of Interior's Soil Erosion Service (SES) for a conservation program. The SES used the money to establish demonstration projects on private lands owned by cooperating farmers who signed five-year contracts in which they agreed to follow the conservation practices inaugurated by the SES. The first wind erosion demonstration unit established was a 15,195-acre project east of Dalhart, Texas. Originally, the federal government allotted thirty-five thousand dollars for the project, but by October 1934 that amount had been doubled and the project had been expanded to 30,000 acres. Similar projects were soon established in several other Texas Panhandle locations and in Colorado, Kansas, Oklahoma, and New Mexico.[13]

Because the SES duplicated many of the activities of the Department of Agriculture, it was incorporated into that department in 1935 and was christened the Soil Conservation Service (SCS). Together the agencies stressed that an effective soil conservation program required the states to initiate land use regulations and encouraged such action by drafting a model state law on May 13, 1936, entitled "A Standard Soil Conservation District Law." This statute provided for the creation of state conservation districts by local petition and referendum. By June 30, 1939, the Dust Bowl states had created thirty-seven soil conservation districts covering 19,036,000 acres.[14]

Within the demonstration projects the SCS, county agents, and the Civilian Conservation Corps provided the necessary technical expertise and equipment to encourage farmers to participate in conservation programs. Contour plowing was one technique they advanced as basic to soil conservation. It enabled the soil to retain a higher percentage of moisture and permitted greater vegetative growth than did land not worked on the contour. But the spring of 1936 saw little contour farming outside the SCS demonstration projects. During that year, however, federal aid enabled Dust Bowl farmers to list 4,469,270 acres—2,469,534 acres of which were contoured. Tests on contoured lands following late May rains indicated that about one inch of additional moisture was conserved and subsoil moisture was more than a foot deeper than on lands not contoured. These results prompted the SCS to predict that the area's grain production would increase 4,500,000 bushels and yield 500,000 more pounds of crop residue for a protective soil covering.[15]

The SCS also stressed the benefits of terraces for Dust Bowl agriculture. Few terraces existed in this region, even though the agricultural experiment station at Spur, Texas, had demonstrated by the summer of 1932 that a two-inch rain could be converted into a seven-inch rain when terraces were combined with contour farming. In December 1932, less than 10 percent of the nearly 4,000,000 crop acres in a twenty-one-county area surrounding Amarillo, Texas, were terraced or contoured. Such treatment of the land increased yearly earnings $2.00 per acre and raised land values $8.26 per acre.[16]

The SCS continually worked to speed and improve the contouring and terracing process. Experiments at the Spur and Goodwell stations increased soil moisture an average of 25 percent on terraced and contoured land. The SCS estimated that such moisture savings increased the chance of a successful wheat crop about 75 percent and increased the average yield 35 percent. In 1934 at Goodwell, terraced plots that received only 3.4 inches of rain throughout the entire growing season produced 185.5 percent more hay than unterraced land. Three years later at the Dalhart station, terraced fields yielded 723 pounds of sorghum per acre, while fields only contoured produced 589 pounds. Here the advantages of contouring and terracing were clearly proven. Where the SCS planted sorghum in straight rows regardless of land slope, the yield was only 461 pounds per acre. The yield on terraced lands was 262 pounds per acre, or 56 percent, greater than that from unterraced fields; and the increase on contoured fields was 128 pounds per acre, or 27 percent.[17]

In May 1936, Baca County in southeastern Colorado received the first beneficial precipitation since September 1935. The rainfall varied from 1.05 to 2.33 inches and provided the first significant test for the demonstration work conducted under the auspices of the SCS. The Springfield Civilian Conservation Corps camp reported that moisture penetrated 41 2/3 inches on terraced lands but only 11 inches on unterraced fields. On land where no soil conservation practices were in effect, the runoff reached 90 percent. With little moisture retained in the soil, conditions were soon favorable for blowing, and ten days after the rain a severe dust storm struck the area. The message was clear: terracing and contouring held moisture in the soil, stimulated plant growth, and decreased wind and water erosion.[18]

The SCS also emphasized strip cropping in order to reduce wind erosion. Strip cropping consisted of planting a close-growing soil-holding crop such as wheat alternately with contoured strips of densely growing feed crops such as sudan grass, cane, sorghum, or small grains. Grain sorghum was particularly effective for stabilizing a field, and sudan grass grew rapidly and provided a dense wind-resistant growth. Both plant varieties were drought-resistant. Dust

Bowl farmers found that sorghum, when planted in strips, protected wheat and fallowed land, collected snow, checked soil drifting, reduced evaporation and transpiration between strips, and provided an adequate soil-holding stubble and root system. The width of the strips depended on the tendency of the soil to erode, the condition of the summer fallow, the type of crop being grown, the wind velocity, and the amount of rainfall.[19]

Generally, Dust Bowl farmers realized success when they planted half of their fields with strip crops and utilized sorghum strips along fence rows to stabilize large drifts. The sorghum strips enabled farmers to remove the fences and stir the drifts so the wind could redistribute the soil. Although strip cropping alone could not end the wind erosion hazard in the Dust Bowl, when farmers combined it with rough tillage practices and contour farming and terracing, it significantly checked soil blowing.[20]

In order to halt dust storms completely, though, grazing lands had to be restored. To accomplish that objective the Department of Agriculture, the Forest Service, and the Soil Conservation Service stressed grazing management, the reseeding of grasslands, and moisture preservation. The SCS advised farmers to rotate and rest pastures, to return at least 25 percent of the vegetative growth to the soil, to graze short grasses no less than two inches from the ground, and to restrict livestock to approximately twenty to thirty head per section of grazing land. Although approximately 65,000,000 acres

Figure 4. This view of a badly drifted Cimarron County, Oklahoma, farm in April 1936 shows the effects of severe wind erosion. The furrows have been almost completely filled with blowing soil. (Photograph from the Library of Congress.)

in the Dust Bowl remained in grass through the 1930s, the carrying capacity of the range was far below normal. Overgrazing and drought had decreased the height and density of the native gramma and buffalo grasses to the extent that the soil had been completely denuded in some areas. E. A. Sherman, associate forester, warned that unless farmers practiced more "conservative" grazing management, soil blowing from the grasslands would help to create a desert in the Southern Plains. By December 1934, nearly the entire native grass cover near Las Animas, Colorado, was smothered by the drifting soil, and by spring 1935 the pasture lands in western Kansas were 35 percent below normal in growth. Similar lands were drifting badly in Texas and Oklahoma.[21]

Dust Bowl farmers also practiced contour furrowing and contour ridging of grazing lands to derive maximum benefit from precipitation. The processes were not yearly operations and could be done efficiently with the implements readily available to the Dust Bowl farmer—the lister, moldboard plow, or chisel. The contour furrow and the contour ridge differed slightly; the plow scattered the furrow slice as widely as possible, while the ridge was left intact or even built up by overlapping two or more slices. The scattered furrow slice slowed runoff by allowing water to flow uniformly across the entire field, thus eliminating the possibility of washing and gullying. Since the furrow was beneath the surface, it was not subject to breaking and so had the added advantage of requiring no maintenance. Furthermore, grass runners extended down the furrow more rapidly than over the contour ridge, and seeds collected in the furrow, enabling rapid vegetation.[22]

In contrast, the contour ridge served to impound water on the grass behind it; if the ridge was above the furrow, it spread the runoff over a wide area. The furrow checked water loss if the ridge broke. The contour ridge, however, required a large amount of maintenance and was slow to revegetate. Contoured pastures that were not overgrazed could hold virtually all of the precipitation that fell, and better growth resulted—approximately 50–100 percent, depending on the sod condition prior to contouring and the adjacent blow areas.[23]

About 5,000,000 acres, 18 percent of the total acreage under cultivation in the Dust Bowl, were submarginal land—land that, given the current price of wheat, did not provide a sufficient return to be profitable. The SCS recommended that all of this land be revegetated with native grasses, either naturally or artificially. The length of time needed for natural revegetation varied greatly, depending on the amount of time the field had been broken, the proximity of seed grasslands, and the amount of grazing and rainfall the field received. It took twenty-five to forty years for the more desirable grasses fully to recover abandoned fields. And farmers and ranchers observed, too, that fields which had been broken only two or three years revegetated much more quickly than lands farmed for a considerable period of time.[24]

The first task in achieving either natural or artificial revegetation was to stabilize blowing land. If natural revegetation was desired, the goal was to obtain a weed growth as soon as possible to hold the soil until more desirable vegetation replaced it. Artificial revegetation, on the other hand, required that weed growth be minimized while seeded grasses became established. To minimize weed growth the SCS advised farmers to plant a cover crop such as sudan grass, sorghum, or broom corn and allow it to remain on the land during the winter. These crops protected the soil from blowing, acted as a moisture-conserving mulch, delayed weed growth, and protected the young grass plants after seeding in the spring.[25]

The SCS suggested seeding a mixture of blue grama, buffalo, side-oats grama, galleta, and sand drop seed grasses on heavy soils and a mixture of blue grama, side-oats grama, sand blue stem, and drop seed grasses on sandy soils. Ten pounds of blue grama and five pounds of side-oats grama mixed with one pound each of the other grasses and seeded per acre produced the best results on heavy soils. Six pounds of sand blue grama and one pound each of the other grasses planted on each acre was more successful on the sandy soils. When the Dust Bowl farmer chose between natural and artificial revegetation, he considered such factors as land value, the cost of seeding operations, the estimated length of time required to reestablish grass by the various methods, the effect of neighboring blow lands, and his financial condition.[26]

During the better part of the decade, efforts to revegetate grasses artificially on submarginal lands met with limited success because rainfall was so far below normal that the grass seed usually failed to germinate and blew out of the soil. Furthermore, many farmers preferred to chance planting feed or wheat because these crops returned higher profits than did grazing lands. As late as spring 1938, the Russian thistle contributed more to the stabilization of submarginal lands than did planned revegetation.[27]

Sand dunes posed a problem for Dust Bowl farmers in some areas, particularly in Curry County, New Mexico, and Seward County, Kansas. The dunes were detrimental not only to the farmers

Figure 5. In spring 1936 these sand dunes formed on land north of Dalhart, Texas, that had not been farmed for three years. With proper soil conservation techniques, dunes like these could easily be controlled. (Photograph from the National Archives.)

who owned the sandy lands but also to neighboring farmers, since the Federal Land Bank would not grant loans on property that was in danger of being covered by sand. Little was done about the sand dunes until early in 1936, when the SCS began experimenting near Dalhart and found that the most effective way to stabilize the dunes was to reestablish plant cover. The SCS recommended breaking down the steep slope on the leeward side of the dune with a tractor and disk or a horse-drawn drag pole. Such a reduction in the height of the slope prevented the wind from forming eddies and allowed the particles of sand to blow beyond the dune. The dunes and the land between them could then be listed to help check soil movement and permit weeds, especially the Russian thistle, to gain a hold. A cover crop of sudan grass, broom corn, kafir corn, or hegari gave extra protection. If such a procedure was followed, almost total stabilization and elimination of sand dunes could occur in a year—even under drought conditions.[28]

By mid-December 1937, Dust Bowl farmers had reduced the amount of seriously eroded land 65 to 70 percent from the previous year. During the summer of 1938 good rains fell over most of the Dust Bowl and allowed farmers to plant soil-holding crops so that by spring 1939 the Dust Bowl had shrunk to the smallest area since 1932. Although dust storms continued in 1939, the wind during the blow months was of lower velocity and shorter duration than at any time since 1934; the lands primarily subject to blowing at this time were those with sandy soils and denuded pastures. Nevertheless, more than 20,000,000 acres of cultivated land needed terracing, and 3,000,000 acres of crop land as well as 34,000,000 acres of grazing land were not yet contoured. Ample rainfall occurred, though, in the summer and autumn of 1940, and for the remainder of the decade the Dust Bowl (and most of the Great Plains) received above-average precipitation. With the return of the rains, the wind erosion problem temporarily ended.[29]

But the rains were not solely responsible for the restoration of agriculture in the Dust Bowl. The work of the Soil Conservation Service was instrumental in helping farmers bring their lands under control. By 1939 most farmers, following the technical advice and practices of the SCS, were using the proper tillage implements, allowing crop residues to remain on the land during the blow season, contour plowing, terracing, strip cropping, planting drought-resistant crops, and following better grazing management practices. The farmers embraced the SCS programs because they were geared to practicality and low cost. Strip cropping, for example, was a simple farming procedure and did not require additional expense. The average cost of cultivating contoured land was 20¢ to 50¢ per acre and of building terraces $2.75 per acre. Most costs were minimal since the SCS and other agencies provided thousands of dollars to help farmers initiate soil conservation programs; and because the farmers had the necessary implements, they could do most of the work themselves.[30]

By 1940, 89 percent of the farmers under SCS contracts credited their conservation practices with increasing land values; for 80 percent it increased their net farm income; and 95 percent intended to continue the programs after the expiration of their contracts. Farmer interest in the formation of conservation districts was high. So much progress had been made on the SCS demonstration projects that the staff previously necessary to maintain operations was reduced to one or two technicians in fifteen of the seventeen projects.[31]

The Dust Bowl of the southern Great Plains was created by a combination of factors—overexpansion, cultivation of submarginal lands, failure to change crops when conditions required it, lack of soil conservation practices, drought, and the relentless wind. The resulting dust storms of the 1930s forced farmers to utilize all of the technical expertise they could command to bring the wind erosion problem under control. When drought and dust storms returned to the Southern Plains in the 1950s, the technology and conservation practices which Dust Bowl farmers had been using for the previous two decades prevented the region from reverting to the severe conditions of the 1930s. The consistent and proper use of technology and the attention to adequate soil protection were significant factors that enabled the Dust Bowl farmers to adapt, survive, and prosper in the harsh environment of the southern Great Plains.[32]

Notes

1. Hugh Hammond Bennett, *Soil Conservation* (New York: McGraw-Hill Book Co., 1939), p. 55; E. E. Free and J. M. Westgate, "The Control of Blowing Soils," *Farmers' Bulletin No. 421* (1910), p. 3; Hugh Hammond Bennett, "Facing the Erosion Problem," *Science* 81 (April 5, 1935): 323; Ivan Ray Tannehill, *Drought: Its Causes and Effects* (Princeton, N.J.: Princeton University Press, 1947), pp. 12, 41.

2. Glenn K. Rule, "Crops against the Wind on the Southern Great Plains," *Farmers' Bulletin No. 1833* (1939), pp. 5-6; Bennett, *Soil Conservation,* p. 737; Message from the President of the United States, *The Future of the Great Plains,* House Document no. 144, 75th Cong., 1st sess., 1937, p. 4; "A Report of the Soil Conservation Service to the Secretary of Agriculture on Problems of the Southern Great Plains and a Conservation Program for the Region," MS, April 1954, p. ii, National Agricultural Library, Beltsville, Maryland.

3. Angus McDonald, *Erosion and Its Control in Oklahoma Territory,* United States Department of Agriculture Miscellaneous Publication no. 301 (1939), pp. 4-6; H. H. Finnell, "Prevention and Control of Wind Erosion of the High Plains Soils in the Panhandle Area" (mimeographed), p. 9, Soil Conservation Service Publications, National Archives, Record Group 114 (hereafter cited as NARG); B. W. McGinnis, "Utilization of Crop Residues to Reduce Wind Erosion," *Land Today and Tomorrow* 2 (April 1935): 12; "The Report of the Eleventh Conference of the Regional Advisory Committee on Land Use in the Southern Great Plains Area," Colorado Springs, Colorado, April 19-20, 1937, pp. 1-2, 5-6, Office of the Secretary of Agriculture, General Correspondence, 1937, Drought File, NARG 16; R. I. Throckmorton, "A Soil Conservation Program for Kansas," *Thirty-first Biennial Report of the Kansas State Board of Agriculture,* vol. 37 (Topeka: State Printer, 1937-38), p. 39; C. C. Isley, "Will the Dust Bowl Return?" *Northwestern Miller* 224 (November 20, 1945): 35; Ben Hibbs, "Reaping the Wind," *Country Gentleman* 104 (May 1934): 45, 48.

4. Ira Wolfert, *An Epidemic of Genius* (New York: Simon and Schuster, 1960), p. 79; *The Future of the Great Plains,* pp. 27, 29; Arthur H. Joel, *Soil Conservation Reconaissance Survey of the Southern Great Plains Area,* United States Department of Agriculture Technical Bulletin no. 556 (1937), pp. 15, 22; B. F. Coen, "A Survey of Baca County Colorado," Federal Emergency Relief Administration, Rural Problem Area Reports, July 14, 1934, pp. 5, 43, NARG 83; K. H. McGill et al., "A Survey of Meade County Kansas," Federal Emergency Relief Administration, Rural Problem Area Reports, July 14, 1934, pp. 5,

43, NARG 83; K. H. McGill et al., "A Survey of Meade County Kansas," Federal Emergency Relief Administration, Rural Problem Area Reports, August 11, 1934, p. 39, NARG 83; H. V. Geib, "Report of the Wind Erosion Survey in the Region of the Oklahoma Panhandle and Adjacent Territory," p. 3, Office of the Secretary of Agriculture, General Correspondence, 1933, Drought File, NARG 16; A. W. Zingg, "Speculations on Climate as a Factor in the Wind Erosion Problem of the Great Plains," *Transactions of the Kansas Academy of Science* 56 (September 1953): 371-77; Bennett, *Soil Conservation*, p. 729; C. Warren Thornthwaite, "The Great Plains," in *Migration and Economic Opportunity*, ed. Carter Goodrich (Philadelphia: University of Pennsylvania Press, 1936), p. 238; *Amarillo Globe*, January 22, 1932.

5. Rule, "Crops against the Wind on the Southern Great Plains," p. 7; *Washington* (D.C.) *Evening Star*, April 15, 1935; Earle G. Brown et al., "Dust Storms and Their Possible Effect on Health," *Public Health Reports* 50 (October 4, 1935): 1370; Soil Conservation Service, *Soil Erosion a Critical Problem in American Agriculture*, pt. 5 of the Report of the Land Planning Committee (Washington, D.C.: Government Printing Office, 1935), pp. 59, 67, 78, 82, 88.

6. Rule, "Crops against the Wind on the Southern Great Plains," p. 32; H. T. U. Smith, *Geological Studies in Southwestern Kansas*, vol. 41, Bulletin of the University of Kansas, no. 18 (September 15, 1940): 178-79; Geib, "Report of the Wind Erosion Survey in the Region of the Oklahoma Panhandle and Adjacent Territory," p. 4; *Yearbook of Agriculture, 1935* (Washington, D.C.: Government Printing Office, 1936), pp. 15-16; "A Report of the Soil Conservation Service to the Secretary of Agriculture on Problems of the Southern Great Plains and a Conservation Program for the Region," p. iii; W. A. Mattice, "Dust Storms, November, 1933 to May, 1934," *Monthly Weather Review* 63 (February 1935): 53.

7. James C. Malin, "Dust Storms: Part I, 1850-1860," *Kansas Historical Quarterly* 14 (May 1946): 129-44; idem, "Dust Storms: Part II, 1861-1880," *Kansas Historical Quarterly* 14 (August 1946): 265-96; idem, "Dust Storms: Part III, 1881-1900," *Kansas Historical Quarterly* 14 (November 1946): 391-413; McDonald, *Erosion and Its Control in Oklahoma Territory*, pp. 25-28; *Topeka Daily Capital*, July 10, 1913; Free and Westgate, "The Control of Blowing Soils," p. 11; Victor C. Seibert, "A New Menace to the Middle West: The Dust Storm," *Aerend* 8 (Fall 1937): 213.

8. E. Morgan Williams, "The One-Way Disc Plow: Its Historical Development and Economic Role (Master's Thesis, University of Kansas, 1962); Rule, "Crops against the Wind of the Southern Great Plains," p. 19; E. F. Chilcott, "Preventing Soil Blowing on the Southern Great Plains," *Farmers' Bulletin No. 1771* (1937), pp. 3-4; *Dodge City Daily Globe*, April 22, 1935; *Abilene Daily Reflector*, March 26, 1935.

9. N. P. Woodruff, W. S. Chepil, and R. D. Lynch, *Emergency Chiseling to Control Wind Erosion*, Kansas State Agricultural Experiment Station Technical Bulletin no. 90 (1957), p. 1; Lawrence Svobida, *An Empire of Dust* (Caldwell, Idaho: Caxton Printers, 1940), pp. 62, 199; Wolfert, *An Epidemic of*

Genius, pp. 73-74; Chilcott, "Preventing Soil Blowing on the Southern Great Plains," pp. 3-12; *Topeka Daily Capital*, August 30, 1936.

10. Hibbs, "Reaping the Wind," p. 48; Chilcott, "Preventing Soil Blowing on the Southern Great Plains," pp. 4-7.

11. Chilcott, "Preventing Soil Blowing on the Southern Great Plains," pp. 7-10; Svobida, *An Empire of Dust*, p. 202.

12. R. S. Kifer and H. L. Stewart, *Farming Hazards in the Drought Area*, WPA Division of Social Research Monograph XVI (Washington, D.C.: n.p., 1938), p. 80; H. H. Bennett, *Handbook of Soil and Water Conservation Practices for the Wind Erosion Area* (Washington, D.C.: United States Department of Agriculture, 1936), pp. 24-25; Margaret Bourke-White, "Dust Changes America," *Nation* 140 (May 22, 1935): 597; *Amarillo Sunday News and Globe*, September 30, 1934, and January 20, 1935.

13. H. H. Bennett, "Memorandum to the Secretary of Agriculture regarding, *A Plan for Control of Wind Erosion in the Region of Southwestern Kansas, Western Oklahoma and Northwestern Texas in Connection with Agricultural Relief*," August 22, 1933, pp. 1-7, Office of the Secretary of Agriculture, General Correspondence, 1933, Drought File, NARG 16; Russell Hatfield, "People on the Plains," *Kansas Water News* 13 (1970): 11-12; Ben Hibbs, "Dust Bowl," *Country Gentleman* 210 (March 1936): 85; *Amarillo Sunday News and Globe*, August 5 and 12, September 9, October 7 and 9, and November 11, 1934, and August 9, 1936.

14. Hatfield, "People on the Plains," pp. 12-15; C. W. Humble, "Nine Counties Have Organized Wind Erosion Districts," in "High Plains Conservationist" (mimeographed), Soil Conservation Service Region 6, Amarillo (March 1936), pp. 3-4, Soil Conservation Service Publications, NARG 114; H. H. Finnell, "Annual Report, 1939-1940," p. 9, Region 6, Soil Conservation Service Publications, NARG 114.

15. Throckmorton, "A Soil Conservation Program for Kansas," pp. 47-48; Rule, "Crops against the Wind on the Southern Great Plains," p. 19; "Emergency Tillage Operations and Results," pp. 1-2, Soil Conservation Service Drought File, 1936-1937, NARG 114; "Program for Rural Reconstruction," pp. 4-5, Soil Conservation Service Drought File, 1936-1937, NARG 114; H. H. Finnell, "The Progress Made in Wind Erosion Control in the Southern High Plains Region," For the Seventh Southwestern Soil and Water Conservation Conference, Stillwater, Oklahoma, July 7-8, 1936, p. 5, Soil Conservation Service Drought File, 1936-1937, NARG 114.

16. H. H. Finnell, "Appraisal of South Plains Agricultural Conditions with Recommendations of a Permanent Program to the Drought Situation," August 17, 1936, pp. 8-9, Soil Conservation Service Drought File, 1936-1937, NARG 114; *Amaraillo Globe*, December 18, 1932.

17. "Emergency Tillage Operations and Results," pp. 1-2; "Program for Rural Reconstruction," pp. 4-5; Rule, "Crops against the Wind on the Southern Great Plains," p. 21; *Amarillo Sunday News and Globe*, February 3, 1935.

18. "SCS Work Tested," Soil Conservation Service Drought File, 1936-1937, NARG 114; "Colorado Conservancy" (mimeographed), Colorado Springs,

Colorado (May and June 1936), p. 1, Soil Conservation Service Publications, NARG 114; H. H. Finnell, "Water Management," Soil Conservation Service Publications, NARG 114.

19. Bennett, *Soil Conservation*, pp. 346, 360-62; Rule, "Crops against the Wind on the Southern Great Plains," pp. 30, 33-37; Bennett, *Handbook of Soil and Water Conservation*, pp. 29, 31-32; R. R. Hinde, "Strip Cropping of Corn, Cotton and Beans," in "High Plains Conservationist" (mimeographed), Soil Conservation Service Region 6, Amarillo (March 1936), p. 8, Soil Conservation Service Publications, NARG 114.

20. Hinde, "Strip Cropping of Corn, Cotton and Beans," p. 8; Chilcott, "Preventing Soil Blowing on the Southern Great Plains," p. 25.

21. Joel, *Soil Conservation Reconaissance Survey of the Southern Great Plains Area*, pp. 6, 8; Rule, "Crops against the Wind on the Southern Great Plains," pp. 39-40; J. C. Whitfield, "Wind Erosion Endangering Colorado Vegetation," *Land Today and Tomorrow* 1 (December 1934): 27-28; "The Recent Destructive Dust Cloud," *Science* 97 (May 25, 1934): 473; H. V. Woodman, "Pasture Development in Texas," *Land Today and Tomorrow* 2 (March 1935): 7; "The Report of the Eleventh Conference of the Regional Advisory Committee on Land Use in the Southern Great Plains Area," p. 8; Bennett, *Handbook of Soil and Water Conservation*, pp. 39-40; "The Drought Situation," p. 4, Office of the Secretary of Agriculture, General Correspondence, Drought File, 1935, NARG 16.

22. "The Use of Contour Furrows and Related Structures on Pasture and Range Land," Prepared by the Section of Agronomy and Range Management, Region 6, Amarillo, Texas, for the Soil Conservation Conference on Agronomy and Range Management, Denver, Colorado, January 13-16, 1937 (mimeographed), pp. 1-6, Soil Conservation Service Publications, NARG 114; Eugene C. Buie, "Contour Furrowing in Region 6" (mimeographed), pp. 1-2, Soil Conservation Service Publications, NARG 114.

23. "The Use of Contour Furrows and Related Structures on Pasture and Range Land," pp. 12-23, NARG 114; Buie, "Contour Furrowing in Region 6," p. 3; "Annual Report," A.S.A.E. Subcommittee on Contour Farming, 1939-1940, Soil Conservation Service Publications, NARG 114; Woodman, "Pasture Development in Texas," p. 11.

24. B. W. McGinnis, "Erosion and Its Control on the Southern High Plains" (mimeographed), p. 16, Soil Conservation Service Publications, NARG 114; Sydney H. Watson, "Natural and Artificial Revegetation in the Southern Great Plains" (mimeographed), pp. 1-2, Soil Conservation Service Publications, NARG 114; F. S. Reynolds, "Seeding Eroded and Cultivated Land to Native Grasses on Dalhart Project," in "High Plains Conservationist" (mimeographed) Soil Conservation Service Region 6, Amarillo (March 1936), pp. 10-11, Soil Conservation Service Publications, NARG 114.

25. Watson, "Natural and Artificial Revegetation in the Southern Great Plains," pp. 2-5; "Program for Rural Reconstruction," pp. 3-4.

26. Watson, "Natural and Artificial Revegetation in the Southern Great Plains," p. 4; Rule, "Crops against the Wind on the Southern Great Plains,"

pp. 45–46; Chilcott, "Preventing Soil Blowing on the Southern Great Plains," p. 27.

27. Roy I. Kimmell, "A Long View of the Wind Erosion Problem," *Quarterly Report of the Kansas State Board of Agriculture*, vol. 57 (Topeka: State Printer, March 1938), p. 86.

28. Charles J. Whitfield, "Sand-Dune Reclamation in the Southern Great Plains," *Farmers' Bulletin No. 1825* (1938), pp. 1-2, 7-9; *Amarillo Sunday News and Globe*, November 17, 1935; Charles J. Whitfield, "Sand Dunes in the Great Plains," *Soil Conservation* 2 (March 1937): 209.

29. *Amarillo Globe*, December 13, 1937; Glenn K. Rule, *Land Facts on the Southern Great Plains*, United States Department of Agriculture Miscellaneous Publication no. 334 (1939), pp. 13, 22; "Report of the Twentieth Conference of the Regional Advisory Committee on Land Use Practices in the Southern Great Plains Area," Amarillo, Texas, April 21-22, 1939 (mimeographed), p. 1, Soil Conservation Service Publications, NARG 114; Tannehill, *Drought: Its Causes and Effects*, p. 51.

30. Untitled MS, Soil Conservation Service Drought File, 1936-1937, NARG 114; Bennett, *Soil Conservation*, p. 738; Hinde, "Strip Cropping of Corn, Cotton and Beans," p. 9; *Amarillo Sunday News and Globe*, September 1 and November 10, 1935, and June 14, 1936.

31. Finnell, "Annual Report, 1939-1940," pp. 4, 12.

32. *Amarillo Sunday News and Globe*, December 12, 1937; "A Report of the Soil Conservation Service to the Secretary of Agriculture on Problems of the Southern Great Plains and a Conservation Program for the Region," pp. 1-6.

Agricultural Risk in the Great Plains

Leslie Hewes

Failure on the frontier of settlement is common. A high turnover of settlers took place well before the plains were reached.[1] By now, even in the Great Plains, the last of the great agricultural frontiers of the United States, the processes of adjusting to a new country and the squeezing out of the unfit should have reduced the risk of failure substantially. Nevertheless, risk remains a characteristic of man-land relationships through much of the region.

Natural hazards are numerous and often severe. In the words of a long-time student, "The droughts, torrential rains, destructive hail storms, crop diseases, insect plagues, and late fall and early spring blizzards combine to make this a high risk region."[2] He might have added wind, and for the pioneer period, rabbits and fire. Drought is usually reckoned the chief natural hazard.

Occupying the New Land

Variability, involving ups and downs, booms and busts, is a part of the regional personality. Hill County, Montana, in the north-central "Triangle" adjacent to the Canadian border, provides an illustration. Its agricultural history includes rapid dryland settlement in the years 1910–17, when one crop commonly paid for the farm. In 1918, reliance on seed loans was common; and in 1919, most operators were forced to sell their livestock. In 1920, 80 percent of the farmers were seeking employment; yet a wheat harvest of 5½ million bushels in 1927 helped pay for the mechanization of the then enlarged farms.[3] Hazards for the unprepared, opportunities for speculators, and the need for the long view for those who play the averages are self-evident. Elsewhere, I have advanced the argument that risk affects not only the dryland farmer, but also the grazier and irrigator.[4]

No doubt, there is merit to Walter Prescott Webb's thesis that unadapted woodsmen made poor settlers in the Great Plains.[5] Actually, the story of who occupied the land and how is not well told, at least by geographers. John Hudson's documentation of the sources of settlers for North Dakota, a striking exception, shows that many were experienced in living in midwestern grasslands.[6] Significant numbers came from other semiarid grasslands—from the Russian steppes, Canadian prairies, and eastern Washington.[7]

It is true that mixed or general farming was pushed westward by pioneers practicing familiar modes of settlement. Early settlers chose farms in or near the valleys adjacent to wood and water. In Nebraska between 1880 and 1885, a time of rapid expansion, farming on the frontier was much like that of settled parts of the state farther east. Corn was the usual first, or sod, crop, but the combination of corn, oats, wheat, and potatoes was almost as common on the margins of settlement. After work stock, dairy cows were the first animals added, but the most common combination also included hogs, beef cattle, and poultry, as in the settled area. A little back of the frontier, perhaps as the necessary infrastructure developed, came some emphasis on dairying and wheat.[8]

Of course, there were exceptions to the rule that midwestern mixed farming was extended westward into the semiarid country. It appears that in both Colorado and Montana dryland farming, commonly with stock raising, was extended from irrigated bases.[9] In the Northern Plains, wheat soon outran corn as the major crop.[10] In the central Great Plains, specialization in wheat came late, apparently after the merits of drought-resistant and hardy Turkey Red wheat were recognized.[11]

Setbacks. The westward advances have been checked and reversed at several times and places. The need for three crops of homesteaders to make settlement stick was one way of putting it. In some localities, as in part of northeastern Colorado, even three such efforts did not bring unmixed success. There the history of settlement was summarized thus: "Within the memory of many of us the lands of eastern Weld County have been settled and abandoned twice—the settlers starved out. . . . Eastern Weld County has been settled for the last time."[12] However, much of that part of the county is now national grasslands, bought by the government in the 1930s. Probably there is validity to the striking assertion that "a panorama of the Great Plains cannot easily disown its carnage of maimed and broken settlement, in a profusion akin to that of the buffalo skeletons which littered the plains in the presettlement period. In no small measure, the material progress of the region was capitalized by the sunk investments of its pioneering generations."[13] Some evidence of the scale of failure and personal loss is seen in the loss between 1890 and 1900 of more than one-half of the population of nine counties in western Kansas and western Nebraska; more farm mortgage foreclosures in the years 1921–25 than farms in four Montana counties; and 80 percent as many abandoned as occupied farmhouses in Baca County, in southeastern Colorado, in 1938.[14]

Poor crops, poor pastures, emergency cattle purchases, and large per capita relief payments during the great drought and depression of the 1930s had somewhat different but overlapping distributions. Especially poor crops and pastures occurred in the mid-1950s mainly in the south-central and southern plains. Farmers made heavy use of the partly temporary land-retirement program of the Conservation Reserve of the Soil Bank about 1960, chiefly on the southwestern dry margin of crop farming in the plains. Thornthwaite's maps of the year-to-year variations in climate suggest a basic reason for both the changing maps of distress and the frequency with which the north-central plains and the Dust Bowl area appear.[15]

It is small wonder that in the introspective atmosphere of the 1930s both official and unofficial calls for retrenchment—a pulling back of agricultural settlement, already demanded in the 1920s—should be made.[16] The changes in land use recommended in the Great Plains were too great to be made by governmental purchase. Instead, what amounted to pilot projects in land use planning and control were undertaken under land utilization projects. More than 5 million acres were acquired by the government in the Great Plains. Today the lands are used for controlled grazing—over 3 million acres as national grasslands, now under the control of the Forest Service, and some 2 million acres in Montana, turned over to the Bureau of Land Management for operation with other government lands even before the program of land purchases was complete.[17]

Taking Stock

Crop Insurance: A Measure of Risk. Wheat is the main dryland crop of the Great Plains. Dryland farming is considered the most hazardous important economic support of the region. Because the Federal Crop Insurance Corporation insures wheat against failure in much of the Great Plains, the rates that it charges (premium as percentage of liability) may serve as a meaningful measure of perceived risk. It is true that some provisions and practices of the wheat insurance program reduce the accuracy of crop insurance rates as a representation of risk.[18] In general, the cost of wheat insurance seems to be a rather conservative appraisal of the record of wheat insurance.[19] Nevertheless, maps of rates charged for wheat insurance provide valuable indicators of the variation of risk from place to place.

The state averages of ratios of premiums to guarantees for Great Plains states and some states to the east (included for purposes of comparison) are shown in figure 1. Costs are about the same in Montana and North Dakota as in more humid states to the east. Only Colorado, Texas, and South Dakota run substantially higher. However, it is only fair to note that more than one-half the counties in Texas where insurance is offered have programs for irrigated wheat only and that many of the counties in Oklahoma having insurance lie well to the east of the Great Plains. New Mexico is omitted from the map because insurance is offered in only one county and there only on irrigated wheat. The discontinuance of wheat insurance in southeastern Colorado resulted in some lowering of the Colorado state average.

The map of insurance rates by counties in the Great Plains shows a rather general increase in rates to the west, although the foothills section of Montana, adjacent to the Rockies, constitutes a major exception (fig. 2). The Dust Bowl, in and about the Oklahoma Panhandle, insofar as insurance is offered, shows up as the chief area of high risk. A second area also stands out from surrounding country as an area of risk—one of fairly high risk—on the western margin of wheat farming in South Dakota. In explanation of the rates shown in some parts of the map, it should be pointed out that if insurance was offered for both summer fallow and continuous wheat and for both winter and spring wheat, the lowest rates were mapped. Despite the use of summer fallow in western Kansas, the 100th meridian seems to continue to warn of higher risk in southwestern Kansas and southward. A cross section showing rates across Kansas, using the second tier of counties north of the Oklahoma border, illustrates the rather abrupt increase as the semiarid country is entered (fig. 3). The marked westward rise in the rates for continuously cropped wheat is indicative of the risks that have caused farmers to stop using the practice almost completely in westernmost Kansas. No figures are available for southeastern Colorado because insurance is no longer offered there.

In general, insurance is offered on unirrigated winter wheat in wheat-growing regions except to the northeast, where only spring

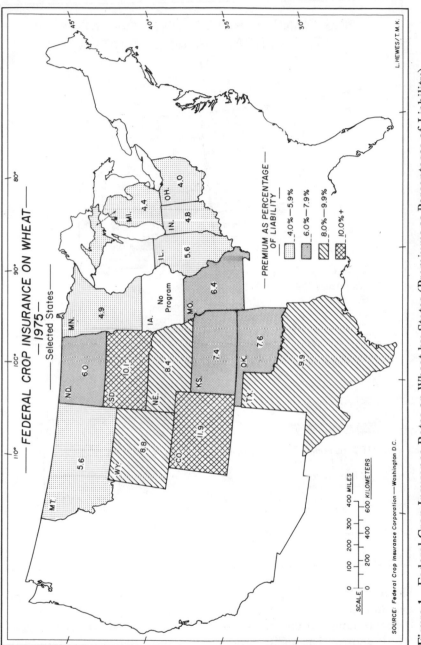

Figure 1.   Federal Crop Insurance Rates on Wheat by States (Premiums as Percentages of Liability)

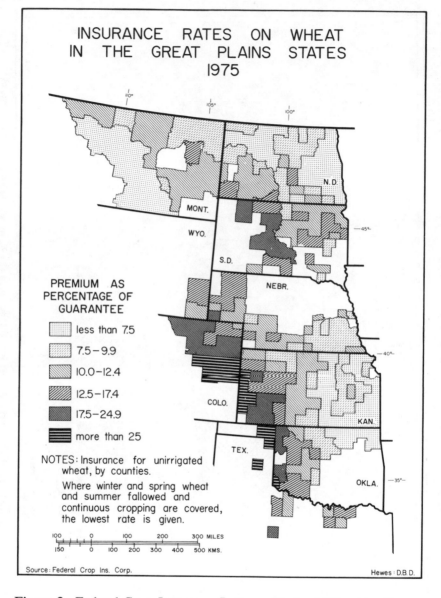

Figure 2. Federal Crop Insurance Rates on Dryland Wheat by Counties. In case different rates apply to winter and spring wheat and/or to continuous cropping and summer-fallowed wheat, the lowest rate is shown. The FCIC gave county figures that were determined on a different (higher) basis than state averages.

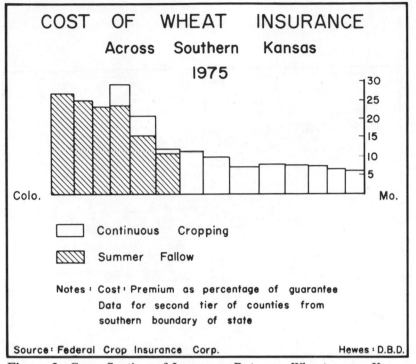

Figure 3. Cross Section of Insurance Rates on Wheat across Kansas

wheat is insured, and in the heart of the Dust Bowl (fig. 4). Continuously cropped wheat is insured in more humid areas to the east and summer-fallowed wheat to the west, again with considerable overlap. Special rates are offered on irrigated wheat in some counties in the southern High Plains (fig. 5).

Variability. Comparison of the map of rates charged for wheat insurance with the maps of variability suggests a partial explanation of the rates.[20] The chief area of very high variability in the Dust Bowl includes the chief area of very high insurance rates, as well as a large area in which no dryland insurance is offered. The fairly high variability of wheat yields in much of the Northern Plains is less indicative of fairly high insurance rates. The map of variability of wheat yields below the regression line, more directly representative of wheat failure, identifies more exactly the regions of very high insurance rates in the Dust Bowl and fairly high rates in South Dakota. Probably it is significant that blank areas in figure 2, representing the lack of insurance on dryland wheat, appear to the west

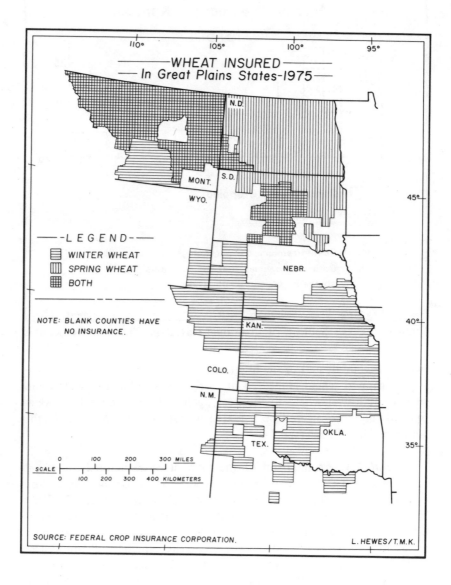

Figure 4. Insurance Offered on Winter and Spring Wheat, 1975

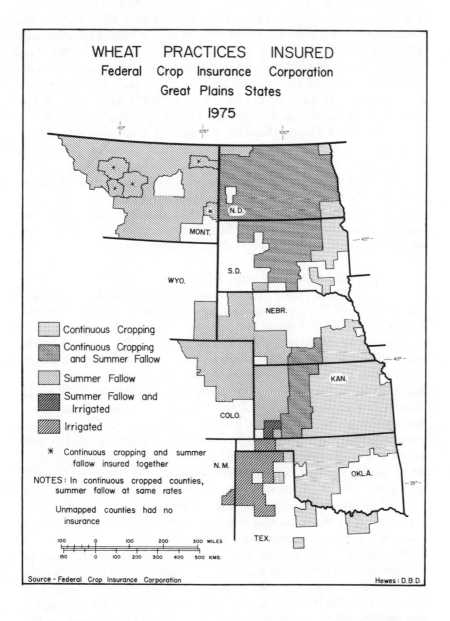

Figure 5. Availability of Federal Crop Insurance on Wheat, by Practice

of the counties having high insurance premiums. As stated elsewhere, the causes of failure or near failure for which indemnities on insured wheat are paid by the Federal Crop Insurance Corporation are thought to be fairly indicative of reasons for the failure of uninsured wheat as well in any particular county in a given year.[21] The chief cause of failure determined from corporation records and the estimates of amount of abandonment of wheat by state-federal agricultural statisticians for the period 1939–57 for a large part of the central Great Plains was drought. Hail was the leading cause in much of the Northern Plains. Drought and related wind, although not as devastating as in the 1930s, still were major risks in wheat growing in the dry 1950s, especially at the southwestern margin of the plains. In the northern wheat country, wheat farmers in the Montana Triangle, where both winter and spring wheat are grown, considered drought the chief hazard, hail second, and winterkilling third. In northeastern Montana, with but little winter wheat, drought and hail were about even, and insects and diseases together were third.[22]

Other Judgments. The maps of premium rates for unirrigated wheat in the Great Plains may be taken as evidence that wheat farming in much of the area is not a high-risk gamble. For much of the region, it appears that wheat failure is no longer a major risk.

As late as 1950, probably because of the failures of the 1930s and earlier, the opinion that survival was more important than high income was probably generally held. An agricultural researcher from North Dakota agreed with that view, arguing that because wheat failures tended to be bunched, the farmer, to protect himself from the recurring years of failure, needed to include subsistence enterprises. Certainly, many early settlers of limited means had discovered, to their sorrow, that a few years of crop failure brought disaster. They could not wait on long-term averages. For those who could afford to take the long view, an agricultural scientist has pointed out, "it is not the unavoidable loss of a crop in the extremely unfavorable years that causes bankruptcy so much as failure to produce maximum yields when conditions are favorable."[23]

Considering the degree to which specialized wheat farming dominates crop farming in the plains, it appears that farmers rather generally agree with the confident assertion of Warren R. Bailey of the Farm Production Economics Division of the USDA Economic Research Service that wheat "is the best adapted crop we have in the Plains." He reached this conclusion despite the high variability of yield, which he said should be accepted as inevitable. For North

Dakota he ranked the return on investment in this order: (1) dryland grain, (2) fertilization, (3) forage crops, (4) livestock enterprises, (5) irrigation. The same author concluded that although grain crops in northwestern Oklahoma were more variable in production than cattle enterprises, they were less variable in income, and that low variability was achieved at the expense of lowered income in Nebraska.[24]

Reducing Risk

The need for protection from the unusually dry years in the plains was recognized early. Summer fallow, the practice of skipping the planting of a crop but tilling the soil often enough to prevent the growth of weeds, resulted in saving part of the moisture of that period for the next year's crop. Probably the chief hazard resulting from this kind of farming was the blowing of dust from unprotected fields, during one winter and spring if winter wheat was grown, or two consecutive winters and springs with spring wheat. In western Kansas, probably with but little summer fallow, whole farms were reported to have blown away by 1910. In northwestern Kansas, where summer fallow was used early, severe wind erosion occurred at that time. In the foothills section of Montana, the practice received a setback from blowing dust about 1915. The problem of soil blowing was widely observed, although damage to growing crops from wind and dust was more likely recognized than damage to the land. Partly as a result, the practice of summer fallowing was not common on the American Great Plains before the 1930s, except locally. Moreover, farmers generally agreed with Agricultural Extension Service workers that fallow did not pay—that two years' crops, wheat after corn or other crops, including wheat after wheat, were more valuable than one year's wheat crop after summer fallow.[25]

Slowly at first, then more rapidly, "protective summer fallow," as it was called by the Agricultural Conservation Program, caught on during the 1930s. In time, the combination of rough, cloddy soil, crop residue left on and near the surface on summer-fallowed ground, and, for much of the wheat country, alternating strips of crop and fallow made summer fallow more effective, both providing some protection against the wind and preserving more moisture in the soil for the next year's crop. The 1974 statement "Strip cropping continues to be the foundation of wind-erosion control but has been augmented during the past two decades with stubble-mulch tillage"[26] is probably accurate for the Northern Plains, less so for the southern part, where strip cropping is not common and the amount of crop residue often falls short of constituting stubble mulch.

Some of the steps by which summer fallow was made more effective can be worked out. Montana, including the Triangle, was the scene of some of the early advance. Partly because of the disaster occurring there about 1920, changes taking place have been chronicled more completely than in most of the plains.

Strip cropping was known in the Triangle earlier, but M. L. Wilson in his 1923 report did not recommend the practice. The use of alternating fairly narrow strips of crops and fallow, begun in neighboring Alberta in 1917, is said to have had some use in Montana within two years, but a report published in January 1935, included the statement that a few farmers had used the practice for three or four years. At the same time, it was asserted that the duckfoot cultivator, an instrument suited to speedy, mechanized power farming that retained crop residue on the surface, was "almost universally used."[27] Farm mechanization during the 1920s and 1930s, increasing the speed at which land could be prepared for crops, cut the need for fall plowing. Thus, the fallow strips left in stubble reduced the hazard to the young wheat alongside in the alternating strips.

Wilson's thoroughgoing report on the Triangle, made in 1923, recommended both listed and plowless fallow. Although the terms *stubble mulch* and *under-tillage* were not used, tools serving that purpose were recognized, among them duckfoots, bar blade weeders, shearing blades, and rod weeders. K. Ross Toole, without citing authority or giving a date, credits the Montana State College Agricultural Extension Service with revolutionizing dry farming in the state. In 1935, before the entry of the federal government into soil conservation on a large scale, important adjustments in Montana agriculture had taken place, among them the adoption of summer-fallow tillage methods, the use of superior drought-resistant varieties of grain, and improvements in tractors and combines.[28]

On the heels of the declaring of the Agricultural Administration Act unconstitutional in 1936 came financial incentives for hard-pressed farmers to engage in a variety of recommended conservation practices. Some of these had been tried out in Montana. An official report of 1938 noted the spread of strip farming into the plains from Alberta by way of Montana, and reported the recent increase in plowless fallow, although acknowledging more blowing from fallow land than from any other. The Field Service Branch of the USDA Production and Marketing Administration showed a total of only 375,000 acres of contour strip cropping and field (across the wind) strip cropping together carried on under agricultural conservation programs in the United States in 1937. Five years later, field strip cropping was done on more than 8,000,000 acres. Much of the big increase in strip cropping took place between 1938 and 1939. The first map of strip cropping I have found, that of 1944, showed the Montana Triangle and northeastern Montana as the chief areas of concentration in the United States. Montana, averaging nearly 4,000,000 acres of strip cropping per year from 1947 to 1951, was far ahead of the second state, North Dakota. The acreage placed under summer fallow under conservation programs in the United States increased from about 3,500,000 acres in 1936 to more than 12,000,000 acres in 1944. In the latter year, the greatest concentration was in the semiarid parts of the central Great Plains, while North Dakota was the leader in the north. In 1947, the plains states leading in summer fallow were North Dakota, Kansas, Colorado, and Nebraska. In 1955, when all the Great Plains states except Kansas included stubble mulching as an approved practice, most of the more than 6,000,000 acres on which stubble mulching was initiated in the United States in that year were in North Dakota and northern Montana.[29]

Summer fallow was recently practiced on some 22,000,000 acres in the Great Plains. Wheat farmers in Montana, Wyoming, and Colorado with few exceptions use summer fallow. Figure 5 is only somewhat representative of where summer fallow dominates. Actually, most wheat is grown on fallow in North Dakota, except in the southeastern part. It is less important in the states to the south, being the exception in eastern South Dakota, eastern Nebraska, and eastern and south-central Kansas. In Oklahoma, it is unimportant except in the Panhandle. The eastward expansion of summer fallow from semiarid into subhumid country has come late, apparently largely as a result of the effort of farmers to maintain wheat production despite the reduction of wheat allotments in effect for about two decades after the Korean War. Perhaps it is significant that the percentage of wheat acreage under summer fallow in North Dakota increased from less than 50 percent in 1953 to more than 80 percent in 1963. In Nebraska, the biggest increase in fallowed acreage in a five-year period occurred between 1960 and 1965; however, in Kansas the largest gain was from 1930 to 1935 (when the practice was apparently encouraged to combat drought). In Colorado the greatest gain occurred between 1945 and 1950, with the big post–World War II plow-up.[30]

It has been asserted that wind erosion has been reduced substantially. Nevertheless, it was stated in 1974 that in the Northern Plains "most of the wind erosion occurs on summer fallow" because of the difficulty of maintaining sufficient crop residues over the second winter of fallow for spring wheat. Long-time researchers in the central Great Plains at the same time said: "One conclusion is that fallow has been a significant contributor to wind erosion mostly because of the way it is tilled; however, this should no longer be true."[31] Field observation indicates, however, that strip cropping is rare in the heart of the Dust Bowl and that subtillage, leaving substantial amounts of residue on the surface, is far from being the rule. Both stripping and stubble mulch are far more characteristic of southeastern Wyoming, the southern part of the Nebraska Panhandle, and the northern Great Plains. Partial stubble mulch with emergency tillage in time of need is resorted to more commonly. Drought-era legislation requiring protective emergency tillage appears to have aided the effort to eliminate the blowing of soil. In West Texas, the spread of irrigation has reduced the hazard of soil blowing.[32]

Wheat yields have increased in much of the plains. No doubt, these increases have contributed markedly to the viability of wheat farming. For the long period 1926–62, however, two large areas averaged less than ten bushels per acre. One included the central, western, and southern parts of the Dust Bowl; the other was located mainly along the North Dakota–South Dakota boundary from about midpoint westward.[33] A large block of counties had increases of more than 50 percent in wheat yields from the 1926–48 period to the 1940–62 period. Most of the area is within the central Great Plains, in and near northwestern Kansas and northeastern Colorado, with an extension along the Nebraska boundary with Wyoming and South Dakota. On the other hand, a considerable part of the old Dust Bowl experienced little or no increase. Although increased yields in good years were important in the overall improvement in yields in much of the central Great Plains, the reduction in failure was also a significant factor. The area showing little or no reduction in abandonment from the 1931–37 period to the 1949–57 period (fig. 6) was much like that in which wheat yields increased very little. Figure 6 should be compared with figure 7, which shows average abandonment in the later period. It is only fair to point out that the increase in failure in the 1950s, a time of drought in the Dust Bowl, was due in part to the great extension of wheat farming after World War II.

Summer fallow is probably responsible for the greatest increase in wheat yields in most of the semiarid portion of the Great Plains. About the time Colorado wheat farmers were adopting summer

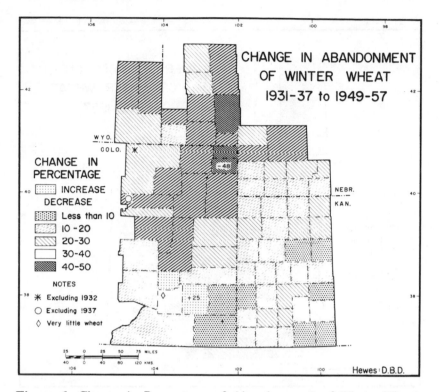

Figure 6. Change in Percentage of Abandonment of Winter Wheat for Two Periods of Drought in the Central Great Plains

fallow as a regular practice, the following assessment was made: "Fallow does not insure a paying crop each year, but the comparative certainty and high average yield of wheat on fallow mark it as the only method of production of winter wheat on the hard-land [nonsandy] soils of the western section of the central Great Plains." Farmers there and in semiarid parts of the northern Great Plains show their agreement. The effectiveness of summer fallow has increased on the lands of wheat farmers as well as at experiment stations. In Montana, state average yields on fallow increased 50 percent from the 1929–51 to the 1952–70 period, although there were about the same number of dry, normal, and wet years.[34]

The substitution of the improved summer fallow for continuous cropping has reduced failure and raised average yields markedly in much of the drier part of the plains. In North Dakota, however, in the fifteen-year period 1949 through 1963, the yield differential in

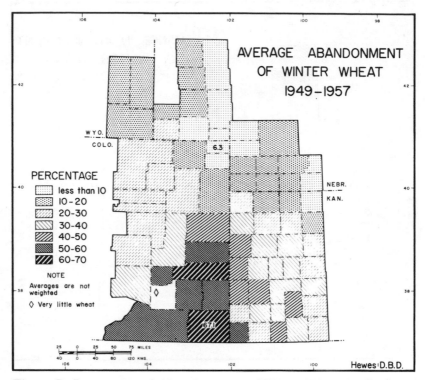

Figure 7. Percentage of Abandonment of Winter Wheat in the Semi-arid Portion of the Central Great Plains, 1949–57

favor of summer-fallow wheat reached 50 percent on a state-wide seeded-acre basis in only four years—1949, 1952, 1959, and 1961. The nine reporting districts analyzed separately for the period 1955–63 show twenty-two instances of eighty-one possibilities in which seeded-acre yields were at least 50 percent higher. In six cases the difference was more than 100 percent.[35]

In Kansas, as in the plains generally, the yield advantage of summer fallow decreases to the east as the performance of nonfallowed wheat improves. In the twenty-year period 1957 through 1976 the average yield of summer-fallowed wheat, on a seeded-acre basis, in the western third of the state was 22.6 bushels, compared to 14.2 for continuous cropping, a difference of almost 60 percent. In the central third the figures were 26.7 and 24.3 bushels, or a 9 percent difference.[36]

Greeley County, located midway on the Colorado border in western Kansas, is a high-risk county. Abandonment remained fairly

high during the windy drought years of the mid-1950s, although the
level of failure was lower than in the 1930s (figs. 6 and 7). In the
twenty years 1957 through 1976, there have been six years in which
abandonment reached 30 percent, including four in which it exceeded 60 percent and two in which it reached more than 90 percent. In those twenty years, wheat on summer fallow outyielded
continuous wheat 18.2 bushels to 11.8 on the average, a gain of
about 56 percent. In only nine of the twenty years did yields on
fallow exceed those from continuous cropping by 53 percent, the
calculated break-even point. Big differences in four good years accounted for almost 60 percent of the difference. Probably, the conclusion is justified that high yields in a few good years, to which
summer fallowing contributed, have kept the average wheat farmer
of Greeley County in business. The importance of a few good years is
probably less in areas of lower risk (where Federal Crop Insurance
rates are notably lower).

The use of improved adapted varieties of wheat has contributed
to the increase in wheat yields in the Great Plains. At Tribune, in
droughty Greeley County, Kansas, 35 percent of the increase in
yields during the years 1919–71 was credited to new varieties. The
head of the USDA regional testing program for hard winter wheat
reports an average increase of 25 percent in experimental yields from
new varieties during the period 1963–76. Scout, the chief variety
grown in Nebraska, showed a gain of 30 percent. Farther north, the
increases due to new varieties were smaller because of the extreme
emphasis on winter hardiness. Much of the increase can be realized
immediately by farmers because of the thorough local testing before
new varieties are released. The experimenting has already been
done.[37]

There are other factors, largely unmeasured, in addition to improved summer fallow and new varieties that have contributed to a
more viable wheat industry in the Great Plains. These include the
farmers' greater control over the timing of their operations because
of improvements in mechanization, the farmers' increased experience, the elimination of many of those without financial reserves,
and the large size of operations. Fertilization, although it has doubtless aided yields in the northern and eastern parts of the plains, has
been used very little in the semiarid central Great Plains, the portion
of the region in which average wheat yields have increased most.

Adjusting Use to the Land. The judgment that wheat is the
best-adapted crop of the Great Plains of necessity is based on the
conclusion that in general wheat is raised where it should be—on

land and in climates suitable for the purpose. Wheat is the chief crop of the plains, especially important near the dry limit of cultivation. Hence, the conclusion that most of land that is in crops should be in crops implies that wheat growing is ecologically quite well adapted to the land that it occupies. If the land classification of 1958 used by the Soil Conservation Service was essentially valid, most of the land then in crops in the plains was suited for that use: only a little over 12 percent (13,800,000 of 113,027,000 acres) of the cropland was judged unsuitable for crops. In addition, 15,463,000 acres in crops were in Class IV, the "least suitable" for cultivation but "suitable for cropping and with reasonably good management much of it can be kept in cultivation if needed."[38]

In a land noted for its booms and busts, the reasonably good fit of use to the land did not take place easily. It is probably impossible to say how great a retreat from formerly cultivated land has taken place, but a 1970 estimate for the central Great Plains that 40 percent of all land was then being cultivated of a total of 55 percent plowed at one time or another gives a "go-back" figure of only 15 percent of all land. If that estimate is approximately correct, the judgment of farmers in the aggregate must be rated as good. Probably there is broad validity to this generalization made shortly after the major homesteading period in southeastern Montana: "Just as there is a tendency for grazing land [land so classified], once homesteaded, to go back into range livestock ranches, so there has been a tendency for the broad stretches of good tillable land, wherever located, to go into wheat farms."[39] Of course, there have been plowups as well as retreats in crop farming. Even at times of low prices for wheat, technology may increase the value of land and encourage expansion.[40] With the lure of high prices for wheat and the availability of farm machinery at the end of World War II came a new major invasion of the grassland of both the northern and central Great Plains, which might well have resulted in the plowing of much of the land bought by the federal government in the late 1930s except for its protected status.

Unresolved Problems

Although the land is generally being put to uses for which it is well suited, there are a number of disturbing exceptions. Probably the best known is in the old Dust Bowl problem area. Another is exemplified in the recent spread of saline seep on summer-fallowed land in the Northern Plains. A third is seen in the overuse of underground water.

Most of the land abandoned in the Dust Bowl in the 1930s was replowed in the 1940s and in large part is still in cultivation, but the long-term outcome must be judged still in doubt. Although a substantial amount of dry farming, including wheat, continues, a number of indicators point out the region as one of extremely high risk. Among them are the widespread participation in the partly temporary cropland-retirement programs of the Conservation Reserve in the late 1950s, the discontinuance of crop insurance after 1955 in a number of counties of especially high loss, the extremely high rates for insurance where coverage on dryland wheat is still in effect, and the considerable number of counties in which only irrigated wheat is insured or no wheat insurance program at all is available (fig. 8). The chief hazard is aridity, not the land in the narrow sense of the word. Although those farms placed entirely in the Conservation Reserve were of substantially lower productivity than those not participating in the program, and substantial amounts of Class IV land are in crops in southwestern Kansas, rather little land "unsuited" or "least suited" for cultivation is mapped as cropland. This area more than any other in the plains experiences recurring drought. Aridity and high winds make it the region of greatest climatic hazard for wind erosion in the Great Plains.[41]

Saline seep is the formation of wet, salty areas in unirrigated soils due to the development of perched water tables, from which excess moisture moves to reach the surface in low places. The failure of crops, usually wheat, to remove all the moisture stored by summer fallowing, especially during humid periods, is considered the main reason for the problem. Saline seep has been considered a serious problem only recently.[42]

The extent of saline seep in the northern Great Plains has been estimated variously. In Montana alone, it was estimated for 1976 that some 140,000–145,000 acres were affected; the figure for North Dakota was 100,000 acres. The chief areas affected in Montana lie in discontinuous fashion within the wheat areas, chiefly in the foothills section and in the northeast. Stillwater County, in the south-central part of the state, had the largest total, 23,000 acres, followed by Chouteau and Fergus counties, in the central part of the state. As mapped by Montana scientists, the area of potential—in part actual—saline seep development includes most of the wheat country of Montana, North Dakota, and South Dakota as well as of the Canadian Prairies. It occurs mainly where glacial till overlies shale but extends beyond the limits of Pleistocene glaciation on the southwest. The rate of increase is given as 10 percent per year.[43]

Solutions to the threat of saline seep call mainly for a more

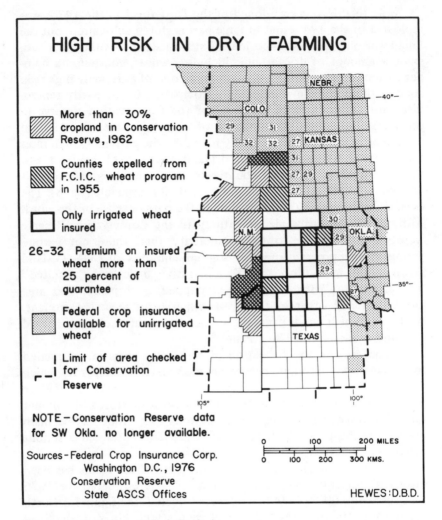

Figure 8. Dust Bowl High-Risk Area

flexible cropping system than now used, including the substitution of continuous cropping for summer fallow, especially when soil moisture is abundant. Evidence that change is occurring is shown by the reinstitution of crop insurance on continuous cropping in five counties in Montana (identified by asterisks in figure 5) after such insurance was dropped in the state because of lack of participation.[44] Three of these counties are ranked second, third, and fourth in acreage affected by saline seep.

A third major kind of ecological imbalance in the Great Plains, which will be only mentioned, is the rapidly increasing overdraft on ground water through the spectacular development of well irrigation. The chief areas affected, mainly in and near the High Plains of Texas, New Mexico, Oklahoma, Kansas, Colorado, and Nebraska, together far exceed saline seep in acreage, and in the aggregate approach the Dust Bowl problem region in extent. Irrigation, held out as a way out of the problem of risk, threatens to become a dead end for much of the well-irrigation country of the Central and Southern Plains.[45]

Conclusion

Despite serious exceptions, the ecological balance in much of the Great Plains is reasonably good. Even so, there remains the question whether the Great Plains experience has been long enough to provide answers to the questions of how to live in the region and use its land. For example, how much of the region has been tested by periods of extreme drought that might occur once in a century? The very fact that summer fallow is a common practice in growing wheat considerably east of the belt in which its use is justified by the increase in yields secured is evidence of defensive farming—an effort to reduce risk, even at the cost of reduced income.[46] Anticipating risk remains common dry farming strategy. Accordingly, some assurance is provided that the dry farming now practiced will stand the test of extreme drought. However, flexibility is one of the more valuable guidelines learned in living in this region of risk. In addition, at least in the more droughty parts, reserves are needed in order for farmers to survive long enough to take advantage of long-term averages.

Notes

This study was supported by the Research Council of the University of Nebraska-Lincoln.

1. Allan G. Bogue, *From Prairie to Corn Belt: Farming on the Illinois and Iowa Prairies in the Nineteenth Century* (Chicago and London: University of Chicago Press, 1963), pp. 25–27.

2. Stanley W. Voelker, "Institutional Adaptations to the Environment of the Great Plains," *Journal of Farm Economics* 40, no. 5 (December 1858): 1266.

3. Neil W. Johnson, *Farm Adjustments in Montana: A Study of Area IV,*

Its Past, Present, and Future, Montana State Agricultural Experiment Station Bulletin no. 267 (Bozeman, March 1939), p. 10.

4. Leslie Hewes, "The Great Plains One Hundred Years after Major John Wesley Powell," in *Images of the Plains: The Role of Human Nature in Settlement*, ed. Brian W. Blouet and Merlin P. Lawson (Lincoln: University of Nebraska Press, 1975), pp. 203-13.

5. Walter Prescott Webb, *The Great Plains* (New York: Ginn and Co., 1931). The theme is elaborated in Walter M. Kollmorgen, "The Woodsman's Assaults on the Domain of the Cattleman," *Annals of the Association of American Geographers* 59, no. 2 (June 1969): 215-39.

6. John C. Hudson, "Migration to an American Frontier," *Annals of the Association of American Geographers* 66, no. 2 (June 1976): 242-65. Also worthy of note are John Hudson, "Two Dakota Frontiers," ibid. 63, no. 4 (December 1973): 442-62; James L. Forsythe, "Environmental Considerations in the Settlement of Ellis County, Kansas," *Agricultural History* 51, no. 1 (January 1977): 38-50; and Louis Carl Brandhorst, "Settlement and Landscape Change on a Sub-humid Grassland: Lincoln County, Kansas" (Ph.D. diss., University of Nebraska-Lincoln, 1974).

7. Hudson, "Migration to an American Frontier"; M. L. Wilson, *Dry Farming in the North Central Montana "Triangle,"* ed. R. B. Bowdsen, Montana State College Extension Service Bulletin no. 66 (Bozeman, 1923), p. 125; J. E. Payne, *Investigation of the Great Plains: Field Notes from Trips in Eastern Colorado*, Colorado Experiment Station Bulletin no. 59 (Fort Collins, 1900), pp. 5-16; Hans D. Badtke, *The Hutterites in Montana*, Montana Agricultural Experiment Station Bulletin no. 641 (Bozeman, August 1971); Cornelius Krahn, "From the Steppes to the Prairies, Part II," *American German Review* 11, no. 4 (December 1944): 30-34, 37, 39; David V. Wiebe, *They Seek A Country: A Survey of Mennonite Migration with Special Reference to Kansas and Gnadenau* (Hillsboro, Kans.: Mennonite Publishing House, 1967); William Sherman, "The Germans from Russia," in *Symposium on the Great Plains of North America*, ed. Carl C. Zimmerman and Seth Russell (Fargo: North Dakota Institute for Regional Studies, 1967), p. 63; Albert J. Peterson, "German-Russian Catholic Colonization in Western Kansas" (Ph.D. diss., Louisiana State University, 1970).

8. Frederick B. Piellusch, "Frontier and Settled Land Use in Nebraska, 1880-1885" (Ph.D. diss., University of Nebraska-Lincoln, 1974).

9. Mary Wilma M. Hargreaves, *Dry Farming in the Northern Great Plains, 1900-1925* (Cambridge, Mass.: Harvard University Press, 1957), pp. 439-40; *Facts about the Fertile Crow Creek Valley and Facts about Bennett Lands* (Denver: W. H. Thompkin Co., ca. 1906).

10. Philip L. Tideman, "Wheat on the Northern Agricultural Frontier" (Ph.D. diss., University of Nebraska-Lincoln, 1967). Also, see Hargreaves, *Dry Farming*, for an account of dryland wheat in the north, including the introduction of dryland crops and equipment.

11. Mark Alfred Carleton, "Hard Wheats Winning their Way," *USDA Yearbook, 1914* (Washington, D.C.: Government Printing Office, 1915), pp. 392-421; Carleton, "Successful Wheat Growing in Semi-arid Districts," ibid., 1900

(Washington, D.C.: Government Printing Office, 1901), p. 534; Carleton R. Ball, "American Wheat Improvement," *Agricultural History* 4, no. 2 (April 1930): 63; H. S. Quisenberry and L. P. Reitz, "Turkey Wheat: The Foundation of an Empire," *Agricultural History* 48, no. 1 (January 1974): 98-110; T. L. Lyon, *The Adaptation and Improvement of Winter Wheat,* Nebraska Agricultural Experiment Station Bulletin no. 72 (Lincoln, 1902), p. 198; Mattie Ellen Mumford, "Geographic Phases of the Wheat Industry of Nebraska" (Master's thesis, University of Nebraska, 1934), pp. 30-38, 51, 86; James C. Malin, "The Adaptation of the Agricultural System to Sub-Humid Environment, Illustrated by the Wayne Township Farmers' Club of Edwards County, Kansas, 1886-1893," *Agricultural History* 10, no. 3 (July 1936): 118-41, specifically pp. 131 and 140.

12. *Weld County* [Colorado] *News,* November 1921, p. 26. See also LeRoy Hafen, *Colorado, the Story of a Western Commonwealth* (Denver: Peerless Publishing Co., 1933), p. 273; Depue Falck, E. R. Greenslet, and R. E. Morgan, "Land Classification of the Central Great Plains, Parts 4 and 5, Eastern Colorado," mimeograph no. 56284, U.S. Department of the Interior Geological Survey, Washington, D.C., 1931, p. 15.

13. H. Van Vleet, "Comment," *Journal of Farm Economics* 45, no. 5 (December 1963): 1099.

14. R. R. Renne, *Montana Farm Foreclosure,* Montana State Agricultural Experiment Station Bulletin no. 368 (Bozeman, February 1937), p. 12; "Land Use in Baca County, Colorado, based on a Field Survey," mimeographed (Land Utilization Program, USDA Bureau of Land Economics, April 1, 1938), Denver Public Library, A 35.2: L/22/22, p. 26 and appendix, pp. 4, 25, 35.

15. Hewes, "After Major Powell," figs. 1-6. A map showing the use of seed loans in a period beginning before the great drought and Depression was another warning signal ("Maladjustments in Land Use in the United States," pt. 6 of the *Supplementary Report of the Land Planning Committee of the National Resources Board* [Washington, D.C.: Government Printing Office, 1935], map on p. 34). C. W. Thornthwaite, *Atlas of Climatic Types in the United States, 1900-1939,* USDA Soil Conservation Service, Miscellaneous Publication no. 421 (Washington, D.C.: Government Printing Office, 1944).

16. Albert Z. Guttenberg, "The Land Utilization Movement of the 1920's," *Agricultural History* 50, no. 3 (July 1976): 477-90; Mary W. M. Hargreaves, "Land-Use Planning in Response to Drought: The Experience of the Thirties," ibid., no. 4 (October 1976): 561-82; "Maladjustments in Land Use," map of projects on p. vi. Also, Carl C. Taylor and Conrad Taeuber, "Wanted: Population Adjustment, Too," *Land Policy Review,* no. 2 (March-April 1939), map of land classification f.p. 24. Fred A. Shannon, *The Farmer's Last Frontier: Agriculture, 1860-1897* (New York: Holt, Rinehart and Winston, 1945), p. 215, expressed the opinion, "Dry-farming cannot flourish where the annual average precipitation is less than fifteen inches. The occasional good years are not enough to make up for the total failure." He spoke for many.

17. H. H. Wooten, *The Land Utilization Program, 1934 to 1964: Origin, Development, and Present Status,* Agricultural Economic Report no. 85, USDA, Economic Service (Washington, D.C.: Government Printing Office, 1965), map

on p. 15. Sherman E. Johnson, of the Bureau of Agricultural Economics, "Land Use Readjustments in the Northern Great Plains," *Journal of Land and Public Utility Economics* 13, no. 2 (May 1937): 152-62, expressed what was probably the official position that the higher-risk areas were probably never self-supporting. M. H. Saunderson and N. W. Monte, *Grazing Districts in Montana*, Montana State College Agricultural Experiment Station Bulletin no. 326 (Bozeman, September 1936), p. 23.

18. Limitations include: (1) The degree of failure may be understated because payment to the insured is based not on failed acreage but on the average yield of the farm unit. (2) Those having good records of low failure are rewarded by obtaining lower premiums or higher guarantees and those with poor records pay higher premiums or may have their insurance discontinued. (3) Substantial reductions in premiums are given on large acreages in wheat, on the expectation that average yields are less likely to go low enough to require payment of the guarantee. (4) The provision in effect in the states of Montana, North Dakota, and South Dakota, where winter wheat is insured, that spring wheat must be replanted upon the failure of winter wheat if such failure is recognized before the time to plant spring wheat. (5) The refusal to accept new customers into the program in occasional years of early recognition of drought.

19. A conclusion based largely on examination of County Analysis Sheets No. 1 for western Kansas and eastern Colorado for the 1950s. Also, according to an analysis of the 1975 Wheat Insurance—Coverage and Rate Summary of the Actuarial Division, it appears that premiums go down slowly in counties in which indemnities paid are low. Apparent overcharges in premiums (premiums more than twice indemnities paid) are not unexpected for counties of short record, but there were some—fifteen were counted—for dryland wheat where the insurance had been in effect the full actuarial period, 1948-73. Four of the nine cases of marked undercharge of premiums (indemnities more than 50 percent greater than premiums) were in counties where insurance began in 1948 or earlier. The conclusion seems warranted that average insurance rates by counties are a somewhat conservative measure of risk, although in most cases close to actuarial experience.

20. Variability, as a statistical device, is a measure of central tendency or, alternatively, of deviation from the mean.

21. Leslie Hewes, "Causes of Wheat Failure in the Dry Farming Region, Central Great Plains, 1939-1957," *Economic Geography* 41, no. 4 (October 1965): 313-30.

22. Warren R. Bailey, *Organizing and Operating Dryland Farms in the Great Plains: Summary of Regional Research Project CP-2*, USDA Economic Research Service, 301, Great Plains Agricultural Council Publication no. 26 (Washington, D.C.: Govermment Printing Office, February 1967), p. 47.

23. Rainer Schickele, "Farmers' Adaptations to Income Uncertainty," *Journal of Farm Economics* 32, no. 3 (August 1950): 362; A. L. Hallsted, "Reducing the Risk in Wheat Farming in Western Kansas," *Thirtieth Biennial Report of Kansas State Board of Agriculture, 1935-1936* (Topeka: Kansas Printing Plant, 1937), p. 109.

24. Warren R. Bailey, "Adapting Farming to the Great Plains," *Proceedings of the Great Plains Agricultural Council*, Bozeman, Montana, July 28-29, 1966, pp. 79-85 (quotation on p. 79; rankings on p. 82); Bailey, *Organizing and Operating Dryland Farms in the Great Plains*, pp. 8, 12.

25. George N. Coffey, Thomas D. Riley, and party, *Reconnoissance* [sic] *Soil Survey of Western Kansas*, USDA Field Operations of the Bureau of Soils, 1910, Twelfth Report (Washington, D.C.: Government Printing Office, 1912), p. 1415. In Thomas County, the extremely dry years of 1910 and 1911 caused complete crop failures, aiding in blowing of some 65,000 acres in three years (L. S. Call, "Culture Methods of Controlling Wind Erosion," *Journal of American Society of Agronomy* 28, no. 1 [March 1936] : 193). Hargreaves, *Dry Farming*, p. 466; A. Osenburg, *Cultural Methods for Winter Wheat and Spring Wheat in the Judith Basin*, University of Montana Agricultural Experiment Station Bulletin no. 205 (Bozeman, July 1927), p. 2. John F. Ross, *Grains for Montana Dry Lands*, USDA Farmers Bulletin no. 749 (Washington, D.C.: Government Printing Office, August 12, 1916), p. 6, said summer fallow "cannot be recommended as a general practice." E. C. Chilcott and John S. Cole, *Growing Winter Wheat on the Great Plains*, USDA Farmers' Bulletin no. 895 (Washington, D.C.: Government Printing Office, September 1917), p. 6. Seeding of winter wheat directly in stubble without prior preparation was advised as protection against blowing and winter killing, but, it may be assumed, at the expense of yields. J. H. Arnold, "Farm Practices in Growing Wheat," *USDA Yearbook, 1919* (Washington, D.C.: Government Printing Office, 1920), p. 140; Osenburg, *Cultural Methods for Winter Wheat and Spring Wheat*, pp. 2-3; Z. L. Zook, *Winter Wheat in Western Nebraska*, Agricultural Experiment Station, University of Nebraska Bulletin no. 179 (Lincoln: February 1922), pp. 20, 24, 29-30; Alvin Kezer, F. A. Coffman, D. W. Robertson, Dwight Koonce, G. W. Deming, *Colorado Wheat Varieties*, Colorado Experiment Station Bulletin no. 329 (Fort Collins: January 1928), p. 5.

26. A. L. Black, F. H. Siddoway, and P. L. Brown, "Summer Fallow in the Northern Great Plains (Winter Wheat)," *Summer Fallow in the Western United States*, Conservation Research Report no. 17, USDA Agricultural Research Service (Washington, D.C.: Government Printing Office, April 1974), p. 41.

27. Wilson, *Dry Farming in the Montana "Triangle,"* p. 81. John S. Cole and George W. Morgan, *Implements and Methods of Tillage to Control Soil Blowing on the Northern Great Plains*, USDA Farmers Bulletin no. 1797 (Washington, D.C.: Government Printing Office, January 1938), p. 18; Black et al., "Summer Fallow in the Northern Great Plains," p. 36; E. A. Starch, *Economic Changes in Montana's Wheat Area*, Montana State College Agricultural Experiment Station Bulletin no. 295 (Bozeman, January 1935), pp. 43, 38.

28. Wilson, *Dry Farming in the Montana "Triangle,"* pp. 81, 74-75, 77; K. Ross Toole, *Montana: An Uncommon Land* (Norman: University of Oklahoma Press, 1959), p. 239; Ronald E. Renne, *The Need and Basis for Readjustment, Part I, Readjusting Montana Agriculture*, Montana State College Agricultural Experiment Station Bulletin no. 306 (Bozeman, December 1935), p. 21.

29. Cole and Morgan, *Soil Blowing on Northern Plains*, pp. 7, 17, 18;

Agricultural Conservation Program Maps, 1944, Field Service Branch, USDA Production and Marketing Administration (Washington, D.C., January 1946), p. 9 and map of strip cropping on p. 10; *Conservation Practice Summary, 1947 to 1951,* Agricultural Conservation Programs Branch, USDA Production and Marketing Administration (Washington, D.C., January 1953), p. 28; *Agricultural Conservation Program Maps, 1944,* p. 13; *Conservation Practice Summary, 1947 to 1951,* p. 32; *Agricultural Conservation Program Maps, 1955* (Washington, D.C., March 1957), p. 29.

30. H. J. Haas, W. O. Willis, and J. J. Bond, "Introduction," *Summer Fallow in the Western United States,* pp. 3–5 (acreage derived by adding state totals); B. W. Greb, D. E. Smika, N. P. Woodruff, and C. J. Whitfield, "Summer Fallow in the Central Great Plains," ibid., p. 56.

31. [Ezra Taft Benson] "Interview from the Dust Country: Secretary Benson Reports on the Big Blow of 1955," *U.S. News and World Report,* May 6, 1955, pp. 26–29; Warren R. Bailey, "The Great Plains in Retrospect with a View to the Future," *Journal of Farm Economics* 45, no. 5 (December 1963): 1096; W. Chepil, F. H. Siddoway, and D. V. Armbrust, "Climatic Index of Wind Erosion Conditions in the Great Plains," *Soil Science Society of America Proceedings* 27, no. 4 (July–August 1963): 449–52. Not nearly as many dust storms occurred at Garden City, Kansas, in the 1950s as in 1930s. "The reason for the relatively low incidence of dust storms during the 1954–1957 period as compared to 1935's may be that farmers had learned more about how to control wind erosion and were in a better economic position to control it" (p. 450). These men seem to agree that despite the high wind erosion estimates of the Soil Conservation Service for recent years, wind damage was not comparable to that of the 1930s: H. J. Haas, W. O. Willis, and J. J. Bond, "Summer Fallow in the Northern Great Plains (Spring Wheat)," *Summer Fallow in the Western United States,* p. 17. Greb et al., "Summer Fallow in the Central Great Plains," p. 64.

32. George S. Wehrwein, "Public Control of Land Use in the United States," *Journal of Farm Economics* 21, no. 1 (February 1939): 77, 84–85; Marvin Jones, "Conservation Legislation Sparked by Dust Bowl," *Soil Conservation* 27, no. 11 (June 1962): 252–53; Hewes, *Suitcase Farming Frontier,* pp. 166–67, 170–74. Greeley County, in westernmost Kansas, had exceptional protection in the years 1938–42, when the locally voted requirement for Triple A Conservation payments included strip cropping (ibid., pp. 87–88). "Farm Management and Demonstration, Northwest [Kansas] District," USDA and Rock Island Railroad Cooperating, February 1–June 30, 1913 (filed with reports of county agents, Extension Division, Kansas State University, Manhattan) stated that the early law passed by the Kansas legislature giving county commissioners authority to regulate blowing had little effect; however, listing of the land was considered effective. W. C. Johnson, C. E. Van Doren, and Earl Burnett, "Summer Fallow in the Southern Great Plains," *Summer Fallow in Western United States,* p. 98.

33. Donald K. Larson and Layton S. Thompson, *Variability of Wheat Yields in the Great Plains,* USDA Economic Research Service in cooperation with the Montana Agricultural Experiment Station, ERS 287 (Washington, D.C.: Government Printing Office, June 1966), fig. 9, p. 12; J. F. Brandon and C. R.

Mathews, *Dryland Rotation and Tillage Experiments at the Akron (Colorado) Field Station*, USDA Circular no. 700 (Washington, D.C.: Government Printing Office, May 1944), p. 17.

34. Black et al., "Summer Fallow in the Northern Great Plains," p. 44, citing *Montana Agricultural Statistics*.

35. *North Dakota Crop and Livestock Statistics, 1963* (Fargo: North Dakota State University, May 1964), p. 12. Haas et al., "Summer Fallow in the Northern Great Plains," p. 20, cite the need for an increase of 50 percent for summer fallow to pay.

36. The 53 percent advantage for summer-fallowed wheat was realized in the thirty-one counties in the western third of Kansas in 304 of a possible 620 times. J. A. Hobbs, professor of agronomy, Kansas State University, in letter of July 13, 1977, gave a 53 percent increase on fallow as the break-even point, lower than that calculated earlier by E. N. Castle, *Effects of Summer Fallow on Wheat Yields in Western Kansas*, Agricultural Economics Report no. 42, Kansas Agricultural Experiment Station (Manhattan, May 1950), p. 6, who considered increases of 60-75 percent economical. T. Roy Bogle, Kansas State University extension economist, in letter of July 19, 1977, gave a figure of 50 percent. Yield data furnished by Kansas Crop and Livestock Reporting Service, Topeka.

37. Roy E. Gwin, Jr., et al., *Making the Most of Soil, Water, Climate in West-Central Kansas through Research at Tribune Branch Experiment Station*, Kansas State University of Agriculture and Applied Science Agricultural Experiment Station Bulletin no. 577 (Manhattan, February 1974), pp. 13, 14; interviews with Virgil A. Johnson, professor of agronomy, University of Nebraska-Lincoln, head of state and regional testing program, hard winter wheat, October 21, 1976, and August 31, 1976. The check variety used was Karkov.

38. Andrew R. Aandahl, Robert W. Eikleberry, and Richard K. Jackson, "Location of 'Low Grade' Croplands in the Great Plains States," presented by Aandahl at Great Plains Council meeting, July 1958, mimeographed, USDA Soil Conservation Service, pp. 5, 6. Kansas, Colorado, and Oklahoma, each with more than 2,000,000 acres of cropland classed as unsuited had the largest amounts. Much of the land so classed in Oklahoma was to the east of the region usually included in the Great Plains.

39. Greb et al., "Summer Fallow in the Central Great Plains," pp. 57, 65-66; Virgil D. Gilman, *Types of Farming in Southeastern Montana, Based on Studies Made in 1926 and 1929*, Montana State College Agricultural Experiment Station Bulletin no. 287 (Bozeman, April 1934), p. 43.

40. O. E. Baker, "Government Research in Aid of Settlers in the Northern Great Plains of the United States," in *Pioneer Settlement*, ed. W. L. G. Joerg, American Geographical Society Special Publication 14 (Worcester, Mass.: Commonwealth Press, 1932), p. 78, wrote, "Land that was submarginal for crops a few years ago has now become clearly super-marginal." Likewise in South Dakota, mechanized farming is reported to have brought lower-quality land into production, according to Kelwyn Krug, "South Dakota Crop Production History," *South Dakota Agriculture, 1975,* Crop and Livestock Production Service Bulletin (Sioux Falls, May 1976), p. 8. See also Leslie Hewes, *The*

Suitcase Farming Frontier, especially pp. 1–82, and, for a later period, pp. 97–120.

41. H. H. Finnell, *Land Use Experience in Southern Great Plains,* USDA Circular no. 820 (Washington, D.C.: Government Printing Office, 1949), p. 4; idem, "The Plow-up of Western Grasslands and Its Resultant Effect upon Great Plains Agriculture," *Southwestern Social Science Quarterly* 32, no. 2 (September 1951): 94–100. The average productivity ratings of farms on the wheat lists of the Agricultural Stabilization and Conservation Service whose cropland was entirely in the Conservation Reserve in 1962 in seventeen communities in south-eastern Colorado was 82.6, while the rating for those farms having no cropland in the program was 99.9. The average productivity rating for a county should be 100. That the average for the 668 farms entirely in the Conservation Reserve program and the 1,264 entirely out is less than 100 is explained by the fact that most of the cropland with very high productivity ratings was irrigated land excluded from the wheat lists because wheat was not grown on it. The seventeen communities checked were Bent County, number 1, 2, and 3 (entire county); Cheyenne County, A, B, C, and E; Crowley County, A, B, and C (entire county); Kiowa County, A, B, C, D, and E (entire county); Kit Carson County, D; Lincoln County, Karvel. If all the cropland except four acres on a given farm was in the program, the farm was considered in. The productivity ratings of the numerous farms partly in the program were not averaged. Aandahl et al., "Location of 'Low Grade' Croplands," pp. 5, 6; Thornthwaite, *Atlas of Climatic Types;* W. S. Chepil, F. H. Siddoway, and Dean V. Armbrust, "Climatic Factors for Estimating Wind Erodibility of Farm Fields," *Journal of Soil and Water Conservation* 17, no. 4 (July–August 1962): 162–65, map, p. 174.

42. James L. Krall and Paul L. Brown, "Cultural Practices for the Control of Saline Seep in the Northern Plains," mimeographed, prepared for the Great Plains Conservation Workshop, Fort Collins, Colorado, August 10–12, 1976, p. 1; E. J. Doering and F. M. Sandoval, *Saline-Seep Development in the Northern Great Plains,* USDA Agricultural Research Service ARS-NC-32 (Washington, D.C.: Government Printing Office, February 1976), p. 7.

43. Krall and Brown, "Cultural Practices for the Control of Saline Seep," p. 1; Doering and Sandoval, *Saline-Seep Development,* p. 8. A map, *Areas Affected by Saline Seep–1974,* by the Montana Department of Lands, gives an estimate, for thirty-four counties, that 140,485–144,585 acres were affected. Loren L. Bahls and Marvin R. Miller, "Saline Seep in Montana," *Second Annual Report,* Montana Environmental Quality Council (Helena, October 1973), pp. 35, 39.

44. Krall and Brown, "Cultural Practices for the Control of Saline Seep," p. 3. Bahls and Miller, "Saline Seep in Montana," p. 42, in addition suggest alfalfa and wheat grasses as "pumps" for drying out the wetter areas. Letter from Neil W. Maxwell, Billings Regional Office, Federal Crop Insurance Corporation, February 28, 1977.

45. William F. Hughes and Wyette L. Harman, *Projected Economic Life of Water Resources, Subdivision Number 1, High Plains Underground Water Reservoir,* Texas Agricultural Experiment Station Technical Monograph no. 6

(College Station, 1969), pp. 5, 31; Gwin et al., *Research at Tribune Branch Experiment Station,* p. 7; D. D. Rohdry, R. L. Anderson, T. B. Grandin, Jr., and D. H. Peterson, *Pump Irrigation on the Colorado High Plains,* Colorado State University Experiment Station Bulletin no. 543S (Fort Collins, May 1970); M. J. Ellis, *Ground Water Levels in Nebraska, 1974,* Nebraska Water Survey Paper no. 40, University of Nebraska Conservation and Survey Division (Lincoln, May 1975).

46. Kenneth Norrie, "Dry Farming and the Economics of Risk Bearing: The Canadian Prairies, 1870-1930," *Agricultural History* 51, no. 1 (January 1977): 138-48, specifically pp. 139, 141-42. Of course, there is an alternative explanation that farmers in the United States were so committed to wheat that they turned to summer fallow in an effort to continue to produce as much wheat as ever despite the reduction in wheat allotments during the years that allotments were in effect.

The Great Plains: Promises, Problems, and Prospects

Gilbert C. Fite

In November 1874, General James S. Brisben returned to Omaha after investigating conditions among desperate pioneer settlers in the Republican River Valley. Drought and grasshoppers the previous summer had left people on the verge of starvation. One farmer told his daughter that when the present meager amount of flour was gone, the family would simply have to starve. His wife, however, said: "God will take care of us."[1] On the front page of the *Wessington Springs* (South Dakota) *Independent* of September 8, 1976, an announcement called for a special prayer service "to request ample rains to break the present drought." In the century between the events reported by General Brisben and the heavenly appeal by the South Dakota editor, residents of the Great Plains have sent up multitudes of prayers for rain, and appealed for charity and relief, when their own best efforts could not overcome the unpredictable climate. Indeed, much of the history of the Great Plains can be written around the uncertain, undependable, and often destructive weather of the region. The cycles of hope and despair, prosperity and proverty have been associated with periods of relatively abundant rainfall or severe droughts. Other factors such as farm prices have also affected the region, but nothing has so dominated life on the plains as rain or the lack of it.

Pioneers gradually encroached on the eastern edge of the Great Plains in the 1870s, but a flood of settlement accompanied the unusually abundant rainfall of the early 1880s. No previous frontier had been settled with such breathtaking speed and amid so much hope and optimism as Dakota and the Central Plains of Nebraska and Kansas. By the latter half of the 1880s farmers were pushing into the Texas Panhandle and the high semiarid plains of eastern Colorado, which one misinformed publicist pictured as a fine corn country. Between 1878 and 1890 thousands of farms and hundreds of small towns sprouted up as if by magic between Bismarck in the north and Amarillo, Texas, more than a thousand miles to the south. The population of North and South Dakota, Nebraska, and Kansas nearly doubled during the 1880s, and the number of farms rose from 219,383 to 357,994. Most of this new settlement was west of the 98th meridian and a good deal of it beyond the 100th. From 72 to 94 percent of the people in those states were considered rural in 1890, and agriculture was the main source of income. Wheat production in the four states jumped from 33,701,437 bushels in 1879 to 83,915,433 in 1889, an increase of about 250 percent.[2] In 1890 cattle numbers, even after the great blizzards of 1886 and 1888, were more than 100 percent above what they had been a decade earlier. The promise of the plains seemed well on the way to fulfillment.

However, disaster lurked in the wings of the great drama taking place on the plains. Contrary to talk about a growing rain belt in western Kansas and eastern Colorado, and Professor Samuel Aughey's pseudoscientific contentions, rain did not follow the plow. Beginning in 1889, and earlier in some parts of the plains, drought struck with deadly fury. And this was only the start of much worse things to come. Drought reached its worst in 1893 and 1894, when burning sun and hot winds so characteristic of the Great Plains left thousands of farmers on the verge of ruin and starvation. Many fled the region and damned it to the hell it seemed to be. Some Great Plains counties lost more than half of their population between 1890 and 1900.[3]

The years between 1878 and 1896 experienced the first boom and bust cycle on the Great Plains. However tragic it may have been for thousands of people, it provided some valuable lessons for those who remained. Farmers learned that the same agricultural crops and practices that had been successful in the more humid Midwest were not suitable for the semiarid plains. They found that acreages larger than the traditional quarter section were required, that they needed to grow drought-resistant crops and utilize cultivation methods that would conserve the limited moisture. Farmers discovered, too, that reserves of livestock feed were necessary to get them over the dry years.

The next boom period occurred during the first two decades of the twentieth century. Farmers pushed into the western Dakotas, eastern Montana, and eastern New Mexico in large numbers for the first time. Although there were droughty times after 1900, in most years rainfall was average or above normal throughout most of the plains. Again, favorable rainfall conditions coincided with better prices, especially for wheat. The demands of World War I brought the average farm price of wheat to $1.60 a bushel in 1916. It had not exceeded $1.00 a bushel since 1881. M. L. Wilson, an expert on Great Plains farming, reported that during 1915–16 wheat on newly plowed ground in Montana made fifty bushels to the acre and sold for $2.00 a bushel. That was the heady stuff out of which boom periods on the Great Plains grew. Between 1915 and 1919, nearly five million new acres of wheat were brought into production in the western Dakotas, Nebraska, and Kansas.[4]

The expansion of agricultural settlement and wheat production on the Great Plains during the decade of World War I marked the second boom period that ended in a bust. The collapse was not as sudden as in the 1890s, but the result was the same for thousands of plains operators. Wheat prices at most interior markets dropped to less than $1.00 a bushel by the fall of 1921, and during the next several years debt-ridden farmers struggled against failure and bankruptcy. The weather was reasonably cooperative during the 1920s, but low farm prices and high costs of operation placed most producers in a cruel cost-price squeeze. It was especially hard to pay debts contracted during the inflationary period of World War I with low-priced farm commodities.

In an effort to make a profit, Great Plains farmers sought to increase their efficiency. They improved their dryland farming practices and turned rapidly to mechanization to cut operating costs. The use of tractors, trucks, combines, and other machines increased dramatically. For example, the number of tractors in the Dakotas, Nebraska, and Kansas increased from 50,464 to 181,150 between 1920 and 1930.[5]

But greater efficiency was not enough. Thousands of Great Plains farmers went broke during the 1920s and others hung on only by a slim margin. Then drought, that mortal enemy of Great Plains residents, struck with renewed devastation. From 1930 to 1938 some parts of the plains suffered from lack of moisture, but the worst drought and dust storm conditions occurred between 1933 and 1936. Even with heavy infusions of federal relief, thousands of families were unable to survive the wrath of Great Plains weather. Many residents again fled the region, the second exodus within a single long generation. Rather than returning east as settlers did in the 1890s, thousands of hopeless farmers migrated westward, mainly to California, Oregon, and Washington.[6]

The Great Plains seemed to alternate between feast and famine. By the middle 1940s the hardships of the "dirty thirties" were only an unpleasant memory. Generally adequate rainfall, wartime prices, and expanded output brought a degree of prosperity to Great Plains farmers after 1941 unlike anything they had ever known. The average value of farm products sold by producers in the Dakotas, Montana, Nebraska, and Kansas increased four to five times between 1939 and 1949. Both farmers and those in the region who depended upon agriculture experienced unusual prosperity.[7]

But it soon became clear that the region's climate was as dangerous and unpredictable as ever. Another severe drought struck large portions of the plains between 1952 and 1956, and again in the mid-1970s. Fortunately, farmers were in a better position to roll with the weather punches in the 1950s and 1970s than they had been in the 1890s or the 1930s.

A series of important farming adjustments had been occurring throughout the Great Plains for a generation or more by the 1970s. Besides improved methods of cultivation, including summer fallowing, planting drought-resistant crops, and deeper and more frequent cultivation, there was a remarkable increase in the size of farms. As many farmers failed, the more successful operators absorbed the land into larger units. By 1974 the average farm size in Montana was 2,510 acres, or nearly what Major John W. Powell had recommended in 1878. In many counties in western Nebraska, Kansas, eastern Colorado, and the Texas and Oklahoma panhandles, the average size of farms ranged from 2,000 to 4,000 acres. The most profitable capital investment by Great Plains farmers was in land. Because of this fact, the more successful operators sought to acquire additional acres, bringing a strong upward pressure on land prices in the 1960s and 1970s. An analysis of land sales in North Dakota in 1974 showed that the major reason behind land purchases was to increase farm size. Four out of every five agricultural tracts sold were bought by active farm operators seeking to enlarge their operations.[8]

Continued advances in agricultural technology made much larger family-type farms possible. The most common size tractor in the 1920s, for example, had only 20–30 horsepower; by the 1970s machines with 150–300 horsepower came into general use. With more basic power the size of all planting, tilling, and harvesting machinery could be increased. As early as 1955 a farmer in the Texas Panhandle rigged up a drill which permitted him to plant a section (640 acres) of wheat a day.[9]

Irrigation was a third major adjustment pursued by Great Plains farmers. During every prolonged drought, there have been strong demands to expand irrigation. If the rain did not come from the heavens, somehow water must be pumped from underground. The first major irrigation movement by plains farmers occurred in the 1890s, but it declined after the return of more normal rainfall. It took nearly another generation and a severe and extended drought before farmers began exploiting the plains' vast underground water resources on a large scale. Farmers on the Southern Plains led the way. During the 1930s, desperate need, advanced pump and well technology, rural electrification, and the availability of capital combined to usher in a large subsurface irrigation movement in West Texas. By 1940 some 250,000 acres were being irrigated from 2,180 wells.[10]

During the next generation, deep-well irrigation gradually spread throughout much of the plains. Every dry period sparked added interest in pump irrigation. During the 1950s the irrigated acreage rose sharply in the Great Plains states and continued to increase during the following decade. Between 1949 and 1969 the amount of irrigated farm land nearly doubled, rising from 10.9 to 19.1 million acres. In some Great Plains states the increase was even more spectacular in the 1970s. Between 1969 and 1974, Nebraska farmers placed more than 2 million new acres under irrigation. Pivot sprinkler irrigation equipment introduced about 1953 provided a substantial advance in deep-well irrigation technology. In eight counties of western Nebraska the number of center-pivot outfits jumped from only 101 in 1972 to 947 in 1975. This was little short of revolutionary. Referring to corn production in western Nebraska by center-pivot irrigation, one writer said it was one of the most "fascinating agricultural stories to come along since Massasoit introduced the Pilgrims to fertilizer." In South Dakota irrigated acreage nearly doubled between 1970 and 1975. The forty counties in the High Plains of West Texas had about 71,000 wells pumping irrigation water to more than 6.3 million acres in 1976.[11]

Individual actions by farmers to adjust to the Great Plains environment have been supplemented by significant help from the federal government. Beginning in the 1930s, Congress enacted a series of agricultural and conservation measures to assist farmers. These included the Agricultural Adjustment Act, the Soil Conservation Act, the shelterbelt program, federal crop insurance, and assistance in building dams and stock ponds. By reducing wind erosion and soil loss, and by providing cash income, the federal government helped substantially to stabilize farm income throughout the plains.

Larger farms, drought-resistant crops and improved tillage,

irrigation, and government price-stabilization and conservation programs have been among the major adjustments and policies inaugurated, mainly since the 1930s, to bring greater stability and a higher degree of prosperity to Great Plains agriculture. Risk has been reduced, but it has certainly not been eliminated. Adjustments to make agriculture conform more closely to the environment, especially the enlargement of agricultural operations so necessary to produce enough income to support a family, have been on balance, however, quite successful.

The success of adjustments in farming and ranching on the Great Plains has helped to create serious institutional problems throughout the region. Larger farms have meant a declining rural population, which in turn has intensified the institutional arrangements affected by space and distance. Such institutions and services as local government, education, health care, and highways have created heavy drains upon the region's resources and in some cases simply have not met people's needs. There may have been good reason, for example, to have the seat of county government within ten to fifteen miles of most residents in the horse and buggy days, but the advent of the automobile and a highway system did away with the need for the traditional small counties. Yet, the structure of county government exists in the thinly settled Great Plains just as if population had continued to grow and the automobile had never been invented.[12]

Space does not permit a full discussion of needed institutional adjustments, but one or two examples will point up the problem. During the Dakota boom of the 1880s, the territorial legislature in Dakota established five colleges and universities in what became South Dakota, and the state lawmakers added two more institutions in 1897 and 1902. This placed South Dakota near the top of the states in the number of colleges and universities per 100,000 population.[13]

After 1930 South Dakota's population began to decline and the state's colleges and universities remained small and operated at relatively high costs. Following World War II the rapid growth in enrollments caused by a higher percentage of young people attending college postponed public recognition that the state had a surplus of institutions. However, some South Dakotans began analyzing the problems and called for change. Officials called in consultants to study the situation, but their reports gathered dust. All of this changed in 1970 when Richard D. Gibb, the commissioner of higher education, developed a master plan for higher education in South Dakota. Gibb said bluntly: "The primary problem in public higher education in South Dakota is that of too many colleges and universities."[14] He recommended that Dakota State College at Madison and Southern at Springfield be closed and that the Black Hills Teachers College at Spearfish become a junior college. Gibb also suggested some other changes such as shifting engineering from South Dakota State University to the School of Mines at Rapid City.

Although a public opinion poll showed that 63 percent of those citizens responding favored reducing the number of colleges and universities, and 69 percent favored a single school of engineering, Gibb's suggestions raised a storm of controversy. Opposition to any substantial change came from alumni, chambers of commerce, students, faculty, and others who had a special interest in maintaining things as they were. Any move to adjust and change higher education in South Dakota to make it more nearly fit the needs, resources, and capabilities of that sparsely populated state has so far met tough resistance and defeat. But this is not just a problem in South Dakota. A study published in 1963 showed that all of the plains states spent a higher percentage of their expenditures on higher education than the national average.[15]

The matter of reorganizing county government in the thinly populated area of the plains states also has been a failure. The population of many counties on the High Plains has dropped to below 5,000, and to even less than 3,000. Of the twenty-three counties west of the Missouri River in South Dakota, only three had more than five people per square mile in 1970; ten, or nearly half the counties, had only two or less. With so few people to bear the expense of county government and services, the individual costs are high. Improved transportation has abolished the need to have the seat of local government within a few miles of farm and ranch families. The suggestion that counties might be combined to cut costs and improve services has so far been rejected. Professor Howard W. Ottoson of the University of Nebraska–Lincoln has proposed that Nebraska be divided into thirteen major divisions, plus Omaha and Lincoln, for purposes of local government. He argues that each division would have enough people and assessed property valuation to provide the necessary services at reasonable tax cost. But he admits that such reorganization in Nebraska's rural areas is not likely to happen. Robert J. Antonides of South Dakota State University has made similar suggestions for South Dakota, but no action has been taken.[16]

The resistance to reorganizing local government is very strong. In 1960 some of the civic leaders in Jerauld County, South Dakota, which lies on the 99th meridian, suggested that their county be combined with Buffalo County adjoining it on the west. The population of Buffalo County was only 1,547 in 1960 and Gann Valley, the county seat, had a mere 105 people. Jerauld County had 4,048 people, and there were 1,488 residents in the county seat of Wessington Springs. Since Wessington Springs had a good courthouse building and very few citizens would have had to drive more than fifty miles, and most people less than thirty, to the seat of local government, it seemed reasonable that Wessington Springs should become the county seat of the reorganized county. Wessington Springs also had a doctor and a hospital and could provide other services. However, the discussions and pressures for combining the counties failed, and Buffalo County continued to maintain county offices and services from a town of eighty people for a population of 1,739 in 1970.[17] Taking the plains states as a whole, they spend considerably more per capita on local government than the national average.

We have pointed to two examples of the too-much syndrome on the Great Plains so clearly outlined more than twenty years ago by Carl F. Kraenzel. The sparse population, declining and even decaying country towns, and professional tastes have combined to leave a void in important services throughout much of the region. One of these is medical care. In 1900 Nebraska had 1,672 medical doctors. Moreover, the spread of doctors over the state was fairly adequate. Only six counties were without a physician and only about one-fourth of the doctors were in Douglas and Lancaster counties, where Omaha and Lincoln are located. While the state had 1,810 doctors in 1967, or 138 more than in 1900, some 62 percent of them were in those two counties. Twelve Nebraska counties had no doctor in 1967. The situation was much the same in the Dakotas. The availability of hospitals, public health services, care for the aged, and other medical services are woefully lacking in many parts of the Great Plains. North Dakotans claim that, although in 1960 about half the doctors were in the state's four largest cities, some 95 percent of the state's citizens are within thirty minutes of medical help. If this is true, people on the state's thinly populated plains still pay a heavy price in terms of time and transportation. It is not easy to measure the social cost of space and distance, but it is becoming an increasingly important item in the expense of living on the Great Plains. For the person who must drive fifty or one hundred miles to get medical attention, the cost of travel might amount to more than the doctor's bill.

The costs of other services and needs are also high in the Great Plains states. Some plains states are spending twice the national average per capita on highways. As mentioned earlier, expenses of state and local government are also high. In 1960 North Dakotans spent 212 percent of the national average on state and local government; in South Dakota the figure was 164 percent. Such costs are bound to require hefty taxes. Property taxes are especially high in some of the plains states. Montana and the Dakotas are among those with the highest property taxes in the nation for each $1,000 of personal income.[19]

The decline and disappearance of so many small towns throughout the Great Plains has become a matter of deep concern to politicians, businessmen, and local residents. While some of the larger towns are growing, hundreds of villages and towns are withering away and becoming little more than retirement communities for aging widows. Of the 382 towns in North Dakota, some 80 percent lost population between 1950 and 1970. For the 1960s in South Dakota the figure was about 68 percent.[20] Even about half of the county seat towns in the Dakotas have been unable to maintain their population. Highly sensitive to decreases in population, small towns meet with outrage any action or policy that tends to hurry their further decline.

One of the criticisms of the Eisenhower-Benson soil bank program in the 1950s was the prospect that some farmers would rent entire farms to the federal government and move away. Any loss of rural population would only add to the problems of local communities. Representative Usher Burdick of North Dakota said in 1960 that the soil bank was "systematically destroying the fabric of North Dakota's small community life." As he put it, when farmers departed, implement dealers and merchants quickly felt the pinch, and finally the social institutions supported by tax money began to suffer. Soon the schools, churches, hospitals, municipal water and sewer services, township and county roads, Burdick declared, started to deteriorate, leaving the community in shambles. He added that he had not been "sent to Congress to legislate the depopulation of North Dakota."[21]

Many Great Plains towns have promoted the idea of attracting industry to reverse their economic stagnation. However, this is mostly a false hope and no amount of promotion and ballyhoo will change the situation. Many plains towns have declined to the point where they cannot provide the services needed by local residents. In order to meet people's needs, discussion in recent years has centered on the development of trade areas that will be large and varied enough to provide for the economic, health care, educational, transportation, and cultural requirements of the citizens of a particular area. To some extent such centers have developed throughout sections of the Great Plains, but mostly without plan or design.[22]

At the heart of the problem facing Great Plains residents is income, or better stated, lack of it. Historically, family incomes throughout the Great Plains have been relatively low. Part of the reason for this is that the chief source of income has been agriculture and returns to farmers nation-wide have lagged behind those received by nonfarm elements of the population. Larger and more efficient farm units have improved this situation to some extent, but the cost-price squeeze prevalent in agriculture during the post–World War II generation reduced profits far below what farmers had a right to expect from their heavy investments and great gains in efficiency. Furthermore, unpredictable weather has contributed to low and uncertain incomes. The smaller farm operators on the plains have been especially hard hit. In 1958, for instance, gross income per farm in Sherman County, Nebraska, averaged only 58 percent of the state average over five census years. In 1969 the residents of Greeley County, Kansas, had 86 percent of that state's average per capita income.[23]

While the people of the Great Plains have faced serious income problems, they have been quite successful in attracting federal largess. At least since about 1930 a heavy flow of funds from Washington has helped the region. These expenditures have taken a variety of forms, including federal outlays for relief, reclamation, military bases, and farm stabilization and conservation payments.

It is not surprising that large numbers of Great Plains citizens, having been hit with the twin blows of drought and low prices in the 1930s, had to rely on federal assistance. In April 1935, some 80 percent of the farmers in one middle county of South Dakota were on relief. In the counties making up the Great Plains portion of ten states, the national government spent $132,663,715 between 1933 and 1936 through the Federal Emergency Relief Administration and the Works Progress Administration.[24]

World War II brought huge expenditures on military installations, especially new air bases. All the way from Sheppard Field near Wichita Falls, Texas, to Grand Forks, North Dakota, air force bases sprinkled the region. The annual expenditures to operate and maintain these installations, as well as the civilian employment, have poured millions of dollars into the economies of several Great

Plains communities. In 1975 eleven such bases employed 29,157 people. Tinker Air Force Base at Oklahoma City was the biggest employer in the state.[25]

But it has been the agricultural programs that have poured the most federal money into the Great Plains region. Payments for agricultural stabilization and conservation purposes have totaled hundreds of millions of dollars since 1933. In 1968 the subcommittee of the Committee on Appropriations of the United States Senate asked the Department of Agriculture to provide an individual listing of all farmers in the United States who in 1967 received stabilization and soil conservation payments of $5,000 or more. That document shows clearly how Great Plains producers benefited.

Since many Great Plains farms are large, it is not surprising that many payments amounted to thousands of dollars. In Chouteau County, Montana, 436 farmers received $4,037,331; in Perkins County in northwestern South Dakota 64 producers drew $513,276; and in Red Willow and Perkins counties, Nebraska, $463,013 and $696,110 went to 58 and 92 farmers, respectively. One hundred and eighty-nine payees in Sherman County, Kansas, received payments of $2,098,492 in 1967, with the top recipient getting $54,460. But things are usually bigger in Texas and that is also true of government payments. Hale County, which lies in the south-central part of the Panhandle, contained 1,310 farms, and 1,110 of those, or 84 percent, received government stabilization and conservation payments in 1967 totaling $15,650,953. Fourteen of that number received in excess of $50,000. Lamb County nearby had 936 farm operators who were paid $11,832,375.[26]

There is no doubt but that the flow of federal money into the Great Plains has kept the region's income considerably above what it would have been otherwise. In seven of the ten states making up the Great Plains, federal expenditures far exceed the United States average. In 1970 the national average was $115 per capita, but North Dakota received $140 and Montana $200.[27] Yet, to depend on federal aid is risky, perhaps not much more dependable than the region's rainfall. The limitation on farm payments for any one crop in 1970 was one indication of this.

The uncertainty of federal expenditures is enhanced with the relative decline of the area's political power. If Texas is omitted, the other nine states that make up the Great Plains have lost ten congressmen through reapportionment since the height of their congressional power. However, in the recent past the region has benefited from an unusually powerful group of spokesmen in Washington who "brought home the bacon." The results of that power are clear. For example, Senate Democrat Robert S. Kerr of Oklahoma and Republican Francis Case of South Dakota teamed up year after year to get votes and money for the Missouri and Arkansas river developments. But the most powerful voices are gone—Sam Rayburn, Lyndon Johnson, Carl Albert, Clifford Hope of Kansas, Francis Case, and Mike Mansfield. With declining power in Washington, the colonial position of the Great Plains will be intensified and the region's welfare may be less well protected in the years ahead. Growing consumer interests, for instance, may weaken the backing for price supports, conservation payments, and other benefits to Great Plains farmers. The objections of cost-conscious taxpayers, and environmental concerns in developing water resources to meet the needs of this semiarid region, undoubtedly increased in the 1970s. In the spring of 1977 President Jimmy Carter eliminated the Oahe irrigation project in South Dakota from his list of water development proposals. Writing about that situation, the editor of the *Huron Daily Plainsman* said: "The battle over Oahe isn't going to be won or lost at a hearing at Pierre but in Washington, and South Dakota doesn't have much clout." The prospects of holding onto regional advantages through political power are not encouraging for plainsmen.

Water is the key to the region's continued economic growth and development. It is a matter of not only the availability of water, but also the competition for this scarce resource. Underground water is at present abundant in some parts of the plains. Areas of western Nebraska are especially well supplied. On the Southern Plains, however, years of heavy pumping have sharply reduced underground water tables. In conservation district number 1 in the Texas Panhandle, the water table fell from one to three feet annually between 1966 and 1976. Recent reports from Ford and Morton counties in southwestern Kansas indicate that the water level there in irrigation wells is falling from five to ten feet a year. With the increased expense of energy for pumping, the cost of subsurface water from some depth will overtake the value of the water itself. Irrigation fuel costs in the Texas Panhandle increased about 400 percent between 1973 and 1977. Also there is the long-run danger of completely exhausting the resource.[28]

Besides having to go deeper and deeper for underground water, there are increasing conflicts over who should be able to utilize particular water. Although the Great Plains states have improved their water resource laws, controversies over water rights still exist.

Two examples will illustrate the problem. In the 1950s the Shell Oil Company developed an oil field in the three farm and ranch counties of Prairie, Fallon, and Wibaux in eastern Montana. In 1961 Shell applied to the Montana Oil and Gas Conservation Commission for permission to water flood some oil wells in connection with secondary oil recovery. Farmers, ranchers, and small-town residents reacted vigorously because they feared that heavy pumping by the oil company would lower the water table. If that happened, it would require deepening their wells and installing larger and more expensive pumps. Nevertheless, the commission approved Shell's request for water which would salvage, the company said, 14,800,000 barrels of oil. When Shell began to pump millions of gallons, the water level fell and a sharp controversy developed between Shell and local residents. There was sufficient water, but the question was who had "economic access to it." The Montana Water Resources Board tried to settle the question, but without much success. As Robert G. Dunbar has written, "The irreconcilable conflict continued between two types of conservation, between the ranchers who wished to conserve the flow of their wells or at least an economic lift and the Shell Oil Company which sought to conserve 14,800,000 barrels of crude oil."[29]

Another conflict seems to be shaping up over the use of water held in Oahe Lake on the Missouri River in South Dakota. A proposal has been made to pipe 20,000 acre feet annually to a coal company near Gillette, Wyoming, to be used for slurry transportation of coal by pipeline to Arkansas. President Ben Radcliffe of the South Dakota Farmers Union said that any proposed diversion of Missouri River water would constitute "selling out of the people's rights and interests" in favor of big business.[30] In all likelihood, controversy over access to Missouri River water will continue for years to come.

From time to time huge diversion projects have been suggested as a means of getting surface water to large sections of the Great Plains. In 1967, R. W. Beck, head of a consulting engineering firm, suggested diverting water from the Missouri River at Fort Randall to the Great Plains through a huge 940-mile canal. Beck proposed pumping water some two hundred miles west up the Niobrara River to a reservoir near Alliance, Nebraska, and then sending it south by canal across the parched lands of western Nebraska, Kansas, Oklahoma, and the Texas Panhandle. Beck estimated that the project would cost $3–$3.5 billion. Another herculean proposal was to pump water from the Mississippi River below New Orleans to West Texas at a cost of some $10 to $12 billion. However grand such projects might be, they have not won popular approval.[31]

The promise of the Great Plains was never as great as the original promoters of settlement claimed. During the last century, natural and man-made disasters have periodically plagued the region. However, the plains recovered from each major crisis and over time the residents adjusted reasonably well to the environmental realities. The people have been tough and resilient, and many of them found good economic opportunities in the region.

Yet the Great Plains region faces difficult problems in the years ahead. These include heavy reliance on agriculture with its highly fluctuating income, the supply and distribution of water, and the question of maintaining adequate social services at a bearable cost. Continued efforts will be made to gain greater stability of agricultural income. Despite much discussion of comprehensive land planning, the principal adjustments will probably result from individual efforts with considerable federal help rather than from national or regional planning. The Great Plains will continue to be a producer of raw materials, and consequently its colonial status in relation to the rest of the nation will not change substantially. As the population continues to decline on the farms and in small towns, lack of support for institutions and essential services will bring a crisis in many communities. However, only crisis and dire necessity are likely to force people to modify their institutional arrangements to meet new conditions. The need for adjustments were clear by the 1970s, but the pressure was only beginning to be strong enough to produce needed change. However, needed change will come and with it a better life on the plains.

Notes

1. General James S. Brisben to Major George D. Ruggles, November 10, 1874, Adjutant General's Office, National Archives, Record Group 94.

2. *Field and Farm* 5 (February 4, 1888): 4; *Historical Statistics of the United States, Colonial Times to 1957* (Washington, D.C.: Government Printing Office, 1960), p. 12, and Bureau of the Census, *1950 Census of Agriculture*, vol. 2, *General Report* (Washington, D.C.: Government Printing Office, 1952), p. 52. See the federal agricultural and population censuses for 1890; Bureau of the Census, *1950 Census of Agriculture*, vol. 2, *General Report*, p. 558.

3. Bureau of the Census, *Twelfth Census of the United States, 1900, Population* (Washington, D.C.: Government Priting Office, 1901), pt. 1, pp. xlviii–xlix.

4. *Yearbook of Agriculture, 1918* (Washington, D.C.: Government Printing Office, 1919), p. 461; Russell Lord, *The Wallaces of Iowa* (Boston: Houghton Mifflin, 1947), p. 297; Lloyd P. Jorgenson, "Agricultural Expansion into the Semiarid Lands of the West North Central States during the First World War," *Agricultural History* 23 (January 1949): 32-33. For expansion in the Texas Panhandle, see Garry L. Nall, "Panhandle Farming in the 'Golden Era' of American Agriculture," *Panhandle-Plains Historical Review* 46 (1973): 68-93; idem, "Specialization and Expansion: Panhandle Farming in the 1920s," *Panhandle-Plains Historical Review* 47 (1974): 47.

5. Bureau of the Census, *1950 Census of Agriculture,* vol. 2, *General Report,* pp. 223, 226.

6. Fred Floyd, "A History of the Dust Bowl" (Ph.D. diss., University of Oklahoma, 1950). The Great Plains Committee estimated that 40,000 families left the drought area of the Great Plains between 1930 and 1936; United States Great Plains Committee, *The Future of the Great Plains,* House Document no. 144, 75th Cong., 1st sess. (Washington, D.C.: Government Printing Office, February 10, 1937), p. 77.

7. *1950 Census of Agriculture,* vol. 2, *General Report,* p. 66.

8. Montana Department of Agriculture and Statistical Reporting Service, USDA, *Montana Agricultural Statistics,* vol. 15 (Helena, Mont., December 1974), p. 8; Bureau of the Census, *Census of Agriculture, 1969,* vol. 1, *Area Reports* (Washington, D.C.: Government Printing Office, 1973), sec. 2, "County Data," pts. 19, 20, 21, 36, 37, 41; Jerome E. Johnson, "1974: Second Year of Sharp Farmland Value Increases," *Farm Research* 33 (May–June 1975): 3-8.

9. Gilbert C. Fite, "The Great Plains: A Colonial Area," *Current History* 40 (May 1961), p. 282.

10. Donald E. Green, *Land of the Underground Rain* (Austin: University of Texas Press, 1973), p. 143.

11. *1950 Census of Agriculture,* vol. 2, *General Report,* pp. 62-63, and *1969 Census of Agriculture,* vol. 4, *Irrigation,* p. 2; Donald M. Edwards, Richard O. Hoffman, and David D. Pape, "Center Pivots Observed Using Satellite Imagery through 1975" (mimeographed; Engineering Research Center, University of Nebraska, 1975). On center-pivot equipment, see William E. Splinter, "Center-Pivot Irrigation," *Scientific American* 212 (June 1976): 90-99; *Farmland News* (Kansas City, Mo.), August 1973; South Dakota Department of Natural Resource Development, "Irrigation Questionnaire Information," 1970, 1974, and 1975 (mimeographed; Pierre, S.Dak.; Leon New, "1976 High Plains Irrigation Survey" (mimeographed; Texas Agricultural Extension Service, Texas A & M University, College Station, Texas).

12. See Carl F. Kraenzel, *The Great Plains in Transition* (Norman: University of Oklahoma Press, 1955), pp. 201-4. Howard W. Ottoson et al., *Land and People in the Northern Plains Transition Area* (Lincoln: University of Nebraska Press, 1966), chap. 14.

13. Richard D. Gibb, "A Master Plan for Public Higher Education in South Dakota" (mimeographed; Regents' Office, Pierre, S.Dak., p. 14. Earlier studies had been made of South Dakota's public higher education by the United

States Office of Education in 1918; by the New York Bureau of Municipal Research in 1922; by Griffenhagen and Associates in 1953; by HEW in 1960; by the state's Board of Regents for Higher Education (the so-called Davis Study) in 1963; and by Max Myers in 1964.

14. Gibb, "Master Plan," no page given.

15. A good discussion of the problems and politics of making reforms in South Dakota's higher education system can be found in Earl Hausle, "The Coordination of Tertiary Education and the Development, Adaption and Implementation of a Master Plan in South Dakota" (Ph.D. diss., University of Nebraska-Lincoln, 1976); Economic Research Service, USDA, Farm Economics Division, *Revenues and Expenditures of State and Local Governments in the Great Plains*, Agriculture Economic Report no. 22, January 1963, p. 6.

16. Marvin P. Riley and Eugene T. Butler, Jr., *South Dakota Population, Housing and Farm Census Facts*, Rural Sociology Department, Agricultural Experiment Station, South Dakota State University, Brookings, Bulletin 611 (May 1973), p. 13; Ottoson et al., *Land and People in the Northern Plains Transition Area*, pp. 321, 342–43; Robert J. Antonides, *Some Guidelines for Organizing Economic Development Efforts in South Dakota along Trade Area Lines*, Cooperative Extension Service, South Dakota State University, Brookings, Extension Circular 651, undated.

17. *Encyclopedia Americana* (New York: Americana Corporation, 1973), 25: 318.

18. Kraenzel, *The Great Plains in Transition*; see chap. 13 especially. American Medical Association, *The Standard Medical Directory of North America, 1903–4* (Chicago, G. P. Engelhart and Co., 1903), p. 353; United States Department of Health, Education, and Welfare, *Health Manpower—A County and Metropolitan Area Data Book* (Rockville, Md., 1971), pp. 97–101; D. Jerome Tweton and Theodore B. Jelliff, *North Dakota: The Heritage of a People* (Fargo: North Dakota Institute for Regional Studies, 1976), p. 214.

19. Economic Research Service, USDA, *Revenues and Expenditures of State and Local Governments in the Great Plains*, pp. 4, 11, 12.

20. Marvin P. Riley and Robert T. Wagner, *Reference Tables, Population Change of Counties and Incorporated Places, South Dakota, 1950–1970*, Rural Sociology Department, Agricultural Experiment Station, South Dakota State University, Brookings, Bulletin 586 (July 1971).

21. *Congressional Record*, 86th Cong., 2d sess., May 17, 1960, pp. 10480–81.

22. Antonides, "Some Guidelines for Organizing Economic Development Efforts in South Dakota along Trade Area Lines."

23. Ottoson et al., *Land and People in the Northern Plains Transition Area*, p. 234; United States Department of Commerce, Social and Economic Statistics, Bureau of the Census, "1973 Population and 1972 Per Capita Income Estimates for Counties and Incorporated Places," *Current Population Reports: Population Estimates and Projections* (Washington, D.C.: Government Printing Office, June 1975). Many Great Plains counties have increased their income per capita in relation to state-wide averages since 1959.

24. The Great Plains Committee, *The Future of the Great Plains*, p. 56.

25. Lt. Colonel Thomas A. F. Conti to Congressman Tom Steed, March 10, 1977, copy in author's file.

26. Senate Hearings before the Committee on Appropriations, *Department of Agriculture and Related Agencies Appropriations*, H. R. 16913, 90th Cong., 2d sess., pt. .2 (1968), pp. 452–54, 676, 753, 1033, 1192, 1206.

27. *Statistical Abstract of the United States* (Washington, D.C.: Government Printing Office, 1971), p. 174.

28. *Cross Section*, May 1976 (published by the High Plains Underground Water Conservation District no. 1, Lubbock, Texas), p. 3; Donald G. Loyd, County Extension Agricultural Agent, Morton County, Kansas, to author, February 23, 1977; and Don K. Wells, County Extension Agricultural Agent, Ford County, Kansas, to author, February 22, 1977; Leon New, Area Agricultural Engineer–Irrigation, Texas Agricultural Extension Service, Lubbock, Texas, to author, March 16, 1977.

29. Robert G. Dunbar, "Completion Report, Groundwater Property Rights and Controversies in Montana" (mimeographed), Montana University Joint Water Resources Research Center, Report no. 76 (Bozeman, Montana State University, April 1976), pp. 42–53.

30. Davis Aeilts, "West River Aqueduct," *South Dakota Farmer* 97 (January 1977): pp. 26–28.

31. *New York Times*, December 9, 1967, p. 39.

Space: Its Institutional Impact in the Development of the Great Plains

Mary W. M. Hargreaves

Analysis of the institutional impact of space presents many of the definitional difficulties which rural sociologists for half a century have explored under the denomination *community*. The importance of establishing some criteria as a basis for local planning, stimulated by the Mount Weather agreement of 1937 and the widespread pressure for school district reorganization in accordance with the recommendations of the President's Advisory Commission on Education in 1938, gave a pragmatic impetus to this inquiry that made it the central issue of their emerging discipline.[1] Yet such definition continues unstable under the impact of change. In the Great Plains spatial environment the element of variability—in physiographic circumstances, in man's perceptions of those circumstances, and in his adjustments to them—has been fundamental to the story of institutional development.

Changing views of the nature of the environment were marked during the nineteenth century in a series of basically different institutional commitments.[2] Until the 1860s, definition centering upon the region as a Great American Desert, unsuitable for permanent settlement, shaped the patterns primarily to those of a population in transit. Even the transcontinental railway construction rested upon governmental subsidy under assumptions that emphasized the enormous barriers to localized settlement.

Penetration, however, brought new insights—recognition that the plains constituted a superb grazing domain and an emerging view that they might also support limited agricultural utilization. As early as 1875 the institutional framework of territories in the transitional zone between the prairies and the plains reflected this ambiguity in conceptualization. Herd laws in Dakota, for example, rested upon local option by county units. During the decade of the eighties the national commitment to safeguard at least the potentiality for agricultural settlement on the plains contributed to the crisis which forced readjustment of the livestock industry.

The severity of the drought of the early nineties, which drove back the line of agricultural advance, seemed to support the argument of those, like Major John Wesley Powell, who called for basic revision of the institutional framework to provide a land system designed in pasturage units with farming limited to a supplementary role under irrigation. In the passage of the Desert Land Act of 1877, the Carey Act of 1894, and the National Reclamation Act of 1902, Congress moved toward such an institutional framework. The Dakotas, however, specifically requested that they be excluded from the Carey legislation, and spokesmen from the transition zone led the way in rejecting Powell's program for mapping and classification of the semiarid region. The borderland commitments were to remain fluid.

At the turn of the century men knew that the dominant view of the western plains was discouraging to farm development; but they knew, too, that the old myth of the Great American Desert had been supplanted. Supported by generally favorable weather conditions for nearly twenty years and assured that dry-farming technology could overcome the climatic handicaps, a new wave of settlers moved to erase the prevailing conception of this land as a grazing domain. They came to claim their heritage under a land system that had preserved for them the opportunity to create the institutions of traditional farm society.

For such settlers space meant loneliness. It signified separation from kinfolk and friends, even from children as they left home for secondary schooling: miles from the nearest neighbor; days, sometimes weeks, between mail delivery; perhaps years of isolation from town, with its stores, medical and dental facilities, and governmental services. It was marked in the high cost of maintaining schools and local government, of hauling grain to market or carrying home supplies, and, at a later day, of stringing telephone or electric lines. For women, by all accounts, space defined as loneliness, separation, distance, emptiness—"Nothing to Make a Shadow," as Faye Cashatt Lewis's mother lamented—was the most oppressive of the hardships.[3] The terror of injury, serious disease, and childbirth remote from doctors appears in all their reminiscences. But for men, too, it represented a stalking fear, in its impact on their families but also in the grueling hardships it imposed upon their labors. Lathrop Roberts's description of his return from the last of twelve thirty-mile grain hauls vividly recounts the agony of toil on an Alberta homestead. Struggling across seventeen miles of trackless plain in drifted snow at temperatures ranging to thirty-six degrees below zero, he had reached Robb's coulee with his oxen and load of coal "at the end of a cruel day." It was only three miles from home, he noted: "But could we get through the coulee? The way down into it was easy, but the way out was hell."[4]

Spatial barriers to customary social interaction were peculiarly relevant to an expanding agricultural settlement, for farms in American tradition represented families. Nannie Alderson, the rancher's wife in *A Bride Goes West,* thought her life more lonely than that of a farm woman, who could count upon the regular return of men from the fields; but she forgot that in the male domain of ranching she held court as a queen, revered as the symbol of domesticity, the center of a fireside that encompassed a numerous crew of cowhands, that she was never left without protection from roaming Indians, and that, isolated from female companionship, she was not expected to remain on the ranch during the crises of child bearing. The ranch family moved to town when the children were ready for schooling. On the other hand, Grace Fairchild, who settled on the Dakota frontier in 1902, came to the claim with two infants and bore seven more—six of them in eight years, all of them at home, and only three of them with the assistance of a doctor, a homesteader twelve miles to the east. For here there were cows to be milked, chickens to be fed and, in the spring, eggs to be incubated, chores that inhibited town residence.[5]

Sparsity of settlement, however, represented a normal phase of the frontier experience. Emigrants onto the plains expected that to be a temporary phenomenon. Because the transcontinental railway system was here established in advance of settlement, they anticipated that the transitional state would be brief. Theirs was not to be a prolonged economy of self-sufficiency but a rapid penetration of the commercial market. The agrarian commitment, with its pressures for the social concomitants of family life—medical facilities, churches, and schools—brought also demands for the supportive adjuncts of economic growth—local roads and bridges, branch lines, shipping centers with credit, supply, and marketing services—all at a cost that permitted competition in terminal exchanges. Neighbors became important as an increase in population that would share the financial burden of institutional development.

Promotionalism, both indigenous and external, fostered the surge of agricultural settlement and engendered the founding of hamlets, towns, and county units as accompaniments of this expansion. Townsites were platted, usually in advance of settlement, at six- to twelve-mile intervals along rail lines. Where railway companies competed for trade territory, such centers proliferated. Enterprising communities, hoping to achieve growth more rapidly and more securely as county seats, exerted persistent pressures for county division. Between 1901 and 1906, 118 new towns sprang up in South Dakota; from 1906 to 1911, 267, over three-fourths of the latter on the plains west of the Missouri River; and from 1911 to 1916, 84 more, over two-thirds in the west-river country. Thirteen new counties were organized in that state between 1900 and 1910 and three more between 1910 and 1920. The pattern was even more sharply delineated in eastern Montana, where fifteen counties were created between 1900 and 1914 and seventeen more in the next decade.[6]

And yet the size of counties in this region remained large by standards elsewhere in the nation. The average area for Montana counties in 1935 was 2,605 square miles, with four exceeding 5,000 square miles, while the national average was only 970. Settlers who had business to transact at the county seat frequently had great distances to traverse—Grace Fairchild's subpoena to provide court testimony in western South Dakota in 1906 required a ninety-mile train ride. There was strong encouragement for multiplication of trading centers, also, in a day when transportation by horses or oxen and wagons limited the economically acceptable range for marketing to a radius of six or seven miles. Throughout much of the plains region, hauling distances as late as 1920 ranged at ten to more than twenty-five miles one way.[7]

The costs of governmental services for expanding community organization were, however, great. In eighteen months Hettinger County, North Dakota, with only 7,000 inhabitants, constructed five large steel bridges, graded many miles of road, culverted all ditches and streams, provided seventy-two schools, and built a courthouse, jail, and sheriff's residence. Expenditures of all Montana counties increased 127 percent between 1914 and 1920, chiefly for roads, schools, social agencies, general government, and debt service. Montana farm real estate taxes during that period increased but 87 percent per acre.[8] Such a balance sheet could be maintained only by an expanding population base that ensured maximum utilization of capital outlay.

Schools entailed the largest proportion of this expenditure. North Dakota permitted an elementary school to be established wherever nine children of school age were living more than two and a half miles from existing institutions and required that one be provided when twelve children were so situated. In South Dakota the optional minimum was as few as seven children living beyond three

miles of an established school. In Montana, school districts encompassed much larger areas, some as large as a thousand square miles,
with the minimum requirement that at least ten children be enrolled.
Yet, as late as 1920, a survey revealed that in Montana 1,841 children of school age lived beyond the reach of elementary institutions.
Under such pressures Ward County, North Dakota, established an
average of over 50 schools a year between 1905 and 1908; Bowman,
Dunn, Hettinger, and Adams counties, a total of over 200 between
1906 and 1908. Stanley County, South Dakota, provided 150 between 1906 and 1910; Fergus County, Montana, nearly 100 between
1908 and 1914.[9] With over 90 percent of all funding for elementary
schools supplied, prior to the mid-thirties, from district property
taxation, only limited facilities could be maintained, frequently sod
houses and abandoned claim shacks. One-room schools with few
students were continued in large numbers throughout the area, even
until recent date. Such institutions need not be badly equipped or
poorly staffed, but during the stringencies of the settlement period,
the depression of the thirties, and the teacher shortages of the forties
and fifties, they commonly afforded minimal structural facilities,
inadequate equipment, and the least qualified instructors in the educational system.

Around 1912, North Dakota and Montana established codes of
standards by which schools could attain approved classification, and
South Dakota instituted such a program in 1919; but relatively few
schools in newly settled districts qualified.[10] As late as 1920 the
Montana superintendent of public instruction reported that 224
"shacks" and 54 ranch houses unsuitable for schools were still in use,
a few in almost every county. Over 1,300 schools in that state then
lacked good wells or springs. The average length of the elementary
school term was but 165 days and in rural areas ranged as low as a
few weeks. The record of attendance was far worse, with Montana
reporting in 1920 that a fifth of the enrolled students were in school
less than four months a year. Almost a quarter of the Montana elementary school teachers were then not even high school graduates.
Montana's certification requirement by legislation effective in 1920
required only two years of general high school education plus twelve
weeks of normal training, available through the high school curricu-
lum; and a North Dakota law of 1921 which required a four-year
high school course or its equivalent as the basis for teacher certification was repealed the following year by popular referendum.[11]

Montana and North Dakota from the turn of the century permitted the organization of free county high schools, one for each

county, with state funding. The Montana superintendent of public instruction in 1914 deplored such concentration of support as institutional legislation designed to serve ranchers, who could send the family to town for the winter, but unfeasible for small-farm society. On the other hand, because the resources had proved inadequate, the South Dakota superintendent in 1920 lamented that state funding was there extended on the narrower basis of township districts. "Owing to the scarcity of population and the low valuation of our pioneer sections of the state," he noted, "proper high school advantages, within reasonable reach, are practically unknown to the boys and girls west of the [Missouri] river."[12]

The movement for consolidation of schools, at the elementary as well as the high school level, began early in states of this region— in North Dakota about 1902, in South Dakota about 1906, and in Montana a decade later.[13] Generally because of transportation costs, it proved a more expensive system than that of local schools; and frequently the consolidated institutions remained one- or two-room facilities. In Montana an accompanying approach to the problem of distance in relation to education was the introduction of dormitories, usually as an adjunct to high schools, beginning at Kalispell in 1914, but in some cases for elementary students, as at Ivanell, in Rosebud County, in 1911. By 1922 twenty-five dormitories were operated in conjunction with Montana schools; and despite the increasing use of automobiles during that decade, eighteen dormitories were still operated in 1928. The superintendent of public instruction the latter year, citing dormitories as "now a well established institution in many of the schools of the state," acclaimed it as "the best solution of the problem of housing of students who live long distances from school."[14]

Yet that official noted, too, in 1930 that in many instances children "too young to be taken away from their homes and boarded at dormitories" required the continuance of a large number of one-room schools. "The long distances to the nearest schools . . . [made] transportation prohibitive," he observed, and concluded: "Montana is such a sparsely settled domain that, in many cases, the problem is how to congregate enough children in one locality to maintain a school." There were then 277 schools with fewer than six pupils enrolled—7 with only one, 33 with two, 40 with three, 74 with four, and 123 with five. "Necessarily," he added, "in such isolated communities the per capita cost of education is high."[15]

The school problem merely typified a wide range of difficulties in institutional adjustment to plains settlement. Small rural churches sprang up even before the schools. While interdenominational meetings served for a time, very quickly the differences of sects, more numerous in an area settled by diverse nationality groups, led to a multiplication of organizations. Fifty-two different religious denominations, 2,217 local church bodies, were operating in South Dakota in 1926. Rural free delivery of mail, which had begun in 1896, was extended in many areas beyond the regulation limit of four families to the mile. In Sumner County, Kansas, rural routes in 1905 averaged twenty-four and a half miles in length but served an average of only forty-five families to the route.[16] Elsewhere the general store of small hamlets derived a large proportion of its business from its service as local post office.

After twenty years of developmental effort, sparsity of population remained characteristic on the plains. The census of 1920 reported 3.76 persons to the square mile in Montana, 9.2 in North Dakota, and 8.3 in South Dakota. A decade later the population of Montana had decreased (to 3.68), and by 1940 the same trend was marked in the Dakotas. On a county basis about a third of Montana, most of Wyoming, a large section of northwestern Nebraska, and a few counties of western South Dakota and the Panhandle of Texas registered less than two persons to the square mile.[17]

Already the premise that this was a land to be developed as a normal evolution of frontier experience had undergone some institutional adjustment. Passage of the Enlarged Homestead Act of 1909, in recognition that the alternating fallow of the dry-farming system required double the acreage of the traditional homestead, had expanded the basic farm allotment from 160 to 320 acres. The Stock-Farming Homestead Act of 1916 had enlarged the primary unit of public land entry to 640 acres. As drought in the Northern Plains from 1919 to 1922 discouraged the more timid and the less successful of the pioneers, their holdings were added to the farms of those who remained. By 1924 the average farm size in eastern Montana was 715 acres; in western North Dakota, 488 acres; in western South Dakota, 643.[18] Institutional organization predicated upon traditional settlement patterns was increasingly difficult to maintain.

With the decline of grain prices after World War I some of the incentive for expanding agricultural development slackened. Areas of the Central Plains from South Dakota southward through western Nebraska and western Kansas underwent a resurgence of growth during the twenties, but they as well as the Northern Plains were caught up in the radical readjustments precipitated by the drought years of the thirties. The initial reaction to this last experience was a renewed attention to the program advocated fifty years earlier by John Wesley Powell.

Irrigation projects heretofore had languished because farmers, producing high yields on virgin land under dry-farming operations during the prolonged period of favorable weather conditions, had been reluctant to pay the high construction costs for reservoirs and the recurring charges for water use. Even refinancing of the project contracts during the mid-twenties had failed to lure settlers onto the irrigated tracts. As drought prevailed in the Northern Plains for nearly a decade from 1929 and extended into the Southern Plains also by the mid-thirties, irrigation won new adherents. Despite national concern over mounting crop surpluses, new reclamation programs were initiated, and farmers were encouraged to enter lands under them. Among the forceful arguments in support of such development was the concentration of settlement and the improvement in institutional organization afforded in areas under the ditch.[19]

The focus of this effort centered upon relocation activities designed to retire from agricultural utilization dry lands judged unsuitable for cropping and to resettle displaced families in irrigated districts. The remaining unoccupied public lands were withdrawn from homestead entry and generally restricted to grazing purposes. Some 36,000,000 acres of private holdings, 46,000 farms, were recommended for retirement from cropping. For vast areas of the plains—more than half the land in one Montana county—this program signified an end to the potentiality of farm development and a reduction of the tax base for the maintenance of institutions already established.[20]

The struggle for preservation of the conception of the family farm had surfaced earlier on the plains, in debates on legislation for the enlarged homestead. James J. Hill; Hardy Webster Campbell, the principal exponent of dry-farming methodology; and even so respected an agricultural scientist as John Widtsoe, of the Utah Experiment Station, had denied that one man could properly cultivate so large a tract. Whatever the merits of their argument, the land hunger which had made speculators of frontiersmen from the founding of the nation had massed support for the larger grants as a projection of agricultural utilization. The program of the Resettlement Administration in 1935, however, challenged the whole development. Protest centering upon this problem contributed to the political pressures that limited and ultimately terminated the work of that agency.[21] Local planning bodies, called upon to formulate plans in 1940 for the future of the region, could not reach agreement on the basic issue of appropriate farm size. While they conceded that holdings as developed under homestead legislation were not adequate, they protested against the views which prevailed in the readjustment program. The debate waxed hottest in the transition zone between the prairies and the plains. Reviewing the proposed unified plan for action in Hand County, South Dakota, Emil Loriks of the Farm Security Administration protested:

> If the . . . land use recommendations were to be carried out, I have been advised that it would mean displacement of about 250 farm families in Hand County alone, and if that same situation should apply over the entire State . . . , we would displace perhaps 12,000 to 15,000 farm families. Talk is cheap and high sounding theory is plentiful, but . . . we still cling to the old-fashioned idea that the farm is a good place to live. We must coordinate our efforts to development of the family sized farm unit, based on a higher degree of self-sufficiency, and keeping farm families on the farm.[22]

Technological changes adopted after World War I were radically altering the practicable scale of family farm operations. The introduction of gasoline tractors, combined harvester-threshers, and motor trucks, together with labor-saving tillage practices such as stubble mulching and chisel plowing enabled a man with one or two sons to cultivate a vastly increased acreage. Farm-management systems recommended in 1925 for eastern Montana called for one and a half to two sections of land. By the mid-thirties most farms in the wheat-producing areas of that state ranged between 500 and 999 acres but many ran above that scale. The trend toward larger units accelerated greatly during the period of favorable weather and high crop prices of the forties. By 1969 farm size in the eastern counties of Montana averaged over 2,800 acres; in western South Dakota, over 2,600 acres; and in western North Dakota, 1,161 acres. A North Dakota Experiment Station analyst expressed again in 1950 the old difficulty of defining a family-sized farm: "The point is simply that modern technology has so revolutionized the capacity of man to handle grain acreage that people may not have grasped its extent."[23]

The impact of this development on regional institutions was drastic. No longer could the sparsity of plains settlement be viewed as a temporary phenomenon. For the most part, the expansion of farm acreage represented an assumption of holdings relinquished by settlers who had abandoned tillage. The number of farms declined between 1924 and 1969 in eastern Montana from 36,591 to 18,220, in western North Dakota from 31,296 to 18,367, and in western South Dakota from 20,511 to 9,386.[24]

A concomitant improvement of transportation significantly affected the situation. On the one hand, it helped to bridge the increasing distance between farms; on the other, it contributed to the disruption of established institutional patterns. The number of automobiles and trucks had increased from 25,000 to over 40,000 in North Dakota and from around 46,000 to nearly 69,000 in South Dakota during the single year 1916–17. By 1920 there were 90,840 in the former state and 121,173 in the latter. Automobiles were found on 80–90 percent of the farms on the plains by the early forties. A South Dakota study reported in 1938 that in the most sparsely settled, western counties more than 10 percent of the value of living was assigned to such expenditure by the average open-country family.[25]

Air travel also became important in the region. As early as 1928 the superintendent of schools in Richland County, Montana, had turned to such transportation as a means by which he could cover his far-flung inspection district. In 1951, South Dakota listed 150 personal landing strips, many of them in the trans-Missouri area.[26] Schools introduced study of the "problems of air-age education" and featured aeronautics departments.

Farm trucks extended the radius of practicable hauling. By the mid-thirties farmers could haul double the load in an eighth the time that had been required with a six-horse team. Motor carriers as early as the twenties had begun to provide effective competition to railways in freighting. The Federal Highway Act of 1956 and the consequent expansion of interstate highways accelerated this development.[27]

As farmers became more mobile, many of them established their residence in town. By the late 1930s as many as a fifth of the farm operators on the High Plains no longer lived in open country. Twenty years later a Montana study found this proportion increasing, particularly in areas of wheat specialization. The greater availability of relief services in towns, and perhaps, too, the operation of farms by townsmen who had exchanged the role of landlord for that of operator as the margin of profit declined, accounted for some of the shift during the thirties; but more than 70 percent of the town farmers during the 1950s attributed their residence to the greater availability of schools. Access to health services, modern conveniences, water, and a richer social life were other factors cited in the move.[28]

Suitcase farming, as defined by Leslie Hewes to apply to residence at least a county away from the farm, in distinction to sidewalk farming, or farming while resident in a nearby town, was not common in the Northern Plains but was found to delineate about a third of the operators along the western border of Kansas in 1935 and as many as 90 percent in northeastern Colorado in the late forties.[29] Since the suitcase farming movement declined markedly as agricultural development matured in the latter areas, it appears to have been an adjustment made possible by transportation as a solution to the problems of sparse settlement under frontier conditions. Town farming, on the other hand, represented an adaptation to a situation that had come to be recognized as relatively permanent.

Declining rural population complicated maintenance of the institutional fabric designed to serve pioneers who had viewed their settlement on the plains as a projection of traditional rural society. As early as 1910–11, when drought was severe in the western Dakotas, railway corporations had ceased construction in those areas, and towns predicated on such expansion had begun to disappear. A decrease of sixty-nine trade centers had occurred west of the Missouri in South Dakota by 1920. During the lean years of the thirties, railway sidings and shipping platforms were closed down and their operations transferred to the larger towns. Nearly 11,500 miles of weekly train service were discontinued in South Dakota between 1931 and 1951, and railway business became increasingly limited to heavy carload hauls between the larger towns and cities.[30] Improved motor transportation heightened the trend toward concentration of social as well as business activity in more distant centers.

In a few instances county governments were eliminated by combination under a single unit. In the Dakotas, notably west of the Missouri, township organization was frequently abandoned. Most numerously, the small hamlets of fewer than fifty residents passed into oblivion. Despite the increased agricultural production of the 1940s, there was in that decade a loss of ninety trade centers in South Dakota, sixty-five of them hamlets and thirty-eight of them west of the river.[31] As RFD routes expanded, the number of fourth-class post offices declined, and the small-town general store lost its attraction as a center of regular visitation. Hamlets with fewer than five business units tended to lose trade as farmers drove to centers where they could find chain stores, retail branches of mail order houses, department stores, and five and ten cent stores. The small-town bank was consolidated in the enterprise of larger towns. Rural churches lost membership and in many cases disorganized. In South Dakota 328 churches, all in small towns or open country, disappeared during the single decade 1926–36.[32] Pressure for improved educational facilities and the impracticability of maintaining existing institutions for a declining population finally brought about a marked diminution in the number of one-room elementary and small high schools.

The number of one-teacher schools decreased in Montana from 2,606 in 1920 to 2,227 in 1938, to 915 in 1948, to 297 in 1968; in North Dakota, from 4,336 in 1929 to 3,655 in 1939, to 2,580 in 1949, to 1,464 in 1959, to 140 in 1969; in South Dakota from 4,647 in 1930 to 3,949 in 1940, to 3,065 in 1950, to 2,136 in 1960, to 582 in 1970.[33] The number of high schools declined in Montana from 228 in 1921 to 205 in 1932, to 175 in 1952, to 170 in 1968; and in South Dakota from 438 in 1930, to 314 in 1948, to 271 in 1963. Twenty-five small high schools in South Dakota closed in two years, 1942–44, in some cases because of the scarcity of teachers, in others, as the state superintendent reported, "because it was economically unsound to maintain a school for such a small number enrolled."[34]

The adjustments that have come about in administrative organization and financing of schools within the region emphasize the trend of institutional change. Consolidation of schools and of school districts was a protracted struggle. The number of rural elementary (common) school districts was reduced in Montana from 2,131 in 1939 to 1,522 in 1948, to 1,067 in 1960, to 738 in 1965; in North Dakota, from 2,113 in 1946 to 1,847 in 1955, to 1,073 in 1960, to 627 in 1965, to 360 in 1975; in South Dakota, from 3,428 in 1945 to 3,067 in 1960, to 2,367 in 1965, to 551 in 1970, to 36 in 1973.[35] Such a reduction did not generally bring about lower pupil costs, but it did distribute the expense more evenly, so that sparsely settled areas and those of low property valuation were given support from other sections. Montana from 1920 to 1927 had authorized an optional county unit organization, but because some districts objected to higher levies the system was abandoned. A popular referendum in that state in 1926 also rejected a proposal to adopt a state levy for public school support. Instead, revenues from special sources, such as inheritance taxes, oil royalties, and a metal mines tax, were allotted as an equalization fund for transportation expenses of districts operating one- and two-room schools.[36] By 1949 Montana provided both county and state support as an equalization fund supplementary to district levies organized into a minimum foundation program.[37] While basic millage rates in conjunction with this system could be legislated, the problem of differing assessment standards remained—and so did the problem of a multiplicity of small districts.

The difficulty of winning popular support for district consolidation was evidenced in South Dakota over the years from 1951 to 1970, as a succession of school district reorganization laws repeatedly revised the program. Initially the law authorized the formation of "community school districts" by consolidation of existing units. After four years and consideration of many plans, the superintendent of public instruction indicated little success: "There is no general agreement as to the particular schools to be closed. Each community wants its school to be continued but favors closing of some other school." His report noted, however: "People in general accept the idea that larger attendance areas are desirable. This principle is supported by the fact that over 850 districts do not operate any school, but assign such resident pupils as they may have, to schools in neighboring districts on a tuition basis." In 1955 the legislature provided for the establishment of county boards of education which, taking into account the total assessed valuation of the county and the combined operational costs of all school districts in the county, might submit reorganization proposals. Four years later the state turned from permissive action to a requirement that master plans for reorganization be submitted by 1962. Now it was hoped that enactment of a minimum foundation program would hasten the process, but still the revision dragged. In 1967 the legislature finally required that all land in the state be incorporated in some independent school district within two years. The South Dakota Stock Growers Association then delayed the effective date by a call for referendum. With endorsement of the voters in November 1968, the measure finally went into operation by 1970.[38]

Meanwhile, states of the plains came under the provisions of a wide range of federal programs in aid of education, from the Smith-Hughes legislation of 1917 through the school lunch funding begun in the 1930s, the Johnson-O'Malley Indian Education Act of 1934, Public Law 874 of 1950 to support the added school costs incurred by the establishment of federal installations, the National Defense Education Act of 1958, and the Elementary and Secondary Education Act of 1965. The radius of commitment to school maintenance which Grace Fairchild had drawn upon as the "Frontier Woman" in 1906, circulating her petition for a local school district, had expanded to national boundaries.

Much that has been noted in the foregoing account is identifiable with development of rural society generally in this country as a result of the improvements of transportation, and of communication in all forms, during the last half century. On the plains, however, the readjustment of institutional organization has acquired impelling force from recognition that the physiographic circumstances are extraordinary, that the change evolves not merely as a betterment of the rural way of life but as a necessity for survival of the agricultural commitment. Where the limits of those spatial pressures may extend remains even yet undefined.

In conceptualization as in institutional forms the people of the plains have been looking to wider horizons. There are social costs in this adjustment, as there were costs to those who surrendered "their school." Carl F. Kraenzel, viewing the regional social organization as increasingly formalized, has seen it as a loss of individual initiative, a transfer of decision making to legal and public channels. On the other hand, Howard W. Ottoson and his colleagues have called upon local and state governments to assert such powers of leadership under a challenge "that they have never really accepted"—through zoning and land-use regulation, for example. Community relationships have become more impersonal, diffuse, and complex. Yet the boundaries are being extended outward to the shared support of a broader base. Even Kraenzel envisioned "national and global significance to this development in the Plains, if steps are taken to make the area a full partner in the democracy of the United States."[39]

Notes

1. Dwight Sanderson, "Criteria of Community Formation," *Rural Sociology* 3 (1938): 373-76, 383-84; Ray E. Wakeley, "Rural Planning: Its Social and Community Organization Aspects," ibid. 6 (1941): 62-63, 66; Charles P. Loomis, Douglas Ensminger, and Jane Wooley, "Neighborhoods and Communities in County Planning," ibid.: 339; Bushrod W. Allin to John Muehlbeier, February 9, 1940, and Muehlbeier to Allin, February 21, 1940, National Archives, Record Group 83, State and Local Planning.

2. For discussion of the changing concepts of the plains, see Mary Wilma M. Hargreaves, *Dry Farming in the Northern Great Plains, 1900-1925* (Cambridge, Mass.: Harvard University Press, 1957), pp. 25-56.

3. Mary W. M. Hargreaves, "Women in the Agricultural Settlement of the Northern Plains," *Agricultural History* 50 (1976): 182-84.

4. Sarah Ellen Roberts, *Alberta Homestead: Chronicle of a Pioneer Family*, ed. Lathrop E. Roberts (Austin: University of Texas Press, 1971), pp. 234-35.

5. Nannie T. Alderson and Helena Huntington Smith, *A Bride Goes West* (1942; reprinted Lincoln: University of Nebraska Press, 1969); Walker D. Wyman, *Frontier Woman: The Life of a Woman Homesteader on the Dakota Frontier, Retold from the Original Notes and Letters of Grace Fairchild* ... (Madison, Wis.: University of Wisconsin-River Falls Press, 1972), pp. 28-30.

6. Douglas Chittick, *Growth and Decline of South Dakota Trade Centers, 1901-51,* South Dakota Agricultural Experiment Station (hereafter cited as SDAES) Bulletin no. 448 (Brookings, 1955), pp. 45-46; W. F. Kumlien, *Basic Trends of Social Change in South Dakota,* pt. 3, *Community Organization,* ibid., no. 356 (Brookings, 1941), pp. 8-9; Paul H. Landis, *The Growth and Decline of South Dakota Trade Centers, 1901-1933,* ibid., no. 279 (Brookings, 1933), pp. 10-11; Roland R. Renne, *Montana County Organization, Services, and Costs: A Study in County Government with Suggestions for Its Improvement,* Montana Agricultural Experiment Station (hereafter cited as MAES) Bulletin no. 298 (Bozeman, 1935), pp. 9-12.

7. Renne, *Montana County Organization,* pp. 12-13, 96 (table 1); Wyman, *Frontier Woman,* pp. 81-83; O. E. Baker, "Agriculture of the Great Plains Region," in *Annals of the Association of American Geographers* 13 (1923): 155-57; Kumlien, *Basic Trends of Social Change in South Dakota,* pt. 3, *Community Organization,* p. 16.

8. *North Dakota Magazine* 3 (January 1909): 23; Renne, *Montana County Organization,* pp. 41, 106 (table 15). See also W. F. Kumlien, *Basic Trends of Social Change in South Dakota,* pt. 7, *Local Government,* SDAES Bulletin no. 347 (Brookings, 1941), pp. 15-16.

9. North Dakota Legislative Assembly, *Laws of the Tenth Session . . . 1907,* chap. 95 (approved March 19, 1907), pp. 131-32; South Dakota Superintendent of Public Instruction (hereafter cited as SDSPI), *Twenty-second Biennial Report . . . July 1, 1932, to June 30, 1934,* p. 42; Montana Superintendent of Public Instruction (hereafter cited as MSPI), *Seventh Biennial Report . . . 1902,* p. 408; idem, *Ninth Biennial Report . . . 1906,* p. 10; idem, *Tenth Biennial Report . . . 1908,* p. 5; idem, *Sixteenth Biennial Report . . . 1920,* p. 21; North Dakota Superintendent of Public Instruction (hereafter cited as NDSPI), *Ninth Biennial Report . . . Ending June 30, 1906,* pp. 256-57, 278-79; idem, *Tenth Biennial Report . . . Ending June 30, 1908,* pp. 17, 298-99, 321-22; SDSPI, *Eleventh Biennial Report . . . July 1, 1910-June 30, 1912,* p. 50; MSPI, *Tenth Biennial Report . . . 1908,* p. 121; *Thirteenth Biennial Report . . . 1914,* folded table.

10. MSPI, *Sixteenth Biennial Report . . . 1920,* pp. 79, 90; NDSPI, *Twelfth Biennial Report . . . Ending June 30, 1912,* pp. 17, 162-204 passim; idem, *Thirteenth Biennial Report . . . Ending June 30, 1914,* pp. 75-102 passim; SDSPI, *Fifteenth Biennial Report . . . July 1, 1918-June 30, 1920,* pp. 30, 31; idem, *Seventeenth Biennial Report . . . July 1, 1922-June 30, 1924,* p. 7.

11. MSPI, *Sixteenth Biennial Report . . . 1920,* pp. 20, 23, 32, 79, 81; idem, *Twelfth Biennial Report . . . Ending June 30, 1912,* pp. 20, 273-75; NDSPI, *Biennial Report . . . Ending June 30, 1922,* p. 160.

12. MSPI, *Thirteenth Biennial Report . . . 1914,* p. 15; SDSPI, *Fifteenth Biennial Report . . . July 1, 1918-June 30, 1920,* p. 11. County high schools were begun in South Dakota in Bennett County in 1921. W. F. Kumlien, *Community School Districts in the Making,* SDAES Bulletin no. 404 (Brookings, 1950), p. 13.

13. NDSPI, *Twelfth Biennial Report . . . Ending June 30, 1912,* p. 285;

SDSPI, *Ninth Biennial Report* . . . *1907-1908*, p. 342; MSPI, *Sixteenth Biennial Report* . . . *1920*, p. 94. The South Dakota program here noted permitted consolidation by realignment of boundaries where small districts were already in operation, but did not provide for the creation of districts on that basis. The latter development was authorized in 1913. SDSPI, *Twelfth Biennial Report . . . July 1, 1912-June 30, 1914*, p. 9.

14. MSPI, *Sixteenth Biennial Report* . . . *1920*, pp. 10, 75-77; J. Wheeler Harger, *Public School Dormitories for Rural Children in Montana*, MAES Bulletin no. 201 (Bozeman, 1927), pp. 6-7; MSPI, *Twentieth Biennial Report* . . . *1928*, p. 81.

15. MSPI, *Twenty-first Biennial Report . . . 1930*, p. 38.

16. W. F. Kumlien, *The Social Problem of the Church in South Dakota*, SDAES Bulletin no. 294 (Brookings, 1935), pp. 10, 12, 14; Wayne E. Fuller, *RFD, the Changing Face of Rural America* (Bloomington: Indiana University Press, 1964), pp. 289, 290.

17. U.S. Department of Commerce, *Fifteenth Census of the United States, 1930*, vol. 1, *Population*, no. 1, *Distribution of Inhabitants* (Washington, D.C.: Government Printing Office, 1931), p. 4.

18. Computed from data in *United States Census of Agriculture, 1925*, vol. 1, *The Northern States . . .*, pp. 1002-9, 1056-64; ibid., vol. 3, *The Western States . . .* , pp. 82-89. Counties identified as eastern Montana run west to and include Toole, Pondera, Teton, Cascade, Meagher, and Park; those of the western Dakotas east to Bottineau, McHenry, McLean, and the Missouri River line southward.

19. P. L. Slagsvold and J. D. Mathews, *Some Economic and Social Aspects of Irrigation in Montana*, MAES Bulletin no. 354 (Bozeman, 1938), pp. 13-14; Marvin P. Riley, W. F. Kumlien, and Duane Tucker, *50 Years Experience on the Belle Fourche Irrigation Project*, SDAES Bulletin no. 450 (Brookings, 1955), p. 30.

20. National Resources Board, Land Planning Committee, *Maladjustments in Land Use in the United States: Supplementary Report*, pt. 6 (Washington, D.C.: Government Printing Office, 1935), p. 14; Roland R. Renne, "Probable Effects of Federal Land Purchase on Local Government," *National Municipal Review* 25 (1936): 401-6, 411; Montana Legislative Assembly, *Laws, 1941*, House Jt. Mem. no. 6, pp. 447-48 (approved February 28, 1941).

21. Hargreaves, *Dry Farming in the Northern Great Plains*, pp. 346-53; Mary W. M. Hargreaves, "The Dry Farming Movement in Retrospect," *Agricultural History* 51 (1977): 160; idem, "Land Use Planning in Response to Drought: The Experience of the Thirties," *Agricultural History* 50 (1976): 571-72, 579-81. By 1950 only about 4,600,000 acres remained in public ownership as a result of the submarginal land purchase. Harry A. Steele and John Muehlbeier, "Land and Water Development Programs in the Northern Great Plains," *Journal of Farm Economics* 32 (1950): 437.

22. South Dakota Land Use Program Committee, Minutes, September 30, 1940, p. 11; cf. also, ibid., March 27, 1940, p. 7, National Archives, Record Group 83, State and Local Planning.

23. Hargreaves, *Dry Farming in the Northern Great Plains*, p. 507; E. A. Starch, *Readjusting Montana's Agriculture*, pt. 3, *Montana's Dry Land Agriculture*, MAES Bulletin no. 318 (Bozeman, 1936), p. 16. 1969 figures computed from *1969 Census of Agriculture*, pt. 18, *North Dakota*, vol. 1, *Area Reports*, sec. 1, "Summary Data," chap. 2, table 1, p. 268; pt. 19, *South Dakota*, vol. 1, *Area Reports*, sec. 1, "Summary Data," chap. 2, table 1, p. 268; pt. 38, *Montana*, vol. 1, *Area Reports*, sec. 1, "Summary Data," chap. 2, table 1, p. 253. Areal boundaries were defined as noted above, note 18. Baldur H. Kristjanson, *What about Our Large Farms in North Dakota*, NDAES Bulletin no. 360 (Fargo, 1950), p. 5.

24. *United States Census of Agriculture, 1925 . . .* , pt. 1, *The Northern States . . .* , pp. 1002–9, 1056–64; ibid., pt. 3, *The Western States . . .* , pp. 82–89; *1969 Census of Agriculture*, pt. 18, *North Dakota*, vol. 1, *Area Reports*, sec. 1, "Summary Data," chap. 2, table 1, p. 268; ibid., pt. 19, *South Dakota*, vol. 1, *Area Reports*, sec. 1, "Summary Data," chap. 2, table 1, p. 268; ibid., pt. 38, *Montana*, vol. 1, *Area Reports*, sec. 1, "Summary Data," chap. 2, table 1, p. 253.

25. USDA, Bureau of Agricultural Economics, *Horses, Mules, and Motor Vehicles, Year Ended March 31, 1924, with Comparable Data for Earlier Years*, USDA Statistical Bulletin no. 5 (Washington, D.C., 1925), pp. 87–89, tables 102, 103; A. H. Anderson, *Changes in Farm Population and Rural Life in Four North Dakota Counties*, NDAES Bulletin no. 375 (Fargo, 1952), p. 18; John P. Johansen, *Population Trends in Relation to Resources Development in South Dakota*, SDAES Bulletin no. 440 (Brookings, 1954), p. 28; W. F. Kumlien et al., *The Standard of Living of Farm and Village Families in Six South Dakota Counties, 1935*, SDAES Bulletin no. 320 (Brookings, 1938), p. 17.

26. MSPI, *Twentieth Biennial Report . . . 1928*, p. 75; Chittick, *Growth and Decline of South Dakota Trade Centers*, p. 38.

27. E. A. Starch, *Farm Organization as Affected by Mechanization*, MAES Bulletin no. 278 (Bozeman, 1933), p. 15; Fred R. Taylor and David C. Nelson, *Factors Affecting the Transportation of North Dakota Grain*, NDAES Bulletin no. 430 (Fargo, 1960), pp. 3, 7, 14, 16, 18–21. While railroads continued to carry much the largest proportion of grain shipments, truck hauling was increasing rapidly during the late fifties and early sixties. Ibid., pp. 15–16, 19, 22. See also David C. Nelson, *Trends in Shipping Grain by Motor Carrier from North Dakota Origins, 1956–57 through 1963–64*, NDAES Bulletin no. 462 (Fargo, 1965), pp. 6, 11–15.

28. Richard Ashby, "Town Farming in the Great Plains," *Rural Sociology* 6 (1941): 342; E. A. Willson, *Off-Farm Residence of Families of Farm and Ranch Operators*, MAES Bulletin no. 530 (Bozeman, 1957), pp. 7, 14, 19–20, 28–29, 53.

29. Anderson, *Changes in Farm Population and Rural Life in Four North Dakota Counties*, 11; Leslie Hewes, *The Suitcase Farming Frontier: A Study in the Historical Geography of the Central Great Plains* (Lincoln: University of Nebraska Press, 1973), pp. 41, 50, 111–12.

30. Chittick, *Growth and Decline of South Dakota Trade Centers*, pp. 16,

34–35; Harald A. Pedersen and Earl B. Peterson, *Market and Trade Center Patronage Patterns in Central Montana*, MAES Bulletin no. 578 (Bozeman, 1963), p. 7. The latter writers, however, find that grain, as distinct from livestock, marketing remains identified with the country elevator and small towns.

31. W. F. Kumlien, *Basic Trends of Social Change in South Dakota*, pt. 7, *Local Government*, SDAES Bulletin no. 347 (Brookings, 1941), pp. 13–15, 24, 29; Chittick, *Growth and Decline of South Dakota Trade Centers*, pp. 13, 19. See also Paul H. Landis, *The Growth and Decline of South Dakota Trade Centers, 1901–1933*, SDAES Bulletin no. 279 (Brookings, 1933), pp. 13, 22–23; Stanley W. Voelker and Thomas K. Ostenson, *North Dakota's Human Resources: A Study of Population Change in a Great Plains Environment*, NDAES Bulletin no. 476 (Fargo, 1968), pp. 49–50; Harald A. Pedersen, *Montana's Human Resources: Number and Distribution of People*, MAES Circular no. 231 (Bozeman, 1960), pp. 3, 5–7; Carl F. Kraenzel, "Sutland and Yonland Setting for Community Organization in the Plains," *Rural Sociology* 18 (1953): 348, 357.

32. Kumlien, *The Social Problem of the Church in South Dakota*, p. 36. Cf. Kumlien, *Basic Trends of Social Change in South Dakota*, pt. 8, *Religious Organization*, SDAES Bulletin no. 348 (Brookings), 1941), p. 12, which places the total loss at 294 churches during that decade.

33. MSPI, *Sixteenth Biennial Report . . . 1920*, p. 9; idem, *Twenty-fifth Biennial Report . . . 1938*, p. 81; idem, *Biennial Report . . . 1949*, p. 24; idem, *Biennial Report, December 1, 1968*, p. 60; NDSPI, *Thirty-first Biennial Report . . . for the Two Years Ending June 30, 1950*, p. 3012; idem, *Thirty-sixth Biennial Report . . . for the Two Years Ending June 30, 1960*, p. 148; idem, *Forty-first Biennial Report . . . for the Two Years Ending June 30, 1970*, p. 237; SDSPI, *Twentieth Biennial Report . . . July 1, 1928 to June 30, 1930*, pp. 325, 421; idem, *Twenty-fifth Biennial Report . . . July 1, 1938 to June 30, 1940*, p. 278; idem, *Thirtieth Biennial Report . . . July 1, 1948 to June 30, 1950*, pp. 294, 322, 352; idem, *Thirty-sixth Biennial Report . . . July 1, 1960 to June 30, 1962*, p. 58; idem, *A Departmental Report . . . June 30, 1973*, p. 45.

34. MSPI, *Twenty-second Biennial Report . . . 1932*, p. 72; idem, *Biennial Report . . . 1952*, p. 25; idem, *Biennial Report, December 1, 1968*, p. 60; SDSPI, *Twentieth Biennial Report . . . July 1, 1928 to June 30, 1930*, p. 15; idem, *Twenty-ninth Biennial Report . . . July 1, 1946 to June 30, 1948*, p. 17; idem, *Thirty-seventh Biennial Report . . . July 1, 1962 to June 30, 1964*, p. 69; idem, *Twenty-seventh Biennial Report . . . July 1, 1942 to June 30, 1944*, p. 18.

35. MSPI, *Biennial Report . . . 1954*, p. 8; idem, *Biennial Report . . . 1949*, p. 10; idem, *Biennial Report, December 1, 1960*, p. 168; idem, *Biennial Report, December 1, 1966*, p. 57; NDSPI, *Twenty-ninth Biennial Report . . . Ending June 30, 1946*, p. 2828; idem, *Thirty-fourth Biennial Report . . . Ending June 30, 1956*, p. 136; idem, *Thirty-sixth Biennial Report . . . Ending June 30, 1960*, p. 220; idem, *Thirty-ninth Biennial Report . . . Ending June 30, 1966*, p. 154; idem, *Forty-third Biennial Report . . . Ending June 30, 1975*, pp. 40–41 (for 1965 and 1975 the data cover total of all districts); SDSPI, *Twenty-eighth Biennial Report . . . July 1, 1944 to June 30, 1946*, p. 66; idem, *A Departmental Report: Department of Public Instruction . . . June 30, 1973*, p. 44.

36. MSPI, *Sixteenth Biennial Report . . . 1920*, p. 94; idem, *Twentieth Biennial Report . . . 1928*, pp. 10-11, 78.

37. MSPI, *Biennial Report . . . 1950*, p. 6. Many years, however, state funding remained below the requirements of the minimum foundation program. MSPI, *Biennial Report . . . 1956*, p. 48; idem, *Biennial Report, December 1, 1968*, p. 4.

38. SDSPI, *Thirty-second Biennial Report . . . July 1, 1952 to June 30, 1954*, pp. 20, 68-76; idem, *Thirty-third Biennial Report . . . July 1, 1954 to June 30, 1956*, pp. 72-73; idem, *Thirty-sixth Biennial Report . . . July 1, 1960 to June 30, 1962*, pp. 58, 59, 66-67; idem, *Fortieth Biennial Report . . . July 1, 1968 to June 30, 1970*, p. 18.

39. Carl Frederick Kraenzel, *The Great Plains in Transition* (Norman: University of Oklahoma Press, 1955), pp. 209-11; Howard W. Ottoson et al., *Land and People in the Northern Plains Transition Area* (Lincoln: University of Nebraska Press, 1966), pp. 348-53 (cf. Hargreaves, "Land Use Planning," pp. 579-82); Kraenzel, *The Great Plains in Transition*, pp. viii, 284.

City and Village Population Trends in the Plains States

Glenn V. Fuguitt

Growth has always characterized the United States population, but it has been very uneven among different parts of the nation. Successive censuses after 1790 have recorded a westward population movement, which is continuing today, and more recently there has been a shift to southern states having a warmer climate. With the transformation from an agrarian to an industrial society has come a massive population concentration in urban and metropolitan areas, accompanied by an increasing tendency for people to live in smaller cities and the open country situated near major centers. Other areas, on the other hand, have experienced considerable population decline in recent decades: notably those rural parts of the South formerly having a large black population, and the Great Plains of the interior extending from the Dakotas to Texas.

By the 1960s, concern about the possible negative consequences of this redistribution led to proposals for population distribution policies to slow down or reverse these tendencies toward concentration. Programs such as those in rural development have been justified in part as ways to change population distribution in desired directions.[1]

More recently, there has emerged a new population trend, which is generating considerable interest. In many parts of the nation for the first time, nonmetropolitan areas are growing and gaining net migrants more rapidly than metropolitan areas.[2] The call for policies to influence distribution to encourage deconcentration, followed shortly by an unanticipated shift of people in that very direction, points up the need for more detailed knowledge and understanding of past and present distribution trends.

Though policy concerns often create the demand for generalizations about national trends, analysis of subregions or states quickly shows considerable variety in distributional tendencies. From a national demographic perspective, the Great Plains region is noteworthy as an area of low population density and relatively low urban and metropolitan concentration. Moreover, it is an area that has experienced slow total growth and net outmigration, along with a rather drastic decline in rural population in recent decades. In this paper, I will examine four states of the Great Plains region—North Dakota, South Dakota, Nebraska, and Kansas—giving particular attention to population changes in incorporated cities and villages. For convenience, these four states will be referred to here as the plains states, although subregional delineations of the Great Plains may leave out some eastern portions of these states and include parts of Montana, Wyoming, Colorado, New Mexico, Oklahoma, and Texas.[3]

The growth and decline of cities and villages have been a very significant part of population redistribution in these four states. In 1970, incorporated centers accounted for approximately 70 percent of the population there, and most of the rapid growth has been found in or near larger population agglomerations, and thus has been associated with the urbanization process. At the same time, many incorporated places have been declining, particularly smaller ones in remote locations. The declining rural village and the growing complex of urban places in metropolitan areas are both central to the problems many people believe to be associated with long-run population distribution trends.

The units of analysis of this study are all the incorporated places reported by the censuses of 1950, 1960, and 1970 for the states of North Dakota, South Dakota, Nebraska, and Kansas. A high proportion of the subregion's cities and villages, even very small ones, are incorporated, and this is in contrast to most other parts of the nation.[4] For each census year, territory designated here as metropolitan includes the nine counties in 1960 Standard Metropolitan Statistical Areas (SMSA's), plus two additional counties given metropolitan status in 1963 on the basis of 1960 census data showing them to have metropolitan characteristics.[5] No new metropolitan counties had been added in these four states by 1970.

Central cities are the major cities of metropolitan areas; the six in these states are Topeka and Wichita, Kansas; Lincoln and Omaha, Nebraska; Fargo, North Dakota; and Sioux Falls, South Dakota. *Urbanized areas* are thickly settled territory, incorporated and unincorporated, surrounding central cities. Incorporated places (called places in this study) in urbanized areas are therefore functionally, though not politically, tied to their central cities. Of the seventeen places in urbanized areas as of 1960, fourteen were in Kansas counties adjacent to Kansas City, Missouri; one (Elwood, Kansas) was adjacent to Saint Joseph, Missouri; another (East Borough) was adjacent to Wichita, Kansas; and the final one (Ralston) was adjacent to Omaha, Nebraska.

Change in Number and Population of Places

There are over 1,800 incorporated centers in the plains states. This is about 10 percent of those reported for the nation, although the four states considered here have less than 2.5 percent of the nation's population. These places are classified by size in table 1 for 1950, 1960, and 1970. There has been a gradual increase in the total number of incorporated places and their population over time. This is true also within every size group over 500 population in the metropolitan counties, but is consistently true only within the 10,000+ size group in nonmetropolitan areas. By definition, the number of central cities did not change, but three new places were added in the territory designated as urbanized areas between 1950 and 1960 and one between 1960 and 1970.

Table 2 shows more clearly the nature of the changes taking place from decade to decade. New places are added at each census and others are dropped because of consolidation or disincorporation. Also, as centers grow or decline in population, they may shift from one size class to another.

For both metropolitan and nonmetropolitan areas, table 2 indicates that the decline in the number and population of smaller centers is not because they are "disappearing," for example, because of disincorporation, for the percentage of places dropping out is never as great as 1 percent. The percentage of new incorporations is likewise low, particularly in nonmetropolitan areas. Clearly most places stayed in the same size class over each period, for the percentage shifting is 29 percent or less (columns 3 and 7). Among those that did shift within metropolitan areas, almost all were shifts due to growth. That is, the places moved to a larger rather than a smaller size class. In nonmetropolitan areas, where growth is slower, only one-half of the shifts overall were to larger size classes (columns 4 and 8). This sorting out of places, however, has resulted in a general tendency for urban growth. As places shifted to the larger size categories, the average place size increased from 1,095 to 1,225 in nonmetropolitan counties, and also increased in metropolitan counties. Yet the average size of places under 500 population in nonmetropolitan counties dropped from 238 to 205 in this period, no doubt because of the decline of the small villages left behind in this class.

Table 1
Number and Population of Metropolitan
and Nonmetropolitan Incorporated Places by Size,
Plains States, 1950, 1960, 1970[a]

	1950		1960		1970	
	No. of Places	Population	No. of Places	Population	No. of Places	Population
Metropolitan[b]						
Central Cities						
(1960)	6	688,023	6	916,429	6	1,023,865
Urbanized Areas						
(1960)	14	146,699	17	208,344	18	356,895
Other:						
10,000+	1	11,037	2	235,510	4	131,212
2,500–9,999	3	13,934	7	36,628	9	49,654
1,000–2,499	6	8,479	11	15,111	15	21,676
500–999	15	9,874	21	14,016	20	14,167
LT 500	58	15,322	48	11,506	45	10,790
Total	103	893,368	112	1,225,544	117	1,608,259
Nonmetropolitan						
10,000+	38	610,698	44	805,928	46	901,738
2,500–9,999	96	432,170	98	443,786	99	442,350
1,000–2,499	223	341,847	231	355,211	228	348,865
500–999	297	208,827	261	185,498	256	183,458
LT 500	1,024	244,573	1,066	236,376	1,084	222,443
Total	1,678	1,838,115	1,700	2,026,799	1,713	2,098,854
All Places	1,781	2,731,483	1,812	3,252,343	1,830	3,707,113

[a]Plains states include North Dakota, South Dakota, Nebraska, and Kansas.

[b]In a Standard Metropolitan Statistical Area as of 1963.

Table 2
Percent Change in the Number of Places by Size and Metropolitan Status, Plains States, 1950–60 and 1960–70

	1950–60				1960–70			
	Of initial places			Shifts due to growth	Of initial places			Shifts due to growth
	drop-out	new inc.	shift		drop-out	new inc.	shift	
Metropolitan outside Urban Areas	0	7	29	100	0	3	21	84
Nonmetropolitan								
10,000+	0	0	3	0[a]	0	0	2	0[a]
2,500–9,999	0	0	10	70	0	0	9	33
1,000–2,499	0	1	11	42	0	1	12	32
500–999	0	(-)	26	36	0	2	20	31
LT 500	(-)	2	3	100[b]	.5	1	2	100[b]
Total	(-)	2	8	51	(-)	1	7	46

(-) Indicates less than .5 percent.

[a] Must be zero.

[b] Must be 100.

The preceding tables reveal the importance of following the same places over time in the study of population change, since the population decline of a size category may actually be due at least in part to the growth of individual places out of the category. In the remainder of this paper, I will consider the growth or decline of groups of places classed by size and location at the beginning of a decade. All centers dropped by the census in either 1960 or 1970 are disregarded. Analysis of change for 1950–60 thus includes the 1,778 incorporated centers reported by the census in 1950 and 1960 that did not drop out in 1970, and analysis for 1960–1970 includes the 1,807 centers reported in both 1960 and 1970 in the four states.

The distribution of places by percent change is given in tables 3a and 3b for centers classified by initial size and metropolitan or

Table 3a
Distribution of Percent Change of Incorporated Places
Classified by Metropolitan Status and Initial Size, Plains States, 1950–60

Metropolitan Status and Size at Beginning of Decade	Number of Places	Distribution by Percent Change					
		Loss		Gain			
		10%+	0–9%	0–9%	10–19%	20%	Total
Metropolitan[a]							
Central Cities	6	0	7	0		100	100
Other in Urbanized Area	14	8	16	16	21	72	100
Not in Urbanized Area	83	7	14	13	16	44	100
Total	103	7	14	13	15	51	100
Nonmetropolitan							
10,000+	38	2	22	25	20	31	100
2,500–9,999	96	3	28	27	22	20	100
1,000–2,499	223	14	35	28	14	9	100
500–999	297	29	28	21	7	15	100
LT 500	1,021	53	21	13	7	6	100
Total	1,675	40	24	17	9	10	100

[a]In a Standard Metropolitan Statistical Area as of 1963.

Table 3b
Distribution of Percent Change of Incorporated Places
Classified by Metropolitan Status and Initial Size, Plains States, 1960–70

Metropolitan Status and Size at Beginning of Decade	Number of Places	Distribution by Percent Change					Total
		Loss		Gain			
		10%+	0–9%	0–9%	10–19%	20%	
Metropolitan[a]							
Central Cities	6			33	67		100
Other in Urbanized Area	17	6	18	6	29	41	100
Not in Urbanized Area	89	13	16	15	15	41	100
Total	112	12	15	14	20	39	100
Nonmetropolitan							
10,000+	44	4	23	34	16	23	100
2,500–9,999	98	18	28	30	11	13	100
1,000–2,499	231	19	35	32	9	5	100
500–999	261	32	28	22	9	9	100
LT 500	1,061	52	20	14	7	7	100
Total	1,695	41	24	19	8	8	100

[a]In a Standard Metropolitan Statistical Area as of 1963.

nonmetropolitan location. The most apparent difference in the tables is the greater tendency for growth in metropolitan areas. For both decades, about three-fourths of the metropolitan places grew, but that was true of only one-third of the nonmetropolitan places. Approximately one metropolitan place out of ten declined more than 10 percent, whereas that was true of four out of ten non-metropolitan places in both 1950–60 and 1960–70.

Many studies have associated initial size with the population change of smaller cities and towns.[6] Most of this research has shown that larger places are more likely to grow, and to grow at a faster rate, than smaller places. This is consistent with the view that smaller cities and towns have suffered because of a centralization of trade and services, particularly since the widespread use of the automobile after about 1920. With improved transportation, rural people have a wider range of shopping choices, while their demands for goods and services have become more varied and specialized. In this kind of changing situation, larger places have a competitive advantage and thus grow more rapidly than smaller ones.

Results here support the research cited above; that is, there is a strong positive association between initial size and the distribution by percent change in both tables 3a and 3b. In earlier nation-wide analyses using 1950–70 data, the North Central region was found to have the strongest positive association between place size and growth, perhaps because small towns are more likely to be farming trade centers there.[7] We also found that the association between size and growth is becoming less marked in some parts of the country (particularly sections of the South) because of the decline in growth levels for larger places and a slight increase for smaller places, when the 1960–70 period is compared with 1950–60. An examination of tables 3a and 3b shows that in both metropolitan and nonmetropolitan segments of the plains states over the 1960–70 period, larger places were less likely to grow, and also were less likely to grow more than 20 percent, than were such places over the 1950–60 period. On the other hand, the smallest places changed little in their growth distributions for the two decades.

In sum there has been: (1) a continuing concentration of population in metropolitan areas, with growth favoring places located in SMSA's over those in nonmetropolitan areas; and (2) a continued urbanization process within the nonmetropolitan areas, with a positive association between growth levels and initial place size.

Results for Individual States

Local variations in the findings just discussed are revealed in table 4. There is general conformity to the pattern of metropolitan concentration, with all states showing a considerably higher proportion of places growing within SMSA's than elsewhere. For the nation as a whole, these differences are smaller, because nationally nonmetropolitan places are more likely to grow than they are in any of the plains states. The most extreme individual state is North Dakota, where only 31 percent of nonmetropolitan places grew over the 1950–60 period and 16 percent over the 1960–70 period.

There tends to be a positive association between size and growth among nonmetropolitan places for each of the plains states, the only exceptions to a completely consistent pattern being in Kansas for both decades and North Dakota for 1960–70. The difference in likelihood of growth between places under 500 populaton at the beginning of each decade and those over 10,000 is always very large. Only in Nebraska in 1960–70 did more than one-third of the places in the smallest size group grow. Again, the lowest proportion is in North Dakota, where only 22 places out of 231 under 500 in 1960 grew over the 1960–70 period, and 76 places out of 303 initially in this size group grew over the 1950–60 period.

Growth levels for individual states generally are lower in 1960–70 than in 1950–60. Exceptions are found for the nonmetropolitan part of Nebraska and the metropolitan part of North Dakota, however. In Nebraska, the percentage growing in each nonmetropolitan size group except the 10,000+ category is larger in the latter decade. In the 1960s, Nebraska and Kansas usually show higher growth levels than North Dakota and South Dakota.

Growth by Location

By distinguishing the growth and decline of cities and villages according to initial size and metropolitan status, I have shown here a congruence between population change of places and the processes of urbanization and metropolitan growth in the plains states. That is, metropolitan places are more likely to grow than nonmetropolitan places, and larger nonmetropolitan places are more likely to grow than smaller ones. This association needs to be examined in greater detail for nonmetropolitan places. We know that the influence of metropolitan centers does not stop at the boundaries of SMSA's,

Table 4

Percent of Places Gaining Population, by Metropolitan Status and Initial Size of Place, United States and Plains States, 1950–60 and 1960–70

	United States		Plains States		North Dakota		South Dakota		Nebraska		Kansas	
	1950–60	1960–70	1950–60	1960–70	1950–60	1960–70	1950–60	1960–70	1950–60	1960–70	1950–60	1960–70
Metropolitan[a]												
Central Cities (1960)	73	54	100	100	100	100	100	100	100	100	100	100
Urbanized Areas (1960)	99	75	93	76	—	—	—	—	100	100	90	73
Other	81	78	76	71	37	53	75	62	85	77	94	78
Total	81	75	79	73	40	55	78	67	87	80	93	77
Nonmetropolitan												
10,000+	81	64	76	73	100	83	100	71	100	100	76	59
2,500–9,999	77	66	69	54	88	86	68	59	75	72	61	36
1,000–2,499	67	64	51	46	58	28	61	43	30	59	62	49
500–999	59	60	43	40	47	18	38	33	37	50	48	46
LT 500	41	47	26	28	19	10	29	22	25	43	30	31
Total	56	57	36	35	31	16	38	29	32	49	42	38
All Places	62	61	39	38	31	18	39	31	35	51	46	41

—— No places in this category.

[a] In a Standard Metropolitan Statistical Area as of 1963.

and also that there should be an interrelationship between larger and smaller nonmetropolitan centers based on their locations.[8]

Nonmetropolitan places in the plains states are considered in table 5, and again the dependent variable is the percentage of places growing. The places are classified by the distance of their county from the nearest central city of an SMSA.[9] Local urbanization is indicated by a further breakdown according to size of the largest place in the county in 1960, and again the cities and villages are distinguished in groups by initial size.

The results are generally consistent in showing a positive association simultaneously between growth and (1) nearness to a central city, (2) size of largest place in the county, and (3) initial size of place. Places, regardless of size, are more likely to grow if they are in counties within fifty miles of a metropolitan center. Such communities undoubtedly have growth advantages because of the possibility of commuting to jobs in the metropolitan area, and by virtue of their location they may also be more attractive as centers for industry and other economic activities. In more remote areas, it is generally true that places are more likely to grow if they are in counties that include larger centers. There is some evidence of an advantage, however, which may be due to lack of nearby competition, for those intermediate-sized places (1,000–2,500) in counties without larger centers. Considering all three variables together, there is a very great range in growth levels. Thus between 1960 and 1970, 93 percent of the places over 2,500 grew if they were less than fifty miles from a central city, but over the 1960–70 period only 21 percent of those places grew that were less than 500 in size, located in entirely rural counties (those in which the largest place is less than 2,500), and more than fifty miles from a central city.

Growth Inside and Outside of Places

These growth patterns for incorporated places indicate an overall concentration of population in the larger centers. Yet the fact that smaller cities are generally more likely to grow if they are in a metropolitan area, near a metropolitan area, or in a nonmetropolitan county having a city over 10,000 indicates that there has also been some local deconcentration around the major cities of the four-state area, which could include migration to the countryside. To consider this possibility, the total population and population of incorporated places were obtained for groups of counties. Then, by

Table 5

Percent of Nonmetropolitan Places Growing, by Size of Largest Place in the County in 1960 (SLP), Distance to a Central City, and Initial Size, Plains States, 1950–60 and 1960–70

	Percent Growing 1950–60 Size in 1950					Percent Growing 1960–70 Size in 1960				
	LT 500	500–999	1,000–2,499	2,500+	Total	LT 500	500–999	1,000–2,499	2,500+	Total
Nonmetropolitan Total[a]	26	42	51	74	36	28	40	46	59	35
Less than 50 miles from a central city	42	63	61	77	52	53	81	64	93	62
More than 50 miles from a central city	24	39	50	74	34	25	34	43	55	32
SLP 10,000	33	42	38	87	44	40	60	52	64	48
2,500–9,999	22	46	59	67	35	25	23	29	52	29
LT 2,500	22	36	50	—	30	21	31	44	—	27

[a]Nonmetropolitan includes places not in Standard Metropolitan Statistical Areas as of 1963.

subtraction, the population living outside incorporated places was determined for each census year.

Table 6 gives the percent change in population in and outside of incorporated places in the region for counties classed by size of largest place in the county and distance from a metropolitan center. For a given category, the population of places first reported in 1960 is considered to be outside incorporated centers in the 1950–60 computations, but is included with other centers for 1960–70. Similarly, the population of places new in 1970 is counted as outside incorporated territory over the 1960–70 decade. Centers dropped after the 1950 census have not been considered in this analysis, and so are counted as outside incorporated centers throughout.

There are contrasting patterns for metropolitan and nonmetropolitan areas over the 1950–60 period. Deconcentration is found within metropolitan areas, with growth outside incorporated places more pronounced than growth inside such centers. For groups of

Table 6

Percent Change in Population in and out of Incorporated Places,
1950–60 and 1960–70, and Total Population Change, 1970–75,
Grouped by Metropolitan Status, Size of Largest Place
in the County in 1960 (SLP), and Distance to
a Central City, Plains States

	1950–60			1960–70			1970–75
	Total	Inside Places	Outside Places	Total	Inside Places	Outside Places	Total
Metropolitan[a]	35.4	31.9	47.9	13.5	18.7	-6.3	3.2
Nonmetropolitan	-.1	9.9	-12.2	-2.8	3.1	-11.8	1.7
Less than 50 miles from a central city	3.2	13.1	-8.0	3.0	13.1	-11.4	3.8
More than 50 miles from a central city	-0.6	9.5	-12.7	-3.5	1.9	-11.8	1.3
SLP 10,000+	13.4	20.1	-1.6	5.6	6.5	3.0	3.5
2,500–9,999	-4.1	5.1	-15.3	-6.6	0	-16.1	-.1
LT 2,500	-10.7	-2.4	-16.6	-11.6	-4.4	-17.7	-.4
Total	8.9	17.1	-3.7	2.4	9.0	-10.8	2.2

[a] In a Standard Metropolitan Statistical Area as of 1963.

nonmetropolitan counties, on the other hand, there is generally growth inside centers but a marked decline outside them.

For 1960–70, however, both metropolitan and nonmetropolitan areas experienced growth in incorporated places and decline elsewhere. Although nonmetropolitan areas changed very little between decades in the level of open-country decline, metropolitan unincorporated territory shifted from a 48 percent growth to a 6 percent decline. This difference between decades is due to a change in the importance of annexation as a component of metropolitan growth in the region. Overall in the plains states, metropolitan urban growth was entirely associated with the annexation of rural territory in the 1960s, whereas two-thirds of the urban growth in the 1950s was in territory already urban at the beginning of the decade. Thus the decline in population outside places between 1960 and 1970 is due to the transfer of rural territory into the incorporated limits of cities, since if no annexation had taken place, the population outside places would have grown 73 percent instead of declining 6 percent. Had there been no annexation between 1950 and 1960, the growth outside places would have been similar, 78 percent, instead of the 48 percent recorded. From a fixed-area perspective, then, local deconcentration continued in metropolitan areas over both decades.

Nationally, a comparison of these two decades shows lower growth levels in the latter ten-year period, consistent with recent fertility declines, and this is also true for the plains states. There is, however, widespread evidence of greater population retention outside incorporated places for the nation as a whole in the latter decade than in the 1950s, despite the practice of annexation. These data indicate, however, that in the plains states, slower growth in the 1960s went along with continuing and even increasing concentration of population in the cities.

Trends since 1970

Actual population counts of cities and villages are obtained only every ten years in the census of population. The Census Bureau now prepares estimates of total county population every year, however, and it is thus possible to obtain the 1970–75 total population growth for the same groups of counties considered in the 1950–70 analysis here, using the 1975 county population estimates.[10] These percentages, in the right-hand column of table 6, are for a five-and-one-fourth-year period and so would be expected to be smaller than other percentages in this table computed for ten-year intervals.

Although they are for total county populations rather than places, the results are significant to this study, for they show a continued slowing of growth for metropolitan counties but overall a shift from decline to growth for nonmetropolitan counties. Metropolitan areas are still growing more rapidly than nonmetropolitan areas as a whole, however, contrary to national norms for this decade, but not as rapidly as more urban nonmetropolitan counties or those adjacent to metropolitan centers. Nonadjacent counties without larger places continue to decline in population, though at a much lower rate than in the previous two decades. On an individual basis, more than 80 percent of these remote rural counties declined over the 1950–60 and 1960–70 peiods, but 57 percent did so in 1970–75. An important element in the moderation of decline and shift to growth in many rural counties may well be a stabilization of the population associated with agriculture. Also the 1975 estimates indicate that many counties in these states with a high proportion of Native Americans have turned from population decline to growth.

Conclusions

This is a study of population change in incorporated cities and villages in four states of the Great Plains region: North Dakota, South Dakota, Nebraska, and Kansas. These states are sparsely populated and not highly urbanized, yet they have a greater prevalence of small incorporated places than most other parts of the nation. Results have shown recent population trends of cities and villages in these states to be closely associated with urbanization and metropolitan concentration. This parallels a long-term national trend, but is in contrast to patterns recently emerging in nonmetropolitan areas of many other sections of the country.

A widely held view is that rural areas are strongly influenced by nearby metropolitan centers, and indeed some social scientists have regarded rural America as the hinterland of a series of metropolitan regions.[11] Generally there is a growth advantage in the plains states associated with nearness to a metropolitan center, but the results here also point to the importance of larger nonmetropolitan cities and towns, because outside metropolitan areas, stability and growth was more likely to be found in or near such places than elsewhere in the 1950–70 period. Thus these findings support the view that rural development programs should be designed to take advantage of urban and metropolitan growth processes and should include consideration of larger nonmetropolitan cities as possible growth points.[12]

Since 1970, there has been a national shift in the pattern of population change, with nonmetropolitan areas now growing more rapidly than metropolitan, and selected completely rural nonmetropolitan counties growing more rapidly than other nonmetropolitan counties that include larger centers. If a goal of rural development policy is to stabilize or reverse population decline, however, the recent increased growth of the nonmetropolitan sector does not necessarily mean that this goal has been achieved, for there are still many areas of population decline, and they tend to be concentrated among the most rural counties in the plains states under study here. Although the levels of decline are generally much smaller since 1970 than before, it is nevertheless true that one-half of the counties in these four states lost population between 1970 and 1975, and a larger number lost more migrants than they gained in this period.

The drawing of further implications from these findings depends upon a more explicit understanding of the relationship between population change and economic and social development. Policy makers have favored a population distribution policy to increase population in nonmetropolitan areas and to slow growth in and around large cities. But people are increasingly questioning the desirability of growth even in nonmetropolitan areas and recognizing that population change may not be the appropriate social indicator of the need for or success of rural development programs.

Slow growth or stability is, of course, different from the sustained rapid decline found in many counties due to the selective outmigration of young people in search of better opportunities. Nevertheless, although the large population decline recorded in nonmetropolitan parts of the plains states has been viewed as a catastrophic process demanding reversal, it has also been seen as a successful adjustment to technological change.[13] The problem is that we still know far too little about the consequences of rapid population growth or extended decline for the community and its institutions, and for both the people who stay and those who go. Further systematic research is needed to cover a wide variety of situations.

But the extent of chronic decline revealed by this study must surely be associated with some severe community adjustment problems at the local level. In these four states, 713 places (four out of every ten), declined more than 10 percent in population from 1960 to 1970, and the situation for 1950–60 was similar. We do not yet know what has happened to places since 1970, but despite a general moderation of total population decline and even shifts to growth in some areas, it seems unlikely that a high proportion of rural centers declining in the previous decade are now gaining residents. Available evidence suggests that at least in some parts of the nation, the nonmetropolitan turnaround is largely an open-country phenomenon.[14]

One may not wish to mount programs to reverse all these population losses, and the sheer number of places involved may be an effective argument against attempting to do so. But such extensive population declines must, in many localities, call for drastic adjustments to maintain local government with decreasing numbers of taxpayers, to supply educational facilities to meet the needs of young people who will soon move, and to provide welfare needs and other public services for an aging population (in South Dakota, the only plains state for which village age data are available, 106 out of 310 incorporated centers in 1970 had at least one person out of four over 64 years of age).

The goals for development programs should differ for different types of communities; these goals cannot and should not always include efforts to gain industry and population. The nonmetropolitan population turnaround is real and widespread, but some population decline is still the rule among most nonmetropolitan counties of the plains states. These areas must not simply be written off or overlooked because of growth elsewhere. Most small towns found in declining areas may continue to decline, but they are not disappearing. The institutional arrangements and the quality of life for citizens in situations of sustained population decline must continue to receive attention by citizens groups, university reseachers, and appropriate units of federal, state, and local governments.

Notes

This research was supported by the College of Agricultural and Life Sciences, University of Wisconsin–Madison, as a collaborator in North Central Region Cooperative Research Project NC-97, and through a cooperative agreement with the Economic Development Division, Economic Research Service, U.S. Department of Agriculture. Analysis was aided by a Center for Population Research grant, no. HD05876, to the Center for Demography and Ecology, University of Wisconsin–Madison, from the Center for Population Research of the National Institute of Child Health and Human Development.

1. U.S. Department of Agriculture, *National Growth and Its Distribution*, proceedings of Symposium on Communities of Tomorrow (Washington, D.C.: U.S. Department of Agriculture, 1968); National Goals Research Staff, *Toward Balanced Growth: Quantity with Quality* (Washington, D.C.: Government

Printing Office, 1970); Henry L. Ahlgren, "Rural Development—Its Dimensions and Scope," paper presented at annual meeting of Rural Sociological Society, August 23, 1971, Denver, Colorado; U.S. Commission on Population Growth and the American Future, *Population and the American Future* (Washington, D.C.: Government Printing Office, 1972).

2. Calvin L. Beale, *The Revival of Population Growth in Nonmetropolitan America,* Bulletin ERS-605, Economic Development Division, Economic Research Service (Washington, D.C.: U.S. Department of Agriculture, 1975); Calvin L. Beale and Glenn V. Fuguitt, "Population Trends in Nonmetropolitan Cities and Villages in Subregions of the United States," Working Paper 75-22, Center for Demography and Ecology, Madison, University of Wisconsin, 1975; Peter A. Morrison with Judith P. Wheeler, "Rural Renaissance in America?" *Population Bulletin* 32 (1976): 1-26.

3. E. Cotton Mather, "The American Great Plains," *Annals of the Association of American Geographers* 62 (June 1972): 237-57; Beale and Fuguitt, "Population Trends."

4. Calvin L. Beale, "Quantitative Dimensions of Decline and Stability among Rural Communities," in *Communities Left Behind: Alternatives for Development,* ed. Larry R. Whiting (Ames: Iowa State University Press, 1974), pp. 3-21.

5. The metropolitan counties are: Cass, North Dakota (Fargo-Moorhead SMSA); Minnehaha, South Dakota (Sioux Falls SMSA); Lancaster, Nebraska (Lincoln SMSA); Douglas and Sarpy, Nebraska (Omaha SMSA); Johnson and Wyandotte, Kansas (Kansas City SMSA); Shawnee, Kansas (Topeka SMSA), and Sedgwick, Kansas (Wichita SMSA). The two counties added in 1963 are Dakota, Nebraska (Sioux City SMSA) and Butler, Kansas (Wichita SMSA).

6. For example, S. C. Ratcliffe, "Size as a Factor in Population Changes of Incorporated Hamlets and Villages, 1930-40," *Rural Sociology* 7 (1942): 318-28; Edmund de S. Brunner and T. Lynn Smith, "Village Growth and Decline, 1930-40," *Rural Sociology* 9 (1944): 102-15; Edward Hassinger, "Factors Associated with Population Changes in Agricultural Trade Centers of Southern Minnesota, 1940-1950" (Ph.D. diss., University of Minnesota, 1956); John F. Hart and Neil E. Salisbury, "Population Change in Middle Western Villages: A Statistical Approach," *Annals of the Association of American Geographers* 55 (1965): 140-60; Glenn V. Fuguitt, "The Places Left Behind: Population Trends and Policy for Rural America," *Rural Sociology* 36 (1971): 449-70; and Glenn V. Fuguitt and Calvin L. Beale, *Population Change in Nonmetropolitan Cities and Towns,* Agricultural Economic Report no. 323, Economic Development Division, Economic Research Service (Washington, D.C.: U.S. Department of Agriculture, 1976).

7. Fuguitt, "Places Left Behind"; Fuguitt and Beale, *Population Change.*

8. See Fuguitt, "Places Left Behind," and Fuguitt and Beale, *Population Change,* for further discussion and analysis of the nation and its regions.

9. This variable was obtained from J. Allan Beegle and used in Dale E. Hathaway, J. Allan Beegle, and W. Keith Bryant, *People of Rural America: A 1960 Census Monograph* (Washington, D.C.: Government Printing Office, 1968).

A distance of fifty miles was drawn from the geographical center of the largest city in each SMSA and nonmetropolitan counties falling within the circle of the fifty-mile radius were classed as being within fifty miles of the SMSA.

10. These 1975 estimates are found in the U.S. Census, *Current Population Reports,* ser. P-26 (1976).

11. See, for example, Hathaway, Beegle, and Bryant, *People of Rural America.*

12. U.S. Commission on Population Growth, *Population and the American Future,* especially pp. 124–26; for a recent review, see also Niles M. Hansen, *Improving Access to Economic Opportunity: Nonmetropolitan Labor Markets in an Urban Society* (Cambridge, Mass.: Ballinger Publishing Co., 1976).

13. See the discussion in Luther Tweeton, *Foundations of Farm Policy* (Lincoln: University of Nebraska Press, 1970), especially p. 374.

14. Calvin L. Beale and Glenn V. Fuguitt, "The New Pattern of Nonmetropolitan Population Change," Working Paper 75-22, Center for Demography and Ecology, Madison, University of Wisconsin, 1975; Stephen J. Tordella, *Urban and Rural Population Change in Wisconsin Counties, 1960 to 1970,* Population Series 70-9, Applied Population Laboratory, Department of Rural Sociology (Madison: University of Wisconsin, 1977).

List of Contributors

Bradley H. Baltensperger is an assistant professor of geography at Michigan Technological University. He is especially interested in the history of agricultural settlement.

Brian W. Blouet is a professor of geography and chairman of the department at the University of Nebraska–Lincoln. He is coeditor of *Images of the Plains: The Role of Human Nature in Settlement* (1975) and author of *A Short History of Malta* (1979).

Gilbert C. Fite is Richard Russell Professor of History at the University of Georgia. Among his many books is *The Farmer's Frontier, 1865–1900* (1966). He is a past president of the Agricultural History Society.

Glenn V. Fuguitt is a professor of rural sociology at the University of Wisconsin–Madison. He has written many articles on population change in nonmetropolitan areas in the United States.

H. Roger Grant is an associate professor of history at the University of Akron. He has written numerous articles on American cultural history.

Mary W. M. Hargreaves is a professor of history at the University of Kentucky. Among her publications is *Dry Farming in the Northern Great Plains* (1957). She is a past president of the Agricultural History Society.

Leslie Hewes is professor emeritus of geography at the University of Nebraska–Lincoln. His publications include *The Suitcase Farming Frontier: A Study in the Historical Geography of the Central Great Plains* (1973).

John C. Hudson is a professor of geography at Northwestern University and editor of *Annals of the Association of American Geographers*. In his recent essays he has focused on the cultural geography of the northern Great Plains.

R. Douglas Hurt is Curator of Agriculture for the Ohio Historical Society. He is the author of several articles published in various western history journals.

G. Malcolm Lewis is a senior lecturer in geography at the University of Sheffield, England. He has published several essays on human perception of the Great Plains region and is an authority on aboriginal maps.

Frederick C. Luebke is a professor of history at the University of Nebraska–Lincoln. His publications include *Immigrants and Politics: The Germans of Nebraska, 1880–1900* (1969) and *Bonds of Loyalty: German Americans in World War I* (1974).

Timothy J. Rickard is an associate professor of geography at Central Connecticut State College. His special interest is the historical geography of irrigation in the United States.

David S. Trask is Dean of Arts and Sciences at Greenville Technical College, South Carolina. He is the author of several articles on Nebraska Populism.

Waldo R. Wedel is archeologist emeritus at the Smithsonian Institution. Among his many books and articles is *Prehistoric Man on the Great Plains* (1961).